The
Civil War
in the
Smokies

Noel Fisher

Published in the United States by Great Smoky Mountains
Association. Great Smoky Mountains Association is a private,
nonprofit organization which supports the educational,
scientific and historical programs of Great Smoky Mountains
National Park. Our publications are an educational service
intended to enhance the public's understanding and enjoyment
of the national park. If you would like to know more about our
publications, memberships, guided hikes and other projects,
please contact:

Great Smoky Mountains Association
115 Park Headquarters Road
Gatlinburg, Tennessee 37738
865.436.7318
SmokiesInformation.org

ISBN # 0-937207-46-2

Editors: Steve Kemp and Kent Cave
Author: Noel Fisher
Cover illustration *Foraging* by Winslow Homer, Library of
Congress
Cover design: Lisa Horstman
Book design: Joey Heath
Editorial assistance by Rebecca Vial, Tom Robbins, Elise
LeQuire and Marianne Wightman
Printed and bound by Maple Press Company,
York, Pennsylvania

06 07 08 09 10

Acknowledgments

I would first like to thank the many local historians, historical societies, and genealogical societies who have labored over the past decades to preserve and interpret the history of the Great Smoky Mountains region. Though they too seldom receive the recognition they deserve, our understanding of the history of this area would be far poorer without their dedication, and works like this would not be possible. Though I do not know and cannot name them all, I would like to mention the following: W. C. Allen, Edwin J. Best, Alberta and Carson Brewer, Inez Burns, Hattie Caldwell Davis, Gertrude E. Collahan, W. Clark Medford, Ruth Webb O'Dell, Duane Oliver, Joseph Sharpe, and Emma Dean Smith Trent. I would particularly like to thank Dr. Elmer Mize for sharing his knowledge of the history of Maryville and Blount County, and Edward R. Walker III for talking with me about his work on East Tennessee. I have also benefited greatly from the excellent histories of Stephen Ash, Charles F. Bryan, Daniel C. Crofts, Durwood Dunn, W. Todd Groce, John C. Inscoe, Gordon McKinney, and Daniel Sutherland.

I also received a vast amount of help with archival sources from the following persons: Steve Cotham, Director of the McClung Collection; Cherel Henderson, Associate Director of the East Tennessee Historical Society; Annette F. Hartigan, Librarian and Archivist at Great Smoky Mountains National Park; Anne E. Bridges and Lisa Travis, Reference Librarians at the University of Tennessee; Duane Frizzell of the excellent manuscript collection at the Hunter Library, Western Carolina University; and the staffs of the Tennessee State Library and Archives, North Carolina State Archives, Southern Historical Collection, University of Tennessee Special Collections, Duke University Library Manuscript Collection, and the Blount County, Cocke County, Sevier County, Haywood County, and Jackson County Public Libraries.

My final thanks go to Steve Kemp, who initiated this work and showed the patience and kindness of a saint while it was being written, and my wife Angela, who performed much research and endured the long and uncertain process of the work's completion.

Contents

Contents   v

List of Illustrations   vi

Introduction   vii

Chapter 1
The Antebellum Smokies   11

Chapter 2
Secession   30

Chapter 3
Early War: Innocence   42

Chapter 4
Innocence Ends: The Chaos of War   61

Chapter 5
The Price of War   85

Chapter 6
The Late War: Confederate Desperation   114

Chapter 7
After the End   143

Notes   152

Bibliography   171

Glossary   177

Index   180

List of Illustrations

Cherokee warriors attack settlements   13

Jacob Harmon and son being hanged   56

War in the mountains   66

Foraging livestock   90

Maps
   East Tennessee   108
   Great Smoky Mountains   110
   Western North Carolina   112

Attack on Fort Sanders   124

Introduction

The American Civil War was, in the truest and fullest sense of the word, a cataclysmic event. In those four years of declared war, and in the ten years of undeclared war that followed, the framework and fabric of life in the United States were permanently altered. Race relations, political structures, economic systems, governmental functions, regional identity, and relations among regions were all ripped apart and remade. Many Americans, North and South, opposed these changes and fought to limit their scope. Others sought far more extensive changes than actually occurred and were disappointed at the war's outcome. Despite the failure of this latter group to achieve their vision of a radically new nation, the changes that the war set in motion, though sometimes hampered and delayed, could not be reversed.

The Civil War also left behind an aggregation of images and symbols that would become embedded in the American psyche. General Robert E. Lee's courtly dignity, General Ulysses S. Grant's common bluntness, President Abraham Lincoln's religious devotion to the Union, the Southern soldiers' grim-humored endurance of hardships, "Pickett's Charge" on the third day of the Battle of Gettysburg, "Sherman's March" through Georgia and North Carolina, these and more all became enshrined in the mythology of the war. Included as well were the war's gallery of heroes—Generals Grant, Sherman, Sheridan, and George Thomas in the North, Generals Lee, Jackson, J. E. B. Stuart, and John Hunt Morgan in the South, and villains—Sherman, General Benjamin "Beast" Butler, and Tories in the South, President Jefferson Davis, General Nathan

Bedford Forrest, and Copperheads in the North.

It is these images, this war of generals and battlefields and causes, that most readily come to mind when the Civil War is mentioned. But the great American conflict had other facets less grand and glittering. Beneath the debates over race and government and territory, beneath the machinations of politics and the panorama of battle, lay the spectacle of daily life during the war, sometimes grim and dreary, sometimes humorous or glorious. This was the struggle of women left alone to manage both farms and homes, to raise children, to make unfamiliar decisions about fields and crops and livestock and finances, and to write cheerful letters to far away husbands and sons while enduring agonizing hours of loneliness and fear and uncertainty and despair. This was the struggle of all Southern families to survive amidst shortages of goods, an increasingly worthless currency, rapacious tax collectors and conscript officers, foraging parties that stripped barns and smokehouses and sometimes the house itself, bushwhackers and thieves who took what little the armies missed, and endless rumors and lies and horrible truths. This was the struggle of ordinary soldiers to endure days of marching in mud and rain and wilting heat and debilitating cold, nights of sleeping on hard ground in crowded tents and makeshift shelters, and more days of drinking, playing cards, searching for better food and better clothes, hoping for letters from home, and looking for a way, any way, to escape the interminable boredom. And this was the struggle of families left to face the loss of husbands and fathers and brothers and sons on battlefields far away, and of others to care for returning soldiers who had been physically, mentally, and emotionally maimed by the war. This struggle had its own gallery of heroes and villains, lesser known and less remembered, but no less remarkable for that, and its outcome would have a profound effect on the fortunes of the Confederacy.

No region of the country, and particularly no region of the Confederacy, escaped the destructive effects of the war. The cataclysm that was the American Civil War reached even into such a seemingly remote and inaccessible region as the Great Smoky Mountains. No large armies marched through these mountains, and no dramatic battles marred the landscape there. The region contributed relatively little in the way of arms and munitions and troops, and it had little say in the decisions affecting the fate of the new nation. Yet the people of the Smokies were no less affected, and their lives no less transformed, than the inhabitants of Richmond or Nashville or Charleston or Atlanta.

The terrain and isolation of the Smokies had contradictory effects. On the one hand, the mountains proved to be a blessing. The rough terrain precluded large-scale campaigning, while the lack of effective transportation and limited production made it impossible to station large armies in the mountains for any length of time. Thus residents of the Smokies were spared the horrors of large-scale fighting in their midst. The mountains could also be a curse. The difficult terrain, and the very remoteness of the region, made the Smokies a prime refuge for deserters, men evading conscription, and criminals. Further, the economic limitations that the mountains had always imposed magnified the war's destructive effects and left families fewer resources to withstand the strains of the war.

The war in the Smokies proved to be an intensely personal conflict. A curious conjunction of terrain, history, politics, and culture bred in the Smokies, as in all the Appalachians, a tragic division of loyalties and a brutal partisan conflict between supporters of secession and adherents of the Union. This was a war where men rode to the house of a neighbor they had known for many years, called him to his door, and shot him dead; where other men left homes and wives and children and trekked north in cold and rain to serve the army and the cause of their choice; and where still others served in poorly supplied, poorly equipped, nearly forgotten units to protect border and home. This was also a war in which many families wanted nothing to do with either side and did everything they could to avoid involvement. The partisan war that flamed in the Smokies was, undeniably, ugly and destructive and full of cruelties, and some have condemned it as pointless and senseless. But the South's partisan conflict cannot be separated from the traditional war, and it was no more nor less senseless than the American Civil War as a whole. The same competing passions and loyalties and visions that produced the national war also produced the partisan conflict, though certainly the peculiar conditions of the Smokies altered the nature of the conflict there.

This work is a history of the Civil War and Reconstruction period in what is now the region of Great Smoky Mountains National Park, or roughly the counties of Blount, Cocke, and Sevier in Tennessee and Cherokee, Haywood, Jackson, and Macon in North Carolina. Events in the Smokies did not occur in isolation, of course, so at times it also takes in the conflict in East Tennessee and western North Carolina. This study considers the nature of antebellum society in the Smokies, the region's response to secession, the recruitment of soldiers for the conventional war, and the conflict between Confederate and Union forces to control this area. Its main purpose, however, is to tell the story of the Great Smoky Mountains' own war: how residents responded to the prospect of secession, how they pursued the conflict in their own ways, how they survived the war's devastating effects, and how that struggle changed both individuals and the society as a whole.

CHAPTER 1

THE ANTEBELLUM SMOKIES

IKE ALL THE SOUTHERN APPALACHIANS IN 1860, THE GREAT SMOKY MOUNTAINS REGION WAS FULL OF CONTRADICTORY CHARACTERISTICS and impulses. It was, at the same time, barely past its frontier period and on the verge of a rapid economic modernization. It was an area where the last Native American removal had taken place just 20 years before and where a remnant of the Cherokee Nation still hung on, aided, curiously enough, by one of the region's richest and most influential white men. It was a region where wealthy families owning hundreds of acres and dozens of slaves lived next to poor families struggling to eke out a living from small plots of rocky land. It was a society that seemed, at once, very like and very unlike the rest of the South, for while Smokies residents considered themselves Southern in institutions and values, often they seemed cut off from the main political and cultural currents of the South by geography, history, and psychology. And it was, at once, a region of great resources and great poverty, of grand visions and failed schemes, of unparalleled beauty and heartbreaking cruelty.

Long before Europeans ever saw the Smokies, the Cherokee had put down deep roots there. No one knows for certain when or why the Cherokee first came to the Smoky Mountains, though their own traditions suggest that the Cherokee left the Ohio Valley and traveled south after losing a decades-long war against the Delaware. Whatever the case, by the eighteenth century the Cherokee had become numerous and powerful, holding at their peak tens of thousands of square miles in what is now Virginia, Tennessee, North Carolina, South Carolina, Georgia, and Alabama. They built networks of towns on the Savannah, Hiwassee, Tuckasegee, and Little Tennessee Rivers, raised corn, beans, squash, and other crops in the rich lands along the rivers (fields which European settlers would later use), took meat, furs and fish from the vast surrounding forests, operated trade networks extending over hundreds of miles, and fought long and indecisive border conflicts with the Iroquis in the north and the Tuscarora, Catawba, and other groups in the south. In 1715 English officials counted 53 major Cherokee towns and estimated the population at 11,200. Echota, located on the Little Tennessee just above the mouth of the Tellico River, held the main council house and constituted the political and religious center of the nation.

By the early eighteenth century English colonists had begun to press on Cherokee territory, and the Cherokee responded with force. In 1715 they made an alliance with the Yamassee and raided all along the Carolinas' frontier, destroying hundreds of homes and farms and nearly overrunning South Carolina. But the American colonies soon rallied, drove the Cherokee back, and forced them to sue for peace. In 1721 Cherokee leaders signed a treaty with colonial officials that fixed the boundary line with South Carolina and established trade regulations favoring the English, and over the next decades English agents made strenuous efforts to keep the Cherokee on their side. This was no easy task, for the Cherokee suspected that the English appetite for land was endless and feared for their remaining territory. Further, while the French and Spanish intermarried with the Cherokee and tended to deal with them on more equal terms, the English held themselves apart and treated the Cherokee as inferiors. Only a combination of threats and trade inducements enabled the English to suppress Cherokee grievances.

Events in the 1750s finally severed these fragile ties. When the English and French again went to war in 1754, only the most arduous English efforts persuaded the Cherokee to enter the conflict on Great Britain's side. But five years of seemingly bungled campaigns left the Cherokee thoroughly disenchanted with their English allies, and in 1759 they joined a confederation of the Iroquois, Mohawk, Delaware, and Shawnee Nations. Once again the Cherokee attacked settlements all along the Carolinas' frontier and temporarily pushed back the European advance. But subsequent colonial counterattacks broke the power of the Cherokee Nation and altered their history forever. In 1759, 1,600 colonial troops under Colonel William Montgomery wrecked a number of towns on the Tuckasegee and Hiwassee Rivers, destroyed crops and food stores, and forced the surviving Cherokee to take refuge in the Smoky Mountains. Undaunted, the Cherokee mobilized new forces, and in June 1760 they surprised a second colonial expedition and forced it to retreat. The Cherokee then besieged Fort Loudon, near what is now Loudon, Tennessee, and compelled the garrison to surrender.

The Cherokee victory was short-lived, however. The following year 2,600 colonial soldiers defeated a Cherokee force near Fort Loudon, recaptured the fort, and destroyed another 15 Cherokee towns. Again the survivors fled to the Smokies, where they lived on what they could gather from the forests. At about the same time Virginia troops marched down the Holston River as far as Great Island, where Kingston, Tennessee now stands. Recognizing that continued resistance was futile, a delegation from the Middle and Upper Towns met the colonials and sued for peace. Cherokee losses in this war were grievous. English estimates of the number of soldiers the Cherokee Nation could field dropped from 5,000 in 1759 to 2,300 in 1762. Unable to contest English demands, over the next ten years the Cherokee ceded their claims to all territory north of the Tennessee River and east of the Blue Ridge, territory that included their best hunting lands.[1]

The first great wave of European settlement into the southern Appalachians, including the Great Smoky Mountains, began just after the Seven Years War. Settlers came in three broad streams: down the Great Appalachian Valley from

In 1776 hundreds of Cherokee warriors attacked white settlements on the frontiers of Georgia and the Carolinas.

Pennsylvania, west from the settled parts of North Carolina, and northwest from South Carolina and eastern Georgia. They were remarkably diverse in origin and included Scotch-Irish, English, Germans, Welch, French Huguenots, and other Western European groups. They were equally diverse in occupation and status, for land speculators, merchants, wealthy farmers with slaves, small farmers, artisans, clergy, hunters, explorers, criminals, rebels, and indentured servants who had served out their time or fled their employment all arrived in the Southern Appalachians. These settlers came for many different reasons and with different means, but two things they had in common were a lack of regard for the Native Americans who held the land and a lack of respect for English treaties and borders.

The first permanent settlements were planted in the Smokies in 1771, when adventurers from southwest Virginia built three tiny villages on the Watauga and Holston Rivers. The settlements all lay within Cherokee territory and beyond the English Proclamation Line of 1763, which had fixed the limit of American settlement. North Carolina had made some claims to this territory, but the settlements had no legal basis, and the state provided no protection and no administrative or legal functions. Unfazed, the expedition leaders organized their own government, the Watauga Association, and paid the Cherokee $6,000.00 in goods in return for an eight-year lease of the territory.[2]

Perhaps because of their recent defeats, the Cherokee initially tolerated the fledgling settlements. But when England and the colonies came to blows in 1775, and when a delegation from the Shawnee, Iroquois, Mohawk, and Delaware Nations came to the council house at Chote to propose an alliance against the Americans, the Cherokee proved receptive. Two older leaders, Oconasta and Atakullakulla, argued against war, but the remainder favored seizing this opportunity to throw back the American settlements. In the spring of 1776 hundreds of Cherokee warriors, armed and supplied by British agents, again fell on the frontier of the Carolinas and Georgia and did great damage, especially in South Carolina. Then in August a smaller force moved secretly against the Watauga settlements, planning to eliminate them. But Nancy Ward, the niece of the Cherokee leader Atakullakulla and an influential spiritual leader, sent warning to Isaac Thomas, a merchant operating a trading post near what is now Sevierville. Thomas passed the warning on to the Watauga leaders, and volunteers from the settlements and Virginia quickly assembled. On August 20, American and Cherokee forces met at Long Island. A day-long battle left many dead and wounded on both sides, but in the end the Cherokee turned back, leaving the Watauga settlements intact.

The colonies-turned-states were quick to take their revenge. In the previous decades of war with Native Americans, European settlers had learned that the way to victory lay not in winning battles but in destroying the enemy's economic foundations. By burning towns, trampling fields, destroying or carrying away food stores, driving off livestock, and selling women and children as slaves, the colonists undermined the ability and the will of Native Americans to continue fighting. The Americans would now put these lessons to use against the Cherokee. In a rare instance of inter-colonial cooperation, Virginia, Georgia, and the Carolinas organized three separate expeditions. In August, General Griffin Rutherford led 2,400 North Carolina volunteers through the Swananona and Balsam Gaps toward the Tuckasegee and Oconaluftee settlements. Cherokee forces attempted to block his advance at Wayah Gap in the Nantahala Mountains, but while Rutherford suffered 40 killed and wounded in the encounter, he eventually pushed the defenders away from the gap. American forces then systematically destroyed 36 towns. Shortly thereafter, 1,800 men from South Carolina under Colonel Andrew Williamson wrecked the Lower Cherokee towns on the Savannah River, while another 2,000 volunteers from Virginia and North Carolina under Colonel William Christian destroyed more towns on the Little Tennessee River.

These expeditions severely diminished Cherokee military power and proved devastating to the whole nation. In 1777 some Cherokee refugees made new settlements on the Coosa River, while hundreds of others abandoned their territory, retreated southeast toward what is now Chattanooga, built new settlements on the Chickamauga River, and took a new name, the Chickamauga. The remainder of the nation determined to make peace before the Americans could organize additional expeditions. In the Treaty of Long Island, signed on July 20, 1777, the Cherokee again ceded all territory east of the Blue Ridge Mountains, along with the disputed lands on the Watauga, upper Holston, Nolachucky, and New Rivers. They also agreed to allow an agent from the American states to live in the nation's new political and religious center, Chote, to .

monitor Cherokee activities.

What appeared to be a decisive settlement proved to be only a truce. In 1780 the Loyalist commander Colonel Patrick Ferguson threatened to bring his force across the mountains and subdue the settlements there. Volunteers from North Carolina, Virginia, and Watauga mobilized in response and marched east. They found Ferguson on King's Mountain and destroyed nearly his entire force. Their departure left the frontier relatively undefended, however, and the Cherokee immediately launched a new series of raids. So in December 1780 Colonel Arthur Campbell and Colonel John Sevier, just returned from King's Mountain, led 700 mounted men from Virginia and Watauga back into Cherokee territory. American forces ambushed a Cherokee army on Boyd's Creek, defeated it decisively, and burned another ten towns, including Tellico, Hiwassee, and Chote, along with 50,000 bushels of stored corn. The following March Sevier took a small picked force of mounted men, crossed the Smoky Mountains over trails barely passable for horses, destroyed six towns near what is now Franklin, North Carolina, and disappeared before Cherokee troops could assemble. And when in the summer of 1781 Cherokee troops again raided new American settlements on the French Broad River near what is now Newport, Tennessee, Sevier took 100 men, surprised the Cherokee camp, killed 12 men, and scattered the rest.

The Cherokee continued to resist American expansion in the 1780s and 1790s, though with little success. While ceding additional lands in the Treaty of Long Island (1781) and the Treaty of Hopwell (1785), lands that the states used

Colonel John Sevier led numerous raids against Cherokee towns on both the east and west sides of the Great Smoky Mountains.

to reward Revolutionary War veterans, the Cherokee continued to harass new American settlements, particularly the fledgling town of Knoxville. Sevier in turn led two final retaliatory expeditions against the Cherokee, one of which penetrated all the way to Cherokee towns in Georgia. Unable to bear the costs of this conflict any longer, in 1798 the Cherokee admitted defeat for the last time. In the Treaty of Tellico they signed away their lands on the Clinch, Little Tennessee, French Broad, and Pigeon Rivers, opening the way for further American settlement in the Smokies. Even so, the Cherokee still held substantial territory in Tennessee, Georgia, and the Carolinas. An American census in 1800 put the Cherokee population at 20,000.[3]

Americans began moving into the Smokies in large numbers in the 1780s.

National Anthropological Archives, Smithsonian Institute

The Shawnee leader Tecumseh argued for joining the British for a fight against the Americans.

The first generations of settlers took lands mostly in the valleys of the French Broad, Pigeon, Tuckasegee, Oconaluftee, Nolachucky, and Little Tennessee Rivers and along smaller waterways such as Scott's Creek and Jonathan's Creek. The lands along these rivers and streams were readily accessible, level, and productive, while the waterways provided cheap transportation for grain, livestock, and other bulky goods. The most successful of these early families acquired thousands or even tens of thousands of acres of the best land, laying the foundations of family fortunes for generations to follow. The children and grandchildren of these wealthy families then tended to marry into other wealthy families, creating kinship networks that would eventually grow into a Great Smoky Mountains elite. Not all the early settlers

succeeded, of course, and certainly there was room for those who came later to make their own fortunes. Even so, many leaders in the late antebellum period were the descendents of these first successful settlers. Perhaps the most remarkable of these early settlers was Colonel Robert Love, one of the many Revolutionary War veterans who came to the mountains when that conflict ended. Love first took up lands near Sevierville, but after a few years he sold his property there, came back across the mountains, and began accumulating holdings in North Carolina. Eventually Love would put together a sprawling empire of 375,000 acres known as the Love Tract and found the town of Waynesville. Love, his sons, and his grandsons would all play leading roles in the affairs of Haywood County.

The other sites favored by the early settlers were the numerous Smoky Mountain coves, including Weir, Tuckaleechee, and Jones coves in Sevier County, Miller and Cades coves in Blount, and Big and Little Cataloochee in Haywood. Coves offered their own substantial advantages: level and fertile land for farming, rich pastures for cattle on the mountain slopes and balds, and protection from the extremes of both summer and winter. But as the favored territory in the river valleys and coves filled, settlers had to take less productive lands on the smallest waterways, on the lower slopes near roads established by the Cherokee and, finally, on the higher and more remote elevations.

Settlement in the Smokies, especially in the early years, was anything but orderly. Speculators staked out huge tracts of land and then sought to resell small parcels to later settlers. Some made fortunes in the process, while others failed disastrously.

Early settlers who were not so affluent made their own claims singly or as members of organized expeditions such as the Watauga enterprise. North Carolina was slow to establish land offices in the Smokies, and many early claims had to be voided or reestablished. More orderly procedures came with the establishment of state land offices, the distribution of land bounties to Revolutionary War veterans, and the formation of county governments. In 1784, while the region was still part of North Carolina, Sevier County was organized from lands in Greene County, and Sevierville became the tiny county seat in 1795. Cocke County was divided off from Jefferson County in 1797, and Blount County was established in 1795. On the North Carolina side, Haywood County was formed in 1808, while Macon followed in 1828 and Cherokee in 1839. Jackson County, laid off from lands in Haywood and Macon, was not organized until 1851.[4]

Having failed to block American expansion, the Cherokee attempted accommodation. When Britain and the United States went to war in 1812, British agents offered the Cherokee arms and supplies if they would enter the conflict against the Americans. The Shawnee leader Tecumseh urged the Cherokee to join his newly formed confederation, but Junaluska argued that war with the Americans would again result in disaster, and the Cherokee rebuffed both the British and Tecumseh. In 1813 they further gambled on American success by sending 800 troops to join General Andrew Jackson's expedition against the Lower Creeks. After Jackson's forces won a series of desperate and costly battles and destroyed several Creek towns, Creek soldiers fell back to Horseshoe Bend

National Portrait Gallery, Smithsonian Institute, artist Charles Torrey

General Andrew Jackson was greatly aided by Cherokee soldiers at the Battle of Horseshoe Bend. However, as president, he ordered the forced relocation of nearly the entire Cherokee nation to Oklahoma.

on the Tallapoosa River and took up positions behind a series of stout breastworks and fortifications. Jackson then brought up his artillery, shelled the Creek positions, and ordered a frontal assault. But when the Creek troops held their lines and threw the Americans back with considerable loss, it appeared that Jackson was stymied. At that moment, however, the Cherokee force that had been sent across the river to block the Creek line of retreat seized a flotilla of canoes, came back across the river, and assaulted the Creek position from the rear. Surprised, the Creek line wavered, and Jackson quickly ordered a second assault. Caught between two forces, the Creek army broke, and most were shot or drowned attempting to flee across the river.

North Carolina Division of Archives and History

Colonel William Holland Thomas commanded a massive and diversified business empire in western North Carolina. He helped the Cherokee buy land near the Great Smoky Mountains and became their appointed leader.

Sadly, the Cherokee received no reward for their service. While many of their soldiers were off with Jackson, white settlers continued to encroach on Cherokee territory, and both the federal government and the governments of Tennessee, North Carolina, and Georgia refused to intervene. Then in 1819 American representatives forced the Cherokee to sign the Treaty of Tellico, in which they abandoned another 6,000 square miles in Tennessee, Georgia, Alabama, and North Carolina. The lost territory included nearly all the remaining Cherokee lands in the Smoky Mountains.[5]

Despite these bitter blows, the Cherokee continued their attempts to meet American demands and conform to American ways. In 1820 the Cherokee Nation, most of which now lay in Georgia, formally adopted a republican government with a national legislature and regional councils. Imitating their white neighbors, the Cherokee also began working their fields with iron plows, horses, and oxen, employing black slaves, pasturing cattle, operating cotton gins and grain mills, mining gold, and building Western style log or frame houses. They also developed a written language, adopted a formal written constitution, established a national press, and allowed white clergy to establish schools and missions in Cherokee towns.

But not all Cherokee left the mountains, and not all chose to accommodate to American ways. In a curious provision, the 1819 Treaty of Tellico set aside 640 acres of land in western North Carolina for each head of household who was considered capable of supporting a family. Yonaguska (or Drowning Bear), who had helped lead Cherokee troops at the Battle of Horseshoe Bend, was granted land near the confluence of the Tuckasegee and Oconaluftee Rivers, near what is now Bryson City. Yonaguska farmed, built a new council house at Soco, and became the political and spiritual leader of the perhaps 60 other Cherokee households who were granted land along the Oconaluftee River and Soco Creek, in what would become Jackson and Cherokee Counties. Eventually these Cherokee assumed an identity separate from that of the main Cherokee nation. They became known as the Oconaluftee or Quallatown or mountain Cherokee, and by most accounts they retained far more of their traditional religious beliefs and cultural practices than the main Cherokee Nation.

So the Cherokee retained a hold in the Smokies, but their lands were poor, their existence sparse, and their position precarious.[6]

It was about this time that a man named William Holland Thomas first entered Cherokee affairs. Thomas was a man of extraordinary talent, energy, and ambition, and for 40 years he would play a leading role in western North Carolina. Born in 1805 on Raccoon Creek, near what is now Waynesville, Thomas left home at age 12 and worked as a clerk in Felix Walker's store in Quallatown. The store failed after three years, and rather than the $100 he had been promised, Thomas received a set of old law books. Undeterred, the following year Thomas opened his own store on Soco Creek. Most of Thomas's business came from Cherokee families who had been forced to move west of the Nantahala Mountains but who still came to Soco Creek to trade. The store (and the farm Thomas's mother bought in 1819) were near Yonaguska's land, and young Thomas soon became friends with the older man. Yonaguska taught Thomas the Cherokee language and Cherokee traditions, and eventually adopted him as his son.

Over the next 30 years Thomas built a business empire in western North Carolina, including a network of stores in Cherokee and Jackson Counties, iron and copper mines, mills, a blacksmith shop, a tannery, a wagon manufactory, a shoe and boot shop, and a fleet of wagons and teams to haul freight to Georgia and South Carolina. He acquired over 100,000 acres in North Carolina, Tennessee, Georgia, and Alabama, operated two small turnpikes, employed dozens of slaves, endlessly loaned and borrowed money, and promoted road- and railroad-building projects. Thomas's business affairs eventually grew beyond his ability to manage, but while his empire survived he enjoyed both wealth and influence. Thomas became business partners with two other important men in Haywood County, James R. Love and William Welch, and in 1858 he married Sarah Jane Burney Love, granddaughter of Colonel Robert Love. James R. Love, the grandson of Colonel Robert Love, was a successful landowner and politician, while Welch was a state senator. Thomas also served in the state legislature from 1848 through 1862, where he tirelessly advocated the interests of western North Carolina.

In 1831 the Quallatown Cherokee appointed Thomas their attorney, advisor, and business manager. Following this appointment, Thomas spent nearly ten years lobbying to secure the Quallatown Cherokee their share of treaty payments. He then used a portion of these payments, along with his own funds, to purchase additional lands for the Cherokee in the Smokies. Because North Carolina law denied the Cherokee the right to own land, Thomas held the deeds in his own name. When Yonaguska was near death, he persuaded the Cherokee to name Thomas his successor. The Cherokee were under increasing pressure to cede all their remaining lands in Georgia and North Carolina, and appointing Thomas their leader gave the Quallatown Cherokee unusual political influence.

Thomas thus enjoyed remarkable latitude over the affairs of the Quallatown Cherokee. But the results of his leadership were mixed. On the one hand, Thomas served a critical role as mediator between

Alonzo Chappel ca. 1850

General Winfield Scott was charged with marching the Cherokee westward along what would become known as the "Trail of Tears."

the Quallatown Cherokee and the federal government, the state of North Carolina, and the Cherokee's white neighbors. He labored to protect their interests and used his business and legal expertise for their benefit. At the same time, Thomas thoroughly mixed his own and the tribe's business affairs and almost certainly profited from his position as leader. And his mismanagement in later years mired the tribe in debts and land claims, involving the Quallatown Cherokee in years of litigation and endangering their holdings.[7]

Andrew Jackson's election as president in 1828 set off the last great conflict between expansionist whites and the Cherokee. Since 1820 the state of Georgia had been pressuring the federal government to remove all remaining Cherokee from the state's boundaries, pressure that increased

considerably when gold was discovered on Cherokee territory. Within a month of Jackson's election, the Georgia legislature summarily extinguished all Cherokee land titles, voided all Cherokee laws, and approved legislation preventing the Cherokee from bringing suit or testifying against whites, holding public assembly, or mining gold. Georgia also required all clergy working in Cherokee missions and schools to take a special oath of allegiance to the state, and immediately imprisoned a dozen ministers who refused to do so. The United States Congress then passed two Removal Acts authorizing the president to force all Native American groups remaining in the East to relocate west of the Mississippi River, and Jackson promptly sent commissioners to the Cherokee and other groups. The Cherokee and their allies fought back, but with little success. In 1832 Samuel Worcester, one of the ministers imprisoned in Georgia, brought suit against the State of Georgia. The Supreme Court ruled that the Cherokee were in fact an established nation and that the State of Georgia had no right to violate its territory, but Georgia defied the decision, and Jackson blatantly refused to enforce it.

In the meantime white residents in Georgia were busy with their own removal campaign. Under the cover of the federal and state acts they seized Cherokee lands and houses, drove off cattle, tore up roads, and whipped, beat, and killed Cherokee inhabitants. Even so the Cherokee held fast, and by 1837 only 2,000, out of an estimated population of 17,000, had agreed to relocate. Among that 2,000, however, was a coterie of leaders who had concluded that once again the only way to survive was by acceding to white pressure. Led by Major

John Ridge, in March 1835 they traveled to Washington, D.C. and negotiated a removal treaty with the Federal commissioner, the Reverend J. F. Schermerhorn. In October, Schermerhorn traveled to Georgia and summoned the whole Cherokee Nation to Red Clay to ratify the treaty. Though only 300-500 Cherokee attended, Schermerhorn considered the treaty final and sent it back to Washington for approval. The Cherokee Nation strenuously protested Schermerhorn's handling of the treaty negotiations, and even Army officers sent to carry out the removal informed Jackson that the treaty was a gross fraud. But Jackson considered the matter closed, declared that the Cherokee Nation no longer existed, and refused any further communications with them. In May 1838 Jackson sent 7,000 Regular Army, militia, and volunteer troops under General Winfield Scott to carry out the removal by force. Scott's men systematically drove Cherokee families off their lands and concentrated them into 12 camps, where they awaited the march west. White families immediately moved in behind to take over the vacated farms.

The Quallatown Cherokee had watched apprehensively as the removal campaign developed. But in a remarkable stroke of policy they had, with Thomas's help, effectively established themselves as a separate entity from the main Cherokee Nation. When the Removal Acts were passed, the Quallatown Cherokee thus claimed that they were exempt from the Acts' provisions. The Cherokee also found some support from their white neighbors, for in 1837 24 men from Haywood County sent a memorandum to Governor Edwin B. Dudley asserting that the Cherokee were "fast improving in civilization, knowledge of the arts and agriculture" and "were becoming good citizens." Though Scott believed it would be preferable for all the Cherokee to relocate, he was uncertain of his authority to move against the Quallatown Cherokee and initially left them alone. But when refugees from the Cherokee Nation who had avoided Scott's troops or escaped the camps began hiding in the Smokies, Scott threatened to drive all the Cherokee from the mountains. The position of the Quallatown Cherokee worsened further when one Cherokee band killed three soldiers and then fled to the Smokies. At this point Thomas intervened decisively. He persuaded the Quallatown Cherokee to sign an agreement not only to deny sanctuary to members of the main Cherokee Nation, but also to assist in apprehending refugees if necessary. Thomas also claimed that he personally went to Tsali, the leader of the band that had killed Scott's troops, and persuaded him to surrender. Unfortunately, Thomas's own account of his actions throughout this period remains thoroughly suspect. At the same time that he was negotiating for the Quallatown Cherokee, he was not only engaged in a land deal with Schermerhorn, but was also operating trading posts near the concentration camps. It seems clear, however, that Thomas's ultimate intent was to protect the Quallatown Cherokee at whatever cost, even if that meant trading on the interests of the Cherokee Nation. The Quallatown Cherokee found other help as well. Levi Caldwell, one of the first settlers in Cataloochee, several times gave food and blankets to Cherokee refugees

TABLE 1			
COUNTY	WHITES	SLAVES	SLAVEHOLDERS
Blount	11,907	1,363	241
Cocke	9,559	849	172
Sevier	8,584	538	96
Cherokee	9,166	520	97
Haywood	5,801	313	61
Jackson	5,501	268	44
Macon	6,004	519	62

during that terrible winter, and others may have done the same.

Thus, in the end, the Quallatown Cherokee remained in the Smokies, joined by perhaps 1,000 refugees from Georgia. Their lands were poor, their opportunities were severely limited, their political position was fragile and ill-defined, and their status was third-class. Even so they remained, and thereby helped create in the Smoky Mountains a curious multi-racial society that, unequal as it was, was rare in the antebellum United States.[8]

The farming economy that developed in the Smoky Mountains was highly diversified. The limitations imposed by climate, terrain, and soil made the large-scale cultivation of cotton and tobacco, the cash crops that drove the economies of other parts of the South and created so much wealth, impractical. Conditions were amenable to many other products, however, and Smoky Mountain farmers cultivated corn, wheat, oats, rye, buckwheat, and other grains, white and sweet potatoes, apples, peaches, apricots, cherries, grapes,

and other fruit, and feed crops such as clover, alfalfa, timothy, and ryegrass. With so many options available, the success of families depended to a considerable extent upon their ability to weigh soil conditions, weather, available labor, and markets and determine how best to use their land every year. Most farm families also owned at least a few cattle and hogs for meat and milk, poultry for meat and eggs, horses or mules for farm work and transportation, and, in some cases, sheep for wool and meat.

The simple realities of climate, terrain, and soil had profound consequences for the Smoky Mountains. The lack of a cash crop, combined with other economic limitations, left the Smokies (and indeed all the southern Appalachians) at a distinct economic disadvantage. Many farmers turned to wheat as an alternative cash crop, and their production found a ready market in Augusta, Charleston, and Savannah. But wheat was not nearly so lucrative as cotton or tobacco, and most Smoky Mountain families were simply unable to generate wealth on the same scale as families in other regions of the South. This, in turn, meant that they owned far fewer slaves and had less capital available to improve farms and invest in roads, railroads, and other enterprises. The end result was a society that differed significantly from other parts of the South, though exactly what those differences were or what they meant remain topics of dispute.

Farming practices in the Smokies varied greatly. In the river valleys, where the land was well watered and the soil rich, farms tended to be larger, generally 200-500 acres, and farmers were more likely to employ additional labor, experiment with different seed types and livestock breeds, and employ progressive techniques such as crop rotation and fertilization. These families were able to produce a considerable surplus beyond their immediate needs and to sell the excess production on the market. Away from the river valleys farms were generally smaller, ranging from 50 to 200 acres. Most production went to the family's immediate needs, and family members provided almost all the labor. And at the far end of the spectrum were the small, barely developed farms found on the higher elevations and in the most remote locations. These farms were generally 50 acres or less, with most of the land left in timber or pasture. Here families lived by raising corn and other crops on small plots, hunting, cutting timber, grazing hogs in the woods, and trading hides, furs, ginseng, and other forest products. It is important to note, however, that these categories are only rough generalizations. Not all large farms were well managed or profitable, and certainly not all smaller farms were backward. Most farm families in the Smokies could expect to produce enough to eat, clothe themselves, buy extra goods such as coffee and tools, and perhaps save to buy additional land.[9]

In the antebellum Smokies, labor beyond the immediate family came from two sources, African-American slaves, and landless whites. Slavery was not at all common in the Smokies, and its role in the economy was limited. This was true not because inhabitants opposed the institution, but rather because most families lacked the resources to purchase slaves. As shown in Table 1, slaveholders made up a tiny percentage of the population, particularly in comparison with other parts of Tennessee and North Carolina, while the number of slaves in the Smokies was also strikingly small. Equally important, slaves and slaveholders were concentrated in particular regions within the Smoky Mountains area: the river valleys, where productive land provided the means and the motive to own slaves; and the larger towns, where professionals and successful merchants employed slaves as house servants and artisans. Slaveholding was also concentrated by family. In Jackson County just eight families owned 170 of the county's 268 slaves. The 15 largest slaveholders held 219 slaves, or 82 percent of the total. In Macon 13 families owned a total of 268 slaves, while the 36 largest slaveholders held 426 of the county's slaves. The Love family figured prominently in this area: Dillard Love of Macon claimed 71 slaves, James R. Love of Haywood held 58, and John B. Love of Jackson owned 49.[10]

White labor, on the other hand, was readily available. The percentage of families in the Smokies who owned their own land was significantly lower than in other parts of Tennessee and North Carolina, and this provided a large pool of farm workers. Most white laborers were employed as tenants, though some also worked for daily wages. Typically a tenant would receive a plot of land to farm, a house to live in, and one-half to two-thirds of the crops raised. In turn, tenants turned the remainder of the crop over to the land-holder, repaired and improved buildings and fences, and, in theory at least, followed the landowner's directions. Tenancy offered laborers some measure of independence and status and eliminated the need for any exchange of money, an important feature in a society in which currency was limited. It may also have contributed to social stabili-ty by partially masking the distinc-tion between landed and landless, by creating a common set of interests between landholder and tenant, and by giving tenants the opportunity to purchase their own land at some point. Too often, however, that opportunity proved to be an illusion, and many tenant families remained poor and landless their whole lives. Further, while tenancy required only limited oversight by landholders, it also limited their ability to mange their property.[11]

Throughout the antebellum period most families in the Smokies attempted to meet as many economic needs as possible from their own holdings. They grew most of their own food, wove and dyed much of their own cloth, made their own clothes, produced candles from beeswax or tallow, and built furniture and other household items. At the same time, most families also managed to produce at least a small surplus beyond their own needs, whether in grain, meat, eggs, butter, hides, or other items

such as ginseng. These they traded for items they could not produce themselves, such as coffee, sugar, farm implements, tools, hardware, shoes, fine cloth, firearms, and luxury items such as books. The trading store, therefore, played a critical role in the economy of the antebellum Smokies. Stores purchased the excess production of the region (barring that of large farmers who marketed their own crops), sold some to nearby town residents, and hauled the rest to large markets such as Augusta, Athens, and Charleston. They also brought in goods from suppliers in Baltimore, Philadelphia, Washington, D.C. and other Eastern cities and sold these to farm and town families. Many merchants further expanded their operations by running craft shops and selling the items produced there in their stores. Trading stores offered extensive cred-it, sometimes settling accounts only once a year, and operated on both a barter and a cash basis.

Merchants, thus, provided vital market-ing and financial services and often provided the only connection Smoky Mountains residents had with other regions. In turn, they tended to be relative-ly wealthy and influential. One of the most prominent merchants in the Smokies was Joseph Cathey, owner of a store at Forks of Pigeon in Haywood County. Cathey sent smoked meat, tanned hides, feathers, apples, and other local products to markets in Charleston, Columbia, Athens, and Savannah, and brought back saddles, tools, salt, gunpowder, paint, glass, and other goods. He also owned several farms and a mill, served as a delegate to the state con-stitutional convention in 1835, was elected to the state senate in 1842, and was one of the wealthiest men in the county. Another successful merchant was Jesse Siler, owner of a store, a tannery, and a blacksmith shop near Franklin.[12]

Some goods did not have to be hauled, but instead moved on their own feet. One of the more remarkable features of the antebellum economy was the vast movement of livestock from East Tennessee and western North Carolina to markets in the Southeast. The cotton growing regions around Savannah and Charleston generated a huge demand for meat as well as grain, and residents of East Tennessee and western North Carolina, including those in the Smokies, soon began driving herds of cattle and hogs to these markets. By the 1850s, 150,000-175,000 hogs passed over the Buncombe Turnpike every year, along with tens of thousands of cattle, and even chickens and turkeys. This trade in livestock offered significant opportunities to residents along the route. Both men and livestock required not only places to stay every night but also substantial amounts of food, so entrepreneurs opened special inns, called stands, about every ten miles along the Turnpike. Stands included pens for the livestock, large stores of corn, and hostels for the drivers, and they bought substantial amounts of corn and other products from local farms.[13]

A third important segment of the antebellum economy in the Smokies was the craft industry. Craftsmen played a critical role by providing goods and services residents lacked the skills to make themselves. Blacksmiths produced basic metal goods, repaired farm implements and household items, and shod horses and mules. Tanners converted cowhides into leather and fabricated a variety of leather

goods. Other craftsmen commonly found in the Smoky Mountains were cobblers, wagon makers, millers, carpenters, and stone masons. In 1860, for example, Jackson County had eight blacksmiths, four carpenters, four commercial millers, two shoemakers, and a tanner. Like merchants, craftsmen operated on trade, credit, and cash, and frequently they owned land and farmed in addition to operating their craft business. Generally they were not so wealthy or influential as merchants, but they made equally vital contributions to their communities.[14]

The final sector of the Smokies' economy was the exploitation of the region's vast resources of timber and ore. The forests were rich in a whole range of valuable hardwoods and softwoods, and the mountains held deposits of copper, iron, and other ores. In the antebellum period, however, mining and lumbering enterprises remained small in scale. By the 1840s, several small sawmills were operating in both the Tennessee and the North Carolina Smokies, but a lack of capital to develop large-scale lumbering operations, and a lack of any means to transport timber to markets cheaply, precluded large-scale cutting until after the Civil War. Mining enterprises were somewhat more common. Daniel D. Foute established an iron forge in Cades Cove in 1827 and for nearly 20 years produced iron blooms and finished products such as wagon wheels, plowshare points, and kettles. Other forges operated in Miller's Cove, in the Pearl Valley, and on the Little Pigeon River. In 1853 William Holland Thomas bought 3,000 acres between Webster and Scott's Creek and opened several iron mines there, while oth-

National Park Archives

Daniel D. Foute of Cades Cove was punished for his alignment with the Confederacy. He was arrested and imprisoned in Knoxville and died there of pneumonia in 1865.

ers established copper mines on Sugar Loaf Mountain, Cullowhee Mountain, and Savannah Creek. Smoky Mountains residents also attempted to exploit more obscure resources. From 1837 to 1842, for example, the Epsom Salts Manufacturing Company took saltpeter, magnesium, alum, and copperate out of Alum Cave. The high cost of transportation forced the company to close, but the mines were reopened in 1862. Other companies profitably quarried marble and slate in Cocke and Blount Counties. The most reliable evaluation of the Smokies' resources came from Daniel David Davis, an engineer for the Pittsburgh mining and engineering firm of John D. Gray and Company. In 1856 the company sent Davis to western North Carolina to evaluate mineral deposits there. Davis found what he believed were substantial deposits of mica and copper in Jackson County and advised his employer to buy the mineral rights. The company declined, citing insoluble transportation problems. Davis then quit the company, formed a partnership with five Jackson County men, and began buying up the rights on thousands of acres. But as always the Smokies' mineral resources remained more a promise than a reality in the antebellum period. The state geologist stated that Jackson County held no known copper deposits, discouraging investment, and the coming of the Civil War put an end to the new company. In 1862 the Confederate government sent Davis to England and Wales to purchase copper smelting equipment. Davis set out for an open port, but he was captured in East Tennessee. When he refused to divulge his business, Union authorities imprisoned him in Indiana. Davis eventually proved his British citizenship and was released.[15]

By far the greatest barrier to the development of lumbering, mining, commercial agriculture and every other economic enterprise in the Smoky Mountains was the lack of effective transportation. Until the railroads penetrated the Smokies, the costs of shipping bulky goods such as ore, timber, and grain on a large scale were simply prohibitive. In other areas of the country rivers provided cheap transport, but in the Smokies the rivers were too shallow and narrow to support large-scale shipping, and in any case they did not connect with neighboring markets. Other regions of the country also built roads surfaced with gravel or stone that reduced the costs and difficulties of freight hauling, but lack of capital, combined with the challenging terrain, limited road building in the Smokies. The lack of effective transportation certainly did not result from an absence of interest or effort. Leaders in the Smokies, as in all the southern Appalachians, fully recognized the value of improved transportation, and the antebellum period was full of schemes for road and rail networks. The vision, however, almost always exceeded the means, and only a small number of these projects was actually completed.

Roads were built, to be sure. One of the chief functions of the county courts at this time was to lay out, build, and maintain local roads, and state law required every voter to contribute several days' labor each year toward this end. Thus most communities had at least some sort of road connection with their neighbors, though these ranged from dirt tracks, sometimes mixed with stone, to mere trails cut through forests. The state governments of North Carolina and Tennessee also chartered a number of toll roads in the antebellum period to connect larger towns and further trade. For example, in 1825 the Haywood County Court chartered a toll road to provide improved access to Cataloochee. Residents could purchase stock in the road, and Court granted two local men a contract to build and maintain the road. The first such road that could serve the Smokies, the Buncombe Turnpike, was completed in 1820. This road began in Greeneville, Tennessee, ran through Madison, Buncombe, and Henderson Counties, North Carolina, and ended in Greenville, South Carolina, where it joined roads leading to Charleston and Augusta. A second toll road originat-

ing in Franklin and running south into Georgia followed in 1830. The Western North Carolina Turnpike, which began in Salisbury, reached Asheville by 1846 and was extended to Murphy a decade later, while smaller branches of the road had reached all the way to the Tuckasegee River by the start of the war. Together these roads gave Smoky Mountain residents improved links to major markets in South Carolina, Georgia, and central North Carolina. Several smaller toll roads were also completed in the 1850s, including one running from Jonathan's Creek through Mount Sterling Gap to Big Creek and Cataloochee, one linking Whittier, North Carolina with Sevierville, Tennessee by way of Indian Gap; one connecting Quallatown with Webster; and one running from Waynesville to Franklin.

Smoky Mountain residents, therefore, were by no means isolated. Regular stage lines ran weekly from Asheville to Clingman, Georgia via Waynesville and Franklin and from Greeneville, Tennessee to Greenville, South Carolina via Sevierville. Most communities also had weekly mail service by the 1830s. But even the best of these roads was slow, rough, and narrow, usually only wide enough for a single wagon. Only railroads offered a real solution to the region's transportation problems, and these were slow in coming. As early as 1835 South Carolina entrepreneurs developed plans for a railroad line that would have originated in Charleston, passed through western North Carolina, and continued on to Knoxville, Louisville, and Cincinnati. If completed, the line could have brought considerable benefits to the mountains. Both South Carolina and

Tennessee refused to charter the proposed company, however, and in any case the project was far too ambitious for the resources available. William Holland Thomas revived the scheme in 1850 and persuaded the North Carolina legislature to charter a railroad that would have connected Charleston and Cincinnati by way of Macon County. The new company managed to lay only 15 miles of track before collapsing, however. Hopes for a railroad connection then turned to the Western North Carolina Railroad, which was to run from Salisbury to Asheville to the North Carolina border. This railroad did not even reach Asheville until 1879 and proceeded no further until years later.

The Tennessee side fared somewhat better. The Great Valley of East Tennessee offered an obvious route for a rail line, and in 1849 the State of Tennessee chartered two rail companies, the East Tennessee and Georgia and East Tennessee and Virginia railroads. Their lines, completed in the mid-1850s, ran the entire length of the Tennessee Valley from Chattanooga to Bristol and connected with other rail lines in Georgia, Alabama, Tennessee, and Virginia. Once completed, these lines gave the Tennessee Valley some of the best rail connections in the South. But the new railroads provided little benefits to the Tennessee Smokies, for most residents remained too far away to haul large amounts of goods to and from the closest depots. As on the North Carolina side, branch railroads were not built into the mountains until after the Civil War.[16]

Churches were a fundamental, though also fragile, element of Smokies society. Given the dispersed population, most churches were small, often with 50 or fewer members, and they met anywhere from once a week to once a month. While some could afford to pay their own pastor, others shared clergy with different churches or depended on itinerant ministers to hold services. Baptists and Methodists predominated, though Presbyterians and many other denominations were present. Periodic revivals partially compensated for the lack of regular church services. One of the most famous revival spots in the Smokies was Shook's Campground, located near Clyde in Haywood County. Jacob Shook, a Revolutionary War veteran and one of the county's first settlers, donated land for the campground and also set aside a room in his house for traveling ministers. The campground held 40 small tents for families along with a large meeting tent, and revivals tended to run for a week or more. Those attending were awakened at daylight and heard preaching at 8:00 a.m., 11:00 a.m., 3:00 p.m., and twilight. Between services they attended prayer meetings, shared meals, and enjoyed the social interactions that revivals offered.[17]

Residents of the antebellum Smokies, thus, were far removed from the squalid, brawling hillbillies of later legend. They were, in fact, probably little different from rural residents all across the South. They cleared land, farmed, built homes, organized communities, established stores, schools, and churches, voted, and sought better economic opportunities. The question that Smokies residents would soon face was which government, the old Union or the new Confederate States, more closely reflected their values, their hopes for prosperity, and their way of life.

CHAPTER 2

SECESSION

N MANY WAYS THE STATE
LINE RUNNING THROUGH THE
GREAT SMOKY MOUNTAINS
WAS AN ARTIFICIAL BOUND-
ARY, FOR THE TENNESSEE
and North Carolina Smokies shared a
common heritage and common economic,
social, and cultural characteristics. Both
regions faced the same economic barriers,
and both were eager for improved
transportation and expanded commercial
opportunities. Both also resented the
perceived dominance of the slaveholding
regions of Tennessee and North Carolina
and their own lack of political influence.
Yet when the states of Tennessee and
North Carolina seceded in May 1861, the
two sides of the Smokies followed remarkably different courses. In North Carolina,
Cherokee, Haywood, Jackson, and Macon
Counties all gave large majorities for
secession, sent a high percentage of their
available men to the new Confederate
armies, and generously supported the troops
with food, clothing, and supplies.
Conversely, the Tennessee Smokies
opposed secession and refused to recognize
the Confederate government, even after
Tennessee separated from the Union. These
divergent courses created great tensions on
both sides of the mountains and eventually
resulted in a vicious cross-border conflict.
Yet as the war progressed the differences

between the two sides diminished. While
the Tennessee Smokies remained adamant-
ly opposed to the Confederate cause,
dissatisfaction with the war and the new
Southern government steadily increased
on the North Carolina side, eventually
resulting in open dissent.

At the beginning of the secession crisis,
few could have predicted the course that
each region would take. A significant proportion of residents in Tennessee, Virginia,
and North Carolina did not view the
election of Abraham Lincoln as an
immediate and intolerable threat to their
interests. They were not ready to abandon
the Union without another attempt at
compromise, and when South Carolina
seceded, many criticized the state for acting
on its own and recklessly precipitating a
crisis. Both Tennessee and North Carolina,
in fact, followed long, difficult, and nearly
parallel routes toward secession.

When the North Carolina legislature
opened its regular session on November 19,
1860 the dominant topic, not surprisingly,
was the state's response to Lincoln's victory.
In his opening address Governor John
Willis Ellis, a staunch Southern rights
advocate, urged legislators to authorize a
state convention to consider secession,
strengthen the state militia, grant him the
authority to accept 10,000 volunteers into
state service, and appoint delegates to a

proposed convention of all the slaveholding states. The legislators, however, were
fiercely divided in their views and were
slow to act. The Committee on Federal
Relations required nearly a month of
intense debate before it could submit a bill
to schedule elections for a state convention, reorganize the militia, and authorize
state volunteers. It also hedged these
measures by requiring that any secession
ordinance the convention might pass be
submitted to the voters for approval. Even
with this provision, conservative legislators
delayed a vote on the convention bill
until January.[1]

In the interim, supporters and opponents
of secession debated the issue in the press,
in public meetings, and in thousands of
private conversations and letters. Advocates
of secession argued that slavery could
survive only in a Southern Confederacy,
that the Union was already fractured
beyond repair, and that North Carolina's
economic interests required that it join the
seceding states. But opponents asserted that
secession would leave slavery more, not
less, vulnerable and insisted that the
Northern and Southern states could still
resolve this crisis peacefully. In western
North Carolina, United States Senator
Thomas L. Clingman and state senator
William Holland Thomas took the lead in
advocating secession, while Representative
Zebulon B. Vance, who would be elected
governor in 1862, was a leading opponent.[2]

On January 7, 1861 the legislators
returned to Raleigh to resume debate.
Passions remained high on both sides, and
several sessions ended in physical con-
frontations. Conservatives realized that
they could not block the convention bill
indefinitely, so eventually they shifted

Library of Congress

Representative Zebulon B. Vance of Buncombe
County, who would be elected governor of North
Carolina in 1862, actually opposed seceding from
the Union.

tactics and forced supporters of the bill to
accept an amendment giving voters the
power not only to elect delegates but also
to determine whether the convention
would be held at all. On January 29 the
convention bill finally passed, and the
election for convention delegates was set
for February 28. In the end, some conservatives joined advocates of secession in
voting for the bill, in the belief that a state
convention would actually reject secession
and that holding the convention might
satisfy the pressure for the state to take
some action.

With the convention bill finally out of

TABLE 2		
NORTH CAROLINA COUNTY	FOR SECESSION CONVENTION	AGAINST SECESSION CONVENTION
Cherokee	149	901
Haywood	504	307
Jackson	250	259
Macon	435	83

the way, the legislature took a number of other steps. With little debate it approved legislation that made all men ages 18 to 45 liable for military duty and authorized the governor to raise and equip 10,000 volunteers, a figure that could be increased to 20,000 in an emergency. It also sent delegates to two different conventions then being organized: the Washington Peace Conference, an unofficial gathering of moderate Northerners and Southerners hoping to find the great sectional compromise that had so far eluded the United States Congress; and a convention of delegates from the seceded states meeting in Montgomery. In keeping with its cautious approach, the legislature instructed the Montgomery delegates to press for a national reconciliation on the basis of the Crittenden Resolutions, but also to consider all measures necessary to "our common peace, honor, and safety."[3]

The results of the February 28 referendum revealed that voters were every bit as divided as their representatives. The secession convention failed by fewer than 1,000 votes, with 46,672 in favor and 47,323 opposed. Some observers speculated that the vote was influenced by reports that the Washington Peace Conference was

preparing to issue sweeping compromise proposals. These reports proved false, but they may have fed conservative and moderate hopes that the crisis could be resolved peacefully.[4] The tallies for the Smokies region are shown in Table 2. Northern leaders found North Carolina's rejection of secession cheering, but the state's appearance of loyalty was deceptive. The February vote was a preliminary judgment, not a final decision, and many of those voting against separation were, as Daniel Crofts has labeled them, conditional Unionists. These voters wanted to preserve the Union, but not at any cost. They shared the grievances that had driven other states to secede, and they wanted a genuine, lasting compromise with firm and permanent guarantees that Southern interests, including slavery, would be protected. They were not allies of the North, and their vote against secession signaled only their desire to give the states every chance to end the crisis and restore the Union. North Carolina's vote against the convention meant only that the state was not prepared to secede at that time, while there was still hope of compromise. It did not mean that voters would always reject secession.[5]

Comments from Joseph Cathey, a prominent Haywood County merchant, farmer, and slaveholder who would later command a company of Confederate troops, illustrate the fluidity of many views at this time. Replying to reports that he supported secession as a means to force the North to make concessions to the South and bring about an ultimate reconciliation, Cathey wrote that he had actually urged that North Carolina take no action until Lincoln clearly revealed the policy he intended to follow toward the South. If the new president refused to make substantial compromises and if reconciliation on an equitable basis proved impossible, Cathey conjectured that Virginia and the other border states would secede and that North Carolina would follow. But Cathey said nothing about what he thought North Carolina should do, and like many in North Carolina his position was more a weighing of possible outcomes than a firm commitment to one course of action. Allen T. Davidson, who would later be elected to the Confederate House of Representatives and help raise an infantry regiment, was also cautious in his views. On April 4, 1861 he wrote his wife "I will send you this on an envelope… with this flag of the Confederate States thereon… not that I bow the knee or even throw up my hat to it, but as a curiosity for you. I could have fought or done anything else honorable this morning when I saw this contemptible rag flying where the Stars and Stripes ought to be." Three days later, however, Davidson warned his son: "If, however, Old Abe does make war on the South, our destiny must be with the South as a state. I would not encourage disloyalty to our section, but only to speak of things from a standpoint at which I am able to form an accurate opinion." [6]

While supporters of separation found their setback painful, they did not cease campaigning. Less than three weeks after the convention's defeat they met at Goldsboro, organized a States Rights Party, and continued to advocate secession in county meetings. Thomas sent out circulars advocating secession, and secessionists in the Smokies became more active after the referendum. In March, for example, Macon County formed an Agricultural Society to encourage home manufacturing and reduce dependence on Northern suppliers, and secessionists in Jackson County attempted to generate support for a similar organization.[7] The events of the next two months strengthened the position of secessionists and eroded the bases of conditional Unionism. Even if they had wanted to do so, the president-elect and Congressional Republicans could offer no substantial compromises without alienating their own political base. Unionist victories in Tennessee and Virginia in February further reduced Republican interest in compromise. Delegates to the Washington Peace Conference found themselves unable to agree on any substantive proposals, and Congress' last efforts to settle sectional differences also collapsed. With all realistic hopes for compromise gone, those who had voted against the convention in February had to consider whether continued opposition to secession made sense. A realignment in loyalties required only an impetus, and the clash of Northern and Southern forces at Fort Sumter provided that push. With the sections now at war, the only question left was which side North Carolina would take, and for most residents the answer was clear.

On May 1 the North Carolina legislature reassembled in special session and, in a single day, authorized elections for a state convention. The bill granted the convention unrestricted powers and specified that its acts need not be submitted to the voters for approval. With that critical step taken, the legislature then authorized the governor to receive volunteers into service and appropriated $5 million for military expenditures. Secessionists then triumphed at the polls with the same seeming ease. In many districts secessionist candidates ran unopposed, while the few remaining Unionist voices were nearly drowned out by the war fever. When the time came to vote, many who still held Unionist convictions either stayed home or voted with the majority. In the Jonathan Creek area of Haywood County, for example, the only person to cast a dissenting vote was Justice of the Peace William Green Berry Garrett, and he was long remembered for this act. Thus, the election results gave a convincing show of solidarity, while obscuring the pockets of Unionism that remained throughout the state. Finally, on May 20 the First Session of the North Carolina Convention met and, with little debate, passed ordinances separating North Carolina from the Union and ratifying the Provisional Constitution of the Confederate States. The convention chose not to submit these measures to another referendum, so Smokies voters were unable to register their final stance on secession. Only the war itself would fully reveal support for, and opposition to, the Confederacy.[8]

The debate over secession in Tennessee followed a nearly identical course. On January 7 Tennessee Governor Isham G. Harris called the legislature into special session to consider Lincoln's election. Like Ellis, Harris agreed that before seceding all the slaveholding states should meet and present a common set of demands to the North. But the governor, an ardent secessionist, did not really believe that any compromise satisfactory to the South could be found, so after reviewing Southern grievances he urged the legislature to authorize elections for a state convention. The legislators agreed, but as in North Carolina they tempered that decision with a provision that voters would not only choose delegates but also determine whether the convention would be held at all.[9]

The specter of secession triggered an outpouring of fervent, nearly violent Unionism in the East Tennessee Smokies. Oliver P. Temple, a Knoxville lawyer who would become one of East Tennessee's foremost opponents of secession, made his first speech on the issue in Sevierville on November 21, 1860, revealing his judgment of the direction the region would follow. Temple then returned to Sevier County in January 1861 to address more than 1,000 Unionists who had gathered at Fair Garden: "A number of the mountain men had their guns with them, significant of the use they were to make of them in the near future…as I unfolded to the people the secession plot to break up the government of their fathers, indignation and determination settled on their brows. A grave and terrible calamity presented itself, which could only be avoided by a united people at the ballot box….They were not learned men, but they had a simple, pure, unswerving love of country.

TABLE 3		
TENNESSEE COUNTY	FOR SECESSION CONVENTION	AGAINST SECESSION CONVENTION
Blount	450	1,552
Cocke	192	1,322
Sevier	69	1,265

They had learned by traditions handed down from father to son, of the great Revolutionary struggle for independence… the Republic was therefore as dear to them as was the Sacred Ark of the Covenant to the Israelites."

Radford Gatlin, the founder of the town first known as White Oak Flats and then Gatlinburg, would soon feel the Unionists' wrath. Gatlin was a successful merchant and the organizer of the New Hampshire Baptist Gatlinites, a splinter group similar to the Primitive Baptists. He was also an outspoken secessionist, however, which proved his undoing. In late 1860 Gatlin's congregation left him, and he was barred from preaching. Shortly thereafter someone burned his barn. Gatlin then sued another man for slander, lost, and was forced to sell his property to pay his legal costs. Finally, a band of Unionists beat Gatlin and ordered him to leave. Gatlin immediately complied, relocating first to Fultonville and then to Atlanta.[10]

On February 2 Tennessee voters not only elected a majority of Unionist delegates, but also refused to authorize a convention. The statewide vote was 69,387 to 57,798, with 33,299 of the nay votes coming from East Tennessee. Blount, Cocke, and Sevier Counties all rejected the proposed conven-

tion by substantial majorities.[11]

As in North Carolina, the February vote in Tennessee did not signal an absolute rejection of secession. Nor did it stop debate over the issue. In mid-March Unionists gathered at Trundle's Crossroads in Sevier County and spent a full day listening to speeches by U.S. Representative T. A. R. Nelson and Knoxville attorneys Connelly F. Trigg and John Baxter. The following week former Mississippi Governor Henry S. Foote, who, along with Alabama Governor William Yancy and Tennessee Senator John Bell, was attempting to rally support for secession in East Tennessee, spoke at Sevierville. Loyalists gave Foote a hostile reception, and one Unionist claimed that the governor barely avoided being mobbed. In Blount County, as in others, a small group of influential men continued to agitate for secession, and in March Elkinah Rader wrote Senator Andrew Johnson that nearly all the county officials were denouncing Johnson and Nelson as Black Republicans. Rader believed, wrongly as it turned out, that Unionists were outnumbered, and he urged Johnson and Nelson to speak there as soon as possible.[12]

Governor Harris called the Tennessee legislature back into special session shortly

TABLE 4		
TENNESSEE COUNTY	FOR SEPARATION	AGAINST SEPARATION
Blount	418	1,766
Cocke	518	1,185
Sevier	60	1,525

after the news of Fort Sumter reached the state. With little delay the legislators approved measures separating the state from the Union and authorizing representation in the Confederacy. Unlike North Carolina, the Tennessee legislature termed the separation a declaration of independence and based its actions on the right of revolution, not on the doctrine of secession. David Vandyke Stakely, the state senator from Greene, Cocke, Blount, and Sevier Counties, and F. A. Armstrong, the state representative from Knox and Sevier voted against both measures. Again in contrast to North Carolina, the Tennessee legislature submitted both acts to the voters for approval and scheduled a referendum for June 8. The legislators clearly considered the referendum a formality, however, for in the following days they voted large sums for military expenditures, sent delegates to the Confederate Congress to coordinate defensive preparations, and authorized Governor Harris to issue officers' commissions, receive volunteers into service, and erect fortifications on the state's waterways.[13]

East Tennessee's second debate over secession was even more intense than its first. The issues were fundamental and beyond compromise, the stakes were

immense, passions were high on both sides, and the threat of violence was always present. Perhaps the most serious conflict occurred at Strawberry Plains on May 5. There a large crowd of Unionists from Sevier, Knox, and Jefferson Counties, reported at anywhere from 2,000 to 5,000, had gathered for a rally on a farm owned by Samuel Meek, a prominent loyalist. The farm happened to be near the Strawberry Plains depot, and while the Unionists were still assembling, a train of Alabama troops happened to be leaving the station. Unionists claimed that as the train passed one soldier seated on top of a car threw a large stone at Meek, while a second fired a revolver. Troops inside the cars then began shooting at the crowd. A number of Unionists had brought their weapons to the rally, and they fired back. After the cars had passed, many loyalists wanted to tear up the tracks, but Meek, Temple, and other leaders persuaded them to desist. Unionists were outraged at this attack on a political assembly and considered it as evidence that the Confederacy intended to deprive them of their liberties. Secessionists, on the other hand, asserted that the loyalists had fired first, without provocation, and that the troops had merely defended themselves.[14]

When the referendum results were

tallied, voters in Middle and West Tennessee gave a decisive majority for secession, though pockets of what Crofts calls unconditional Unionism remained in both regions. But in East Tennessee about two-thirds of voters rejected the measures for independence from the Union and representation in the Confederacy. In Blount, Cocke, and Sevier the results were similar to those of the February referendum.[15]

Historians have advanced a number of theories to explain why Unionism persisted so strongly in East Tennessee when it evaporated in most other areas of the South. Some argue that, because the region had relatively few slaveholders and slaves, it felt less threatened by the emergence of the Republican Party and Lincoln's election than other parts of the South. Others believe that the continuing influence of Whig Party principles created a lasting attachment to the Union and a desire for a government that would promote commercial and manufacturing interests. Still others credit East Tennessee's Unionism to superior leadership, to the region's supposed isolation from Southern political currents, or to long-standing resentments against the rest of the state over East Tennessee's declining influence in the state government.

It is likely that all these factors influenced East Tennessee's vote on secession. But other areas of the South, including western North Carolina, had similar economic and political characteristics and yet supported secession. So what made East Tennessee different? John C. Inscoe, recognizing the numerous similarities between East Tennessee and western North Carolina, concluded that the primary difference between the two regions was psychological. Inscoe argued that in the late antebellum

United States Senator Thomas L. Clingman, for whom Clingmans Dome is named, was a strong Southern Rights advocate who favored secession for North Carolina.

period western North Carolinians were generally optimistic about their future and believed that their continued prosperity required close economic ties with neighboring Southern states. They therefore determined that secession would benefit their region. Thomas, for example, prophesied that western North Carolina would "become connected with every part of the state by railroad. It will then become the center of manufacturing for the Southern markets, the place where the Southern people will spend their summers, spend their money, educate their children, and very probably make laws for the nation." East Tennesseans, conversely, tended to be pessimistic about their future prospects and saw no economic advantage in joining the Confederacy. Inscoe and Gordon B. McKinney also assert that certain leaders, particularly Thomas Clingman, effectively propagated strong Southern Rights views in western North Carolina in the decade before the war, preparing the region for secession. East Tennessee, conversely, had no powerful Southern Rights advocate in the antebellum period to counteract its natural tendency to remain loyal to the Union.[16]

The difficulty with this first argument is that in the absence of polling data any conclusions about East Tennessee's or North Carolina's state of mind in 1860 are based more on impressions than hard data. The problem with the second theory is that in any period it is impossible to determine how much leaders shape, and how much they reflect, the views of their followers. Was East Tennessee Unionist because it had strong Unionist leaders, or did it have strong Unionist leaders because the population had deeply entrenched loyalties to the old Union? It is also important to note that, while western North Carolina initially supported secession, a substantial portion of the population later turned against the Confederacy, raising strong suspicions that the loyalties of East Tennessee and western North Carolina were not so different as they appeared initially. In short, no explanation of East Tennessee's Unionism, or of western North Carolina's support for secession, has proven convincing, and perhaps none ever will. But that fact should not prove surprising, for even with all the resources available to them, political scientists still struggle to explain contemporary voter behavior. Rather, the difficulty in explaining one region's rejection of secession and another

region's support should serve as a reminder of how complex and changeable Civil War loyalties actually were.

While the roots of Unionist loyalties remain difficult to trace, the arguments East Tennessee Unionists made against secession were remarkably consistent and reveal profound suspicions of Confederate intentions. Major John Henry Fowler, a Louisville merchant who represented Blount and Sevier Counties in the state senate in the 1840s, provided a classic formulation of these arguments in a letter written to his son-in-law. Fowler claimed that for over a decade Southern politicians had foreseen that their dominance of the Federal government would soon end. Unwilling to continue living in a nation they could no longer rule, they had been plotting to take their states out of the Union by any means necessary and to form a new government they could control. Secession, therefore, had nothing to do with slavery or the security of the South, and Lincoln's election had simply provided a pretext for Southern leaders to execute plans they had already made. Fowler also argued that the majority of Southerners actually opposed separation from old government, and that secessionists had carried their states out of the Union only by suppressing debate, intimidating voters, and grossly misrepresenting Northern intentions.[17]

Other Unionists claimed that, in a Confederacy dominated by slaveholders, nonslaveholders would become second-class citizens and would eventually lose their rights and liberties. Johnson defiantly proclaimed that whatever secessionists attempted, "they never can, while God reigns, make East Tennessee a land of slaves." William G. Brownlow, editor of the *Knoxville Whig*, insisted that East Tennessee loyalists would "never live in a Southern Confederacy and be made the hewers of wood and drawers of water for a set of aristocrats and overbearing tyrants." He also warned, prophetically, that if secession passed war would come, and the burden of that war would fall on "the honest yeomanry of these border states, whose families live by their hard licks, four-fifths of whom own no negroes and never expect to own any." Temple likewise argued that secession would inevitably worsen the position of Southern yeomen, for "large slaveholding communities were always inimical to non-slaveholding men." Unlike secessionists, therefore, many East Tennessee Unionists concluded that they could preserve their rights only by remaining within the Union, and they were willing to fight to do so.[18]

Thus, despite the state's strong support for secession, East Tennessee loyalists were not prepared to accept the results of the referendum. Two days after the vote, representatives from 30 East Tennessee counties and one Middle Tennessee county assembled at Greeneville to consider their next step. Blount County sent seven delegates, Cocke ten, and Sevier 18. Almost immediately the convention split between radicals who favored outright defiance and conservatives who advocated a more cautious approach. On the second day of the convention the Business Committee, which was controlled by radicals and which included Samuel Pickens of Sevier, W. T. Dowell of Blount, and P. H. Easterly of Cocke, released a stunning set of resolutions. Written by T. A. R. Nelson, the resolutions declared that the June referendum had been corrupted by

William G. "Parson" Brownlow was editor of the *Knoxville Whig*. He foresaw that secession for Tennessee would lead to war, the waging of which would be carried out by people in East Tennessee and western North Carolina who did not own slaves and were not part of the Southern aristocracy.

voter intimidation and falsification of poll results and was therefore nonbinding. East Tennessee, along with the loyal counties of Middle Tennessee, would remain in the Union as the true state of Tennessee. If left alone, the Unionist counties would avoid involvement in the conflict and would not interfere with Confederate recruiting or with military transport on the railroads. However, if state or Confederate authorities attempted to arrest Unionists or occupy the loyal counties, Unionists would ask the Federal Government for protection and defend themselves by whatever means necessary. Toward this end, the Business Committee recommended that each county organize its own Home Guard and that the convention raise a central army of 15,000 men.

This brazen challenge to state and Confederate authority carried huge risks. But initially most delegates, still caught up in the defiant spirit that the referendum campaign had created, were prepared to approve the resolutions. The more conservative delegates were appalled at the document, however, believing that if it passed the Confederate government would immediately send forces to East Tennessee, arrest the delegates, and crush any resistance. The fact that several Confederate units passing through Greeneville had threatened to break up the Convention made these fears more plausible. After two days of rancorous debate the conservatives won their point, and the Convention set aside Nelson's document and approved a far more moderate set of resolutions. This new document still asserted that Tennessee's act of separation was fraudulent and that East Tennessee intended to remain in the Union, but it did not directly challenge Confederate authority. Instead, the Convention agreed to petition the state legislature for authorization to separate from Tennessee and form its own new state. The Convention agreed to reconvene in August at Kingston, presumably to organize the new state, and named five men to a secret Executive Committee to oversee the Unionist movement in the interim.

It is unlikely that many of the delegates at Greeneville believed that the petition to form a separate state had any chance of success. It was, however, the only remaining course between open rebellion and acceptance of Confederate rule. Further, many delegates believed that Northern forces would soon enter East Tennessee and wrest the region from Confederate control. Given that hope, temporary acquiescence certainly seemed preferable to a violent rebellion that would not only result in great suffering but almost certainly fail. While all the delegates formally approved the new resolutions, however, a number left the convention bitter and dissatisfied, and at least two secretly agreed to begin raising Home Guard units in their counties.[19]

In July the Unionist delegates, Temple, John Netherland, and James P. McDowell, presented their memorial to the state legislature. The legislature politely acknowledged the request; then immediately tabled the petition on the grounds that the matter should be left to the new legislators who would be elected in August. With that action Unionists and Confederates reached an impasse, and there they remained throughout the summer and fall of 1861. Unionists showed no signs of wavering in their loyalties, while Confederate authorities were as yet unwilling to use force to bring East Tennessee into the new nation. In July the Reverend J. M. L. Burnett, an outspoken secessionist and a Baptist minister who had recently taken a position in Jonesville, expressed his fears for East Tennessee's future: "Distrust and hate among the more violent, and an awful sense of impending peril among the reflecting portion of the people—these are all the prevalent feelings here. Not a single community in which families are not divided: father crying long live the Union, and death to traitors—the son cheering 'Liberty and South.' This, too, more than a month after it is known that the State has seceded by a majority of 61,000. Rebellion is openly avowed."

Burnett's sense that a momentous conflict was taking shape in East Tennessee would prove all too correct.[20]

CHAPTER 3

EARLY WAR: INNOCENCE

HE FIRST MONTHS OF THE WAR IN THE SMOKIES WERE CHARACTERIZED BY TRAGIC NAIVETE ON ALL SIDES. CONFEDERATE VOLUNTEERS cheerfully marched off to camps with little sense of how long the war would last or how many hardships they would suffer. Families and communities enthusiastically saw them off, seemingly oblivious to the months of loneliness, deprivation, and grief that lay ahead. Loyalists hatched ambitious plots to throw off Confederate rule, while Southern authorities dismissed Unionists as inconsequential malcontents. The war cruelly destroyed all these illusions, and by the spring of 1862 both soldiers and civilians, Confederate and Unionist alike, began to recognize the magnitude of the struggle in which they had engaged.

Because North Carolina held no referendum in May 1861, it is impossible to gauge support for secession in the North Carolina Smokies. But the actions of the population in the war's first months revealed both widespread enthusiasm for the cause and significant pockets of opposition. In June 1861 James Whitaker, who would later command a company in the Sixty-ninth North Carolina Infantry, complained that in Cherokee County "The war excitement has engaged the minds of every man in the county. The preachers have quit preaching,

the churches are lingering under a fatal disease... it seems that they are all gone astray mixing and mingling with the world."[1]

Indeed, every county in the North Carolina Smokies made an impressive contribution to the war effort. Haywood County's first company, organized by Robert A. Love, was designated Company A of the Sixteenth North Carolina Infantry. The unit served in West Virginia for a few months before being transferred to the Army of Northern Virginia. After surviving the Seven Days Battles, Second Manassas, Harper's Ferry, and the Battle of Antietam, the company was sent back to western North Carolina and became Company E of the Sixty-ninth North Carolina Infantry. Haywood's next two companies, raised by Sam C. Bryson and Thomas I. Lenoir, became Companies C and F of the Twenty-fifth North Carolina Infantry under Colonel Thomas Clingman. The Twenty-fifth North Carolina was also sent east and fought at the Battles of Seven Pines, Malvern Hill, Sharpsburg, and Fredericksburg. It returned to North Carolina briefly in the spring of 1864, but was then ordered back to Virginia, where it remained until the war's end.

Haywood County also supplied one company in Colonel Robert Vance's Twenty-ninth North Carolina Infantry and four companies in the hard luck Sixty-second North Carolina Infantry. The Twenty-ninth North Carolina was sent to Cocke County in late November 1861 to put down the Unionist rebellion there. It was then stationed along the East Tennessee railroads until February 1862, when it was sent to Cumberland Gap. In September 1862 the regiment joined the unsuccessful invasion of Kentucky, after which it was sent to Middle Tennessee and fought in the Battle of Murfreesboro. The regiment also endured the Battles of Chickamauga and Chattanooga before being ordered to Mississippi. The Sixty-second North Carolina Infantry was also stationed along the East Tennessee railroads until July 1863, when it had the very bad luck to be sent to Cumberland Gap. In September the Sixty-second and other Confederate regiments were surrendered at Cumberland Gap, and many men spent the remainder of the war in Northern prisons. In all, the county raised 925 regular troops, of which about 100 died in service.

Jackson County, similarly, supplied Company L of the Sixteenth North Carolina Infantry, Company B of the Twenty-fifth North Carolina Infantry, and two companies in the Sixty-second North Carolina Infantry. It also sent a considerable number of men to the Thirty-ninth North Carolina Infantry, which fought at the Battles of Chickamauga and Chattanooga and then campaigned in Alabama, South Carolina, and Georgia. Somewhere around 84 men from Jackson died in Confederate service.[2]

Confederates had far more trouble recruiting in the Tennessee Smokies, but units were organized there as well. In Cocke County, Thomas Gorman, who had served two terms as county sheriff and one in the state legislature, organized a cavalry company. When 27 of his men could not provide horses, Gorman signed notes for them to purchase mounts, and the men agreed to pay him back out of their pay. Sadly, Gorman was badly wounded when the company was sent out to operate against Unionists in November 1861, and he resigned soon after. Cocke County also provided Company C of the Twenty-sixth Tennessee Infantry under Colonel John M. Lillard and sent men to the Sixtieth and Sixty-ninth Tennessee Infantries and the Fifth Tennessee Cavalry. The Twenty-sixth Tennessee Infantry was surrendered at Vicksburg in July 1863, and many men spent eight months at a prison camp in Indiana. In Blount County, William C. Holden and A. L. Mims both recruited cavalry companies, while James McCamy, Will Holland, and J. E. Toole raised infantry companies. Other men from Blount entered the First, Second, Fifth, and Eighth Tennessee Cavalries and the Third, Thirty-seventh, and Thirty-eighth Tennessee Infantries. Sevier County provided parts of Company A, Thirty-ninth Tennessee Mounted Infantry, Company I, Thirty-seventh Tennessee Infantry, Company L, Fourth Tennessee Cavalry, and Company I, Sixty-ninth North Carolina Infantry. Of course Blount, Cocke, and Sevier would also send substantial numbers of men to the Union armies.[3]

Recruiting at this stage was haphazard, but zeal for the war largely made up for the lack of system. Wealthy merchants and farmers, county officials and legislators, Mexican War veterans, and other influential men took it upon themselves to raise companies. A desire to defend their homes and join the grand adventure brought them recruits with little effort. Companies were mustered in Asheville or Raleigh or Nashville, armed and equipped, and pieced together into regiments by the State Adjutant General's office. Regiments then elected officers, received additional equipment, and drilled. This, at least, was how the system was intended to work, though too often a lack of supplies, experienced officers, and time left the equipping and training woefully inadequate. Alfred Bell, a wealthy farmer who recruited one of the first companies in Macon County, bought most of the company's equipment with his own funds. When he applied for reimbursement, the state Adjutant General's office settled only part of his expenses and refused to pay for utensils, cups, "and a good many other things." They also insisted on reimbursing him in state notes payable in 1865: "I don't know whether the merchants will take them or not but it was the best that could be done."[4]

In these first months the war was more a festival than a grim reality. When Haywood's second company, the "Haywood Sharpshooters," marched off to Asheville, a crowd of men and women accompanied them and remained in town until the company moved on. When another Haywood company was detained at Asheville for the summer, the men expressed their disappointment that they could not immediately go on to the fighting in Virginia. In November 1861 Alfred Bell reported with great satisfaction that his company had finally been mustered in Asheville. Since the men had no tents, they had been comfortably housed in an academy near the town. They received ample rations and were given beef every day. Similarly, H. T. Mingus of Cherokee wrote happily in August 1861 that his unit had "plenty to eat and…sleep in rooms on blankets," while John Sutton reported "the boys are all in good heart and want to get in a fight…I think that we are going on a good cause and the Lord will be on our side." Captain J. D. Bryon, stationed near Wilmington, was primarily fascinated with his first view of the ocean: "You can stay in the encampment and see all the steam boats and steam ships running all the time it is a grand seen…you may stand on the beach and look as far as your Eyes can see and it is nothing." The Confederates were expecting a landing by 6,000 to 10,000 Northern troops at any time, but Bryon did not seem worried at the prospect.

R. B. Edmonston, who had also been sent to the coast, was even more sanguine, predicting that there would be no fighting there that winter and that peace would be made by February 1, 1862.[5]

But not everyone viewed the war so lightly. In June, Robina Norwood of Haywood expressed her private satisfaction that the county's first company had been delayed at Asheville. She hoped that the United States Congress would override Lincoln's actions, end the war, and let the Southern states go in peace. A month later, when the company was preparing to move east, Robina still thought the conflict might end before the men had to fight. But by September she had given up that hope, and now predicted that "this generation is destined to bear every variety of trouble such as generally accompany revolutions." Other women left behind also expressed their misgivings about what was to come. Shortly after Alfred Bell left home with his company, Mary wrote of her difficulties adjusting to his absence: "I almost dread for night to come and wish it could be day all the time if I could do without sleep—I cannot sleep sound like I do when you are at home I do not know how I am to make out this winter and while you are gone I tell you 12 months is a long while…I do not know how I can even stand it I shall try and work hard and pass the time the best I can." And Sarah Mingus, the sister of H. T. Mingus, was deeply disturbed when she heard that several men in her brother's regiment had died: "Brother do you ever think of dying in such a multitude of people. Forget not your prayers, you are in the mud and illy clothed, do your duty while in the service, but do no put yourself in danger…. It appears that every man will have to leave and none left to support the lame and needy."[6]

The distinctive society of the North Carolina Smokies also produced one of the war's most distinctive units, a collection of combined white and Cherokee companies that would become known as "Thomas's Legion." The Legion was the brainchild of William Holland Thomas, and its difficult history mirrors the experience of the Smokies during the war. Shortly after North Carolina seceded, Thomas convened a council of Cherokee leaders to discuss the crisis. No doubt reflecting his influence, the Council voted to support the Confederate war effort, and 200 Cherokee volunteered for state service. Thomas then wrote directly to President Jefferson Davis to offer the Confederacy a Cherokee battalion. Thomas planned to keep the battalion in the Smoky Mountains to defend the border against invasion and suppress dissent, though he did not include this

Confederate President Jefferson Davis approved the request by William Holland Thomas to form a battalion of Cherokee Indians.

information in his letter. Davis agreed to accept the battalion, though inexplicably he proposed using the Cherokee as scouts in the swampy areas of eastern North Carolina. But when a mustering officer arrived in Quallatown in October 1861 to enroll the companies, Thomas refused to proceed unless the state legislature granted the soldiers state citizenship. The legislature refused, and no troops were mustered.

At some point Thomas changed his mind about the state citizenship issue, and in April 1862 Major General Edmund Kirby Smith sent Major Washington Morgan to enroll Thomas's first company, made up of 120 Cherokee and 12 white recruits. Morgan was the son of Major Gideon Morgan, who had helped lead the Cherokee assault at the Battle of Horseshoe

Confederate Major General Edmund Kirby Smith sent Thomas's Legion to Strawberry Plains in East Tennessee to guard the Holston River Bridge.

North Carolina Governor Henry T. Clark requesting permission to recruit a full regiment. Thomas argued that western North Carolina would be defenseless if Union forces seized East Tennessee, and he proposed to use his regiment as a "guerrilla force" for the "defense of the Carolinas, Virginia, and East Tennessee." Thomas promised to complete the regiment by August. But Clark, who suspected Thomas's motives and lacked confidence in his military abilities, rejected the request. Refusing to be bound by military protocol, Thomas then sought support from Kirby Smith. Starved for troops, and facing serious threats from Union forces in Kentucky and Tennessee and from loyalist partisans at home, Kirby Smith endorsed the idea. Secretary of War Judah P. Benjamin then not only authorized Thomas to raise three additional companies but also promised him three units already in existence: Companies A and L of the Sixteenth North Carolina Infantry, which had been recruited in Haywood and Jackson Counties, and a new company being raised by Elijah Johnson in Haywood County. Thomas's recruiters worked quickly, and in July Captain William Williams Stringfield was sent to muster in the new companies.

When Stringfield arrived at Valleytown where the recruits had gathered, he found the kind of bizarre situation that the personalized and politicized Civil War recruiting system sometimes created. Colonel Allen T. Davidson, one of Thomas's old political rivals, was also attempting to organize a regiment, and he had come to Valleytown for recruits. Stringfield found Davidson telling the recruits that Thomas had no authority to receive them into service and urging them

Bend. Predictably the company elected Thomas captain. Thomas's enemies charged that he took the commission to further his political career, but Thomas insisted that he accepted the command only to make certain that his troops' interests would be protected. Shortly after their enrollment, Kirby Smith had the Cherokee troops armed with firearms taken from East Tennessee loyalists and ordered the company to Strawberry Plains to guard the Holston River Bridge. Soon thereafter Thomas received more recruits, and the company was divided in two.

Though pleased with his success thus far, Thomas had another reason for staying at home. He had not given up his vision of a much larger force, and in April he wrote

to join his regiment instead. After listening for a few minutes and debating what to do, Stringfield interrupted Davidson and read his mustering orders to the assembly. Davidson, defeated, left the area, and Stringfield won Thomas's lasting gratitude. Stringfield then mustered three companies for Thomas's regiment and an additional two for a separate battalion to be commanded by Lieutenant Colonel William C. Walker. By July Thomas had acquired eight companies, six of white troops and two of Cherokee. Shortly thereafter Thomas was ordered to send two additional companies to Walker's Battalion, but as compensation he was given two new companies, one being raised by James A. McKinney in Blount County and one by Stephen Whitaker in Cherokee and Clay Counties, North Carolina.

In late September Companies A and L were finally released from the Sixteenth North Carolina, and Thomas had nine companies. Though this was one short of the usual contingent, the War Department organized the companies into a regiment and designated the new unit the Sixty-ninth North Carolina Infantry. Thomas, naturally, was elected colonel, while James R. Love, captain of the former Company A of the Sixteenth North Carolina, became lieutenant colonel. James R. Love was not only the grandson of Colonel Robert Love, he was also Thomas's business partner and brother-in-law. Stringfield was chosen major, while James Terrell, another of Thomas's business partners, became assistant quartermaster. In October Thomas received a tenth company that had been raised in Blount, Roane, and Union Counties, Tennessee. Still not satisfied, Thomas sent President Davis

notice of his intention to expand the regiment into a "Legion" by adding cavalry and artillery. Thomas nearly achieved this goal in October, when Major General John P. McCown, temporarily in command of the Department of East Tennessee, sent him three companies of cavalry. Walker, meanwhile, had enlarged his battalion to seven companies. Together the regiment, the battalion, the attached cavalry, and the artillery Thomas would later acquire would become known as Thomas's Legion.[7]

But Thomas would never be able to put the unit to the uses he had envisioned. Military needs elsewhere continually took precedence over the interests of western North Carolina, and Thomas's companies were soon scattered and put to uses he had never envisioned. Three white companies were sent to the Army of Northern Virginia, where they participated in the Seven Days Battles and the fighting at Second Manassas and Sharpsburg. Other companies were sent to East Tennessee to guard bridges and rail lines, hunt down bushwhackers and conscripts, and perform other garrison and police tasks. Guard duty was dull and unrewarding, and Thomas's men suffered repeated outbreaks of measles, smallpox, and mumps that took many lives. The other duties were far more deadly and unpleasant, but Unionists found Thomas's men to be dangerous enemies. Daniel Ellis, a Unionist who led a partisan band in Carter County, noted that loyalists particularly feared the Cherokee troops for their skill and persistence in tracking escapees and bushwhackers. Unionist spokesmen such as William G. Brownlow scourged the Confederate government for using Cherokee troops to track white

North Carolina Division of Archives and History

Confederate Lieutenant Colonel James R. Love was Colonel Thomas's business partner and brother-in-law.

Southerners, though Ellis noted that the Cherokee companies' white officers were more "cruel" than their men.[8]

On the other side of the border, Thomas used his remaining companies to improve the road connecting Sevierville and Webster, to mine alum, saltpeter, and other minerals from Alum Cave, and to keep order in Cherokee and Jackson Counties. Thomas also organized a "company of sappers and miners" to aid in the road building. Led by Robert Collins, the man who had guided Arnold Guyot's surveying parties in 1856, 1859, and 1860, the company was made up largely of East Tennessee loyalists who would not enroll in combat units but who would perform other duties. When Confederate authorities ordered the men moved to regular regiments in late

1862, nearly all deserted. Thomas's men built crude barracks on Mount LeConte near Alum Cave and surrounded them with a wooden fortification built of felled trees. The complex, which became known as Fort Harry, was intended to house the miners and road builders, protect Alum Cave, and prevent Federal forces from crossing into North Carolina. Northern troops burned the fort in 1864.[9]

While the Confederacy mobilized for war, Unionists in East Tennessee were also preparing to fight, either on the side of the Federal forces gathering in the North or on their own at home. Almost immediately after the Greeneville Convention, loyalists began leaving East Tennessee to join the small Union army that was forming at Camp Nelson, Kentucky. Although Confederate troops were now stationed at Knoxville and along the railroad, they made few attempts to stop the exodus. By September enough Tennessee Unionists had reached Kentucky to form four regiments.[10]

Many more Unionists who were not yet ready to leave home gathered into Home Guard units, militia-type companies that could mobilize quickly to confront Confederate troops and East Tennessee secessionists. Oliver P. Temple, who probably knew more about Unionist activities than any other person in East Tennessee, asserted that in Blount County Unionists began drilling in early April. In Sevier County loyalists formed a mounted company the same day the referendum was held, and formally organized their Home Guard in August. Secessionists identified Willie Homer, a brick mason, as the chief organizer in both Sevier and Blount, but also blamed Andrew Fleming, a Knoxville lawyer, for helping set up Home Guard units in several counties. When Cocke County formed its Home Guard is unclear, but later events would prove that it was active by late summer. Initially Unionists drilled openly, but as Confederate authorities became more threatening, Home Guardsmen hid their activities. Will McTeer, who would later serve with the Second Tennessee Cavalry (Union), remembered that Unionists in Blount met several times in a little-known cove near Little River Gap on Chilhowee Mountain. As many as 1,500 armed men would gather there, raise a large American flag that some of their wives had made after the referendum, and spend a full day listening to speeches and drilling. In Blount County six young women, Cynthia Dunn, Harriet McTeer, Eva and Dora Jackson, and Samantha and Adalia Miller, formed their own Home Guard unit. Though often dismissed as a joke, these women performed many of the same tasks as men, carrying word of enemy units, distributing letters from Union soldiers, arranging meeting places for men planning to go to Kentucky, and helping escaped prisoners.[11]

Confederate supporters also took up arms. One of the earliest bands was the Templer Lewis Scouts, a Home Guard unit apparently organized by Captain A. L. Mims and Confederate officers to suppress loyalist sentiment in Cocke County. The Scouts were aggressive and well led, and Unionists soon came to fear them. Sometime in the summer of 1861 the Lewis Scouts came to the home of George Schultz, a prominent opponent of secession in Newport. They demanded food, and when Schultz replied that he had none they accused him of making speeches

Confederate Brigadier General Felix K. Zollicoffer's sympathies did not lie with the Tennessee Unionists, however, he did show compassion for them, and promised them full protection if they behaved as peaceable citizens.

against the Confederacy, tied him to a wagon wheel, and whipped him until he fainted. Schultz's family claimed that his screams could be heard a half mile away. That same summer a second Unionist, William Allen of Cosby, was on his way home from Sevierville when he had the misfortune to meet the Scouts near Jones Cove. Fearing for his life, Allen took out a jug of whiskey, passed it around, and made friendly conversation. After a time the Scouts let Allen go, and he rode on. Allen may have thought he was safe, but he was wrong. Before he was out of sight one or more of the Scouts shot and killed him.[12]

Many East Tennessee secessionists

Dr. J. G. M. Ramsey was a prominent seccession-ist who urged the governor to cancel state elections for fear the Unionists would win. He was right.

ly urged the new commander to use all available means to bring Unionists over to the Confederate side.

The editor of a large Whig newspaper in Nashville, Zollicoffer was personally acquainted with many loyalist leaders in East Tennessee. Like other Tennessee Whigs, he had initially opposed secession, and he was disposed to be patient and conciliatory with Unionist holdouts. Immediately after reaching East Tennessee, Zollicoffer issued a general proclamation. He reminded Unionists that the state had expressed its final wish in the referendum, and he insisted that the time for political debate was over. Tennessee was now part of a new nation that was at war, and all its citizens had to unite. At the same time, Zollicoffer stressed that he was only asking Unionists to become peaceable citizens, not to give up all affection for the Union. If loyalists complied, they would receive his full protection. Zollicoffer then issued strict orders to his troops to respect private property, invited loyalist leaders to his headquarters to discuss affairs in the region, and confidently reported to Richmond that, given a little time, East Tennessee Unionists would fall in line.[13]

Zollicoffer's hopes were sadly disappointed. Tennessee held state elections in early August, and in all three East Tennessee districts the Unionist candidates, T. A. R. Nelson, Horace Maynard, and George Bridges, openly declared that if elected they intended to take their seats in the United States Congress. Dr. J .G. M. Ramsey and other influential secessionists urged Governor Harris to cancel the elections in East Tennessee and appoint representatives instead. Harris, Davis, and Zollicoffer all agreed, however, that allowing the elec-

suspected that Unionists were preparing for armed conflict, and they insisted that the only way to end the resistance was to imprison Unionist leaders, break up the Home Guard units, and disarm loyalists. Despite secessionist warnings, however, neither Governor Isham G. Harris nor President Jefferson Davis believed that Unionists posed a serious threat, and both were convinced that if handled properly loyalists would come over to the Confederate side. Confederate authorities, therefore, chose to play a waiting game in East Tennessee. Davis signaled this policy by choosing Brigadier General Felix K. Zollicoffer to command the Department of East Tennessee. Davis ordered Zollicoffer to stamp out any resistance, but he particular-

tions to proceed would prove to Unionists that the Confederate Government represented no threat to their rights as a free people. When the elections were over, all three Unionist candidates had won by wide margins, proving, it seemed, that loyalists had not moderated their position at all.[14]

Faced with such intransigence, Confederate authorities adopted more confrontational policies. Southern troops arrested Nelson and Bridges before they could reach Kentucky and gave them the choice between taking an oath of allegiance to the Confederacy or imprisonment for the length of the war. Both chose the oath, though Bridges would later escape Tennessee. The Confederate District Attorney for East Tennessee, John Crozier Ramsey, also now felt free to act. Ramsey had been advocating harsh measures against loyalists since June, and following the election he had over 100 influential Unionists arrested and sent before a special session of the Confederate District Court. One of those seized was William H. H. Duggan, a Methodist minister in Sevier County. Unionists claimed that Confederate troops actually arrested Duggan in his own church during a quarterly meeting and forced him to walk behind their horses. The day was particularly hot, and Duggan, who was a large man, collapsed after seven miles. Brownlow attributed the arrests to old political resentments: "The truth is, they had voted the Union ticket, and they had voted for years against certain men, and this explains their arrests."[15]

But these attempts to deprive the Unionist movement of its leadership were largely frustrated. Both Horace Maynard and Andrew Johnson eluded Confederate

Union Major General George B. McClellan supported the plan of Tennessee partisans to burn railroad bridges in East Tennessee to halt Confederate military traffic.

troops and reached Washington, D.C., where they pressured President Lincoln and Union commanders to occupy East Tennessee as soon as possible. In Knoxville, District Court Judge William H. Humphreys rejected Ramsey's argument that the war conferred extraordinary powers on the new government, and he refused to allow the Confederate District Attorney to prosecute Unionists based on their political views or suspected activities. Humphries offered nearly every man sent before him release in return for taking a loyalty oath and giving a bond for good behavior. Ramsey's arrests, therefore, did little damage to the Unionist movement, while strengthening the belief of loyalists that they could never be safe under Confederate rule. Secessionists, in turn, became even more frustrated with the refusal of the Confederate government to act decisively in East Tennessee.[16]

Zollicoffer also took sterner measures,

ordering his cavalry to patrol the most disaffected counties, confiscate arms, break up Unionist meetings, and arrest loyalist leaders. Confederate troops nearly came to blows with Blount County loyalists when a cavalry detachment based in Maryville was sent to Tuckaleechee Cove. Judge Williams of Maryville warned the detachment commander that on the way to the cove he would pass a large flagpole with an American flag and that he should leave it be. This was the same area where the Unionist Home Guard had been drilling. As they approached, some of the Confederate troopers saw the flag and raised their muskets to shoot it down. But the detachment commander stopped them and ordered his men to form a circle around the flag and salute it before riding on. The captain would later thank the judge for his advice, when he learned that Unionists had been con-cealed in the slopes surrounding the cove and had been waiting to fire.[17]

The standoff between Unionists and Confederate authorities finally ended in early November, thanks largely to the work of William B. Carter. Carter, a Baptist minister and a member of one of northeast-ern Tennessee's leading families, had helped lead the fight against secession and had supported Nelson's proposals at the Greeneville Convention. Distressed at the growing threats to Unionists, Carter apparently feared that federal troops would not enter East Tennessee before winter set in, and he was determined to help them along. Sometime in September Carter slipped across the border, met with Brigadier Generals William T. Sherman and George Thomas at Camp Dick Nelson, and then traveled on to Washington, D.C.

Through the influence of Johnson and Maynard he won an audience with Lincoln, Secretary of War Simon Cameron, and Major General George B. McClellan, and there laid out a breathtaking plan. Carter proposed to organize bands of East Tennessee partisans to destroy a number of bridges on the East Tennessee railroads, halting military traffic in the region and eliminating the threat of Confederate reinforcements. Unionist Home Guard units would then harass the few Confederate troops in East Tennessee, enabling Federal forces in Kentucky to take and hold the region. McClellan favored the plan as a diversion for his pending operations in Virginia, and Lincoln, who from the beginning had hoped to use East Tennessee as a base to rally Unionist sentiment elsewhere in the South, issued orders for Union forces to seize positions on the rail line near Knoxville the first week of November. Cameron apparently gave Carter $2,500 to finance the operation.

As so often happened this early in the war, Lincoln and his advisors badly under-estimated the considerable operational and logistical difficulties involved in invading East Tennessee. But the decision was made, and Carter went back to Kentucky, met a second time with Sherman and Thomas, and came back over the border undetected. He then traveled the entire length of East Tennessee from Elizabethton to Chattanooga, found seven men to lead the operations against the bridges, and secreted himself in Morgan County to wait for the Federal army. Remarkably, all this took place without Confederate authorities having anything more than vague suspicions of Unionist threats against

**The railroad bridge at Strawberry Plains, Tennessee was unsuccessfully attacked
by pro-Union partisans on November 8, 1861.**

the railroads. Whether Carter shared his plan with other Unionist leaders is a secret that has remained buried to this day. Temple claimed that the conspiracy did not involve more than 300 people, and he denied that he or any other prominent leader had received advanced warning of the operation.[18]

Carter's bands struck late on the night of November 8. They burned five bridges in Hamilton, Bradley, Greene, and Sullivan Counties, tore down telegraph lines in numerous places, and temporarily cut communications between Knoxville and Richmond. Although loyalists failed to bring down four other bridges, Carter had made good on his promise. All traffic on the railroads was temporarily halted, and

Zollicoffer, who had moved his main force to Jacksborough to watch for a Union invasion, was unable to send orders to his officers in Knoxville. Further, word of the bridge burnings spread with remarkable speed, and by morning hundreds of armed Unionists had assembled in camps scattered around at least a dozen counties. Their appearance distracted Confederate officers, and terrified secessionists besieged authorities with demands for protection, further adding to the confusion. Colonel William B. Wood, who commanded the troops at Knoxville, reported "I need not say that great alarm is felt by the few Southern men. They are finding places of safety for their families, and would gladly enlist if we had arms to furnish them."[19]

Union General William T. Sherman ultimately reneged on plans to invade East Tennessee, fearing his troops would be unable to find adequate supplies in the lean countryside.

One of the leaders Carter chose was William C. Pickens, a Methodist minister from Sevier County and the son of state senator Samuel Pickens. William Pickens was brave, adventurous, and a natural leader, but he was also impetuous and reckless, traits that would doom his operation. Carter assigned Pickens the bridge that crossed the Holston River near Strawberry Plains, a critical target close to Knoxville and the Strawberry Plains depot. On the night of November 8 Pickens and 12 other men crossed the French Broad River at Underdown's Ferry and hiked undetected to the Holston. They approached the bridge cautiously, but when they saw no guards Pickens and two other men climbed up on the bridge abutment and lit a torch. Unfortunately for them, the bridge was in fact guarded by a single man, James Keelin. Apparently Keelin saw Pickens' band approach from his post in the guardhouse, and as soon as the torch flared he fired, hitting Pickens in the thigh. Keelin then rushed out and attempted to pin Pickens on the bridge. One of Pickens' men pulled a large knife and repeatedly attempted to stab Keelin, but in the dark he hit Pickens instead, nearly cutting off one hand and giving him several other deep wounds. More loyalists then swarmed up on the bridge and plunged into the confused fight. Eventually they shoved Keelin off the bridge and fired several shots at him. But Keelin survived the fall, avoided the gunfire, and ran for help.

Pickens' men then assessed their situation and found, unbelievably, that they had no matches. Pickens had lost his during the fight with Keelin, and none of the other loyalists had thought to bring any. The conspirators considered running to the nearest house for fire, but they feared giving themselves away and were also concerned that Keelin might return with reinforcements at any time. They were also anxious about Pickens, who was badly in need of care. So in the end they gave up the botched operation, took Pickens to a nearby loyalist farm, and found a doctor, James Ellis of Trundle's Cross Roads, to treat him. After a few days they placed Pickens on a sled, covered him with corn shocks, and smuggled him back to Sevier County. There he was hidden at various farms, moving every few days for safety. Pickens eventually recovered from his wounds, escaped to the Federal lines in Kentucky, and rose to the command of the

Third Tennessee Cavalry (Union).[20]

Despite Carter's initial success, the whole venture collapsed with frightening speed. On November 2 Sherman, who had been pressured into the operation from the beginning, at last listened to his own judgment—or his own fears—and canceled the invasion. His small force was short on arms, supplies, and transport, and Sherman concluded that, even if his men managed to hold positions in East Tennessee, they could not be supplied throughout the winter. He also considerably overestimated the Confederate forces facing him. Thomas, conversely, firmly believed that the operation was feasible, and he strenuously protested the cancellation order. Johnson and Maynard, who had returned to Kentucky to accompany the invading force, also begged Sherman to reconsider, and then threatened to lead the East Tennessee regiments across the border on their own. Sherman would not relent, however, and he threatened to arrest Johnson and Maynard if they interfered. Whether Sherman or Thomas was correct can never be known. Given the difficulty Union forces had maintaining themselves in East Tennessee two years later, Sherman's decision was certainly defensible. Yet the consequences for East Tennessee loyalists were catastrophic.[21]

Confederate retribution against Unionists was swift and harsh. Work crews restored railroad traffic more quickly than anyone expected, and within a week the War Department was able to send reinforcements from Middle Tennessee and Georgia. Secretary of War Judah P. Benjamin telegraphed orders directly to Colonels Daniel Leadbetter and William B.

Wood, both of whom had criticized Zollicoffer for excessive leniency, instructing them to arrest the leaders of the revolt, anyone connected with the bridge burnings, and anyone found in arms against the government. Benjamin made it clear that they were expected to crush the uprising quickly and decisively and could use any means necessary.[22]

In the next few weeks Confederate troops systematically moved through East Tennessee. They broke up the Unionist camps, confiscated weapons, impressed supplies, and arrested and imprisoned hundreds of Unionists on suspicion that they were involved in the revolt or simply because they were known to have loyalist sentiments. Confederate officers claimed that their men acted with discretion and restraint and arrested only men known to be a threat to the government, but Unionist spokesmen such as Brownlow asserted that Confederate troops shot suspected Unionists without trial, beat women to force them to reveal where their husbands and sons were hiding, and stole horses, money, and other private property. Over 200 loyalists who were considered particularly dangerous were sent to military prisons in Alabama and Georgia, while the rest were confined in Knoxville or in county jails.[23]

In those terrible days following the bridge burnings, the Smoky Mountains in Tennessee became a center of the uprising and suffered the unhappy consequences of Confederate attentions. On November 10 400 men from Sevier County marched on the Strawberry Plains bridge to make a second attempt at destroying it. By the time they reached the bridge, however,

Parson Brownlow's book

Jacob Harmon and his son, Henry, were hanged in Knoxville for burning a railroad bridge over Lick Creek.

they found it guarded by 200 infantry, a company of Confederate cavalry, and about 100 volunteers from Knoxville. The two ragged forces exchanged shots for a day and a half before the Unionists gave up and withdrew. But they did not go home. Instead, the loyalists set up camp near the Sevier-Knox county line, only ten miles from Knoxville, and continued to menace both the bridge and the city. On November 11 Wood reported that dozens of additional Unionists from Sevier, Blount, and other counties further up the Valley were streaming into the camp to reinforce the loyalists already there. Two secessionists had warned Wood that "if an attempt is made to take [William C.] Pickens it should be sudden and in sufficient force to overcome all opposition—the Unionists are well organ-ized in Sevier, and if notified beforehand, will in all probability resist." A few days later Confederate troops marched on the camp and broke it up with little difficulty, eliminating that threat to the railroad. But they brought back few prisoners, for the loyalists "retired without a shot where our troops [were] not able to find them."[24]

But the operation did not end there. Confederate authorities had sufficient information to suspect several prominent Sevier Countians, and they moved aggres-sively against those men. On November 10 Wood informed Zollicoffer that R. H. Hodgson, state representative from Sevier and Knox counties, had made a "treasonous speech" in Sevierville and was suspected of having helped to organize the bridge burnings. Wood had in fact attempted to

Strawberry Plains, Tennessee, battlefield, 1864.

arrest Hodgson the previous day, while he was still in Knoxville, but Hodgson had slipped away. Hodgson eventually gave himself up and was forced to take an oath to the Confederacy before being released. Confederate troops also arrested Samuel Pickens, Edward Hodges, and William Hodges. These three men were considered particularly dangerous and were sent to the Confederate military prison in Tuscaloosa, Alabama. Pickens was over 70 years old and in poor health, and in February 1862 he succumbed to the harsh prison conditions. Edward and William Hodges survived and were released that same month. The Reverend William H. Rogers, a Methodist Episcopal minister from Blount County who was also imprisoned in Tuscaloosa, described prison conditions this way: "In the room above us prisoners were dying with the small pox and their urine would run down into where we were confined… we were fed with bread made of meal in which the corn; cob and shuck had all been ground up together, and on rotten meat…I am free to assert that Tuscaloosa was to the Union men of East Tennessee what Andersonville was to Federal soldiers." Rogers gave this testimony after the war and may have exaggerated for effect, but certainly Pickens was not the only loyalist to die in Tuscaloosa.[25]

At least 400 rebellious Unionists also assembled in Cocke County following the bridge burnings. They established a camp on the heights near Parrottsville, threw up makeshift fortifications, and even built a crude wooden cannon. Despite these preparations, in mid-November Brigadier General William Carroll brought up troops from Knoxville, easily overran the camp, and captured about 100 loyalists. Confederate authorities detained the prisoners in a small stockade in Parrottsville, where reportedly they received little food and had no sanitary facilities. Shortly after their arrest Hamilton Yett, a wealthy secessionist from Cocke County, came to the stockade and asked to see "them animals." One of the prisoners, Robert Reece, hurled a brick from the fireplace at Yett, hitting him squarely in the head and knocking him out. The soldiers guarding the prison immediately took Reece outside and hanged him. The fate of the other prisoners varied. Some managed to escape, others were shot trying, and still others were sent to Confederate military prisons.[26]

Unionist trials did not end there. Immediately after the bridge burnings Colonel Daniel Leadbetter took a strong force to Greene County, the home of both Andrew Johnson and T. A. R. Nelson. Two bridges had been burned there, and Leadbetter believed that the county was a center of the Unionist resistance. After arresting a number of loyalists and hanging three suspected bridge burners, Leadbetter marched on a camp of perhaps 300 Unionists. These loyalists fled toward Cocke and Sevier Counties where, as Leadbetter stated, "they seem to have many friends." Leadbetter soon learned that the Unionists were near Parrottsville, where "the inhabitants were in instant expectation of an attack." Hoping to trap the elusive enemy between two forces, Leadbetter continued south with his regiment toward Newport and Parrottsville,

while Confederate cavalry under Captain Monsarrat rode north from Morristown. When the two forces met near Parrottsville, however, they closed on empty air. Leadbetter admitted that the mountains had defeated him: "That country consists of a tumultuous mass of steep hills wooded to the top with execrable roads winding through the ravines and often occupying the beds of the water courses.... At the farm houses along the more open valleys no men were to be seen and it is believed that nearly the whole male population of the country were lurking in the hills on account of disaffection or fear. The women in some cases were greatly alarmed throwing themselves on the ground and wailing like savages. Indeed the whole population is savage....These people cannot be caught in that manner." Determined to salvage something from the expedition, Leadbetter sent three companies to Parrottsville and two to Warrensburg with orders to impress provisions, seize horses, and arrest "troublesome men." "The whole country is given to understand that this course will be pursued until quiet shall be restored to these distracted counties." This lesson would, indeed, be repeated again and again until the war's end.[27]

Other events drew Confederate eyes toward the Smokies. As the debate over secession had intensified in East Tennessee, William G. Brownlow, editor of the *Knoxville Whig*, had become one of the leading prophets of the Unionist movement. Brownlow was a master agitator, and his open contempt for Confederate leaders, his uncompromising Unionism, and his enormous influence throughout the region made him, in Confederate eyes, the most notorious and hated Unionist in East Tennessee. Brownlow continued to publish defiantly loyalist editorials throughout the summer and fall of 1861, but by late October he realized that he had pushed the game to the limit. On October 26 Brownlow released his last issue, closed his press, and rode east in the company of the Reverend James Cummings of Sevier County. Brownlow claimed that he left Knoxville to attend the chancery court session at Maryville and to collect debts for his paper in Sevier. But the coincidence of his disappearance with the bridge burnings was too much for Confederate authorities to accept.

What Brownlow actually did during this time is unknown, but local secessionists and Confederate officers leveled numerous accusations against him. On November 9 Wood reported that Brownlow had made a "treasonable speech" in Sevierville and that many in attendance were suspected of involvement in the bridge burnings. Confederate Attorney General John Crozier Ramsey also thought it significant that Brownlow had gone to Blount and Sevier Counties, which Ramsey referred to as "the residence of the malcontents who are known as the incendiaries" and "the home of the most hostile population to the Southern Confederacy that we have in East Tennessee." Most damning, J. G. Wallace, one of Brownlow's old political enemies, wrote Ramsey that when Brownlow appeared in Maryville on November 8, an unusually large number of men, mostly Unionists, were in town. Brownlow and Cummings immediately went to the home of the Reverend W. T. Dowell and spent the whole day meeting with small groups of men, many of whom

were armed. "We discovered very clearly that there was something going on that pleased the Union men exceedingly. They seemed in very good spirits, and more confident and defiant than they had been for months." The next day, when news of the bridge burnings reached Maryville, Brownlow and Dowell immediately saddled their horses and rode out through Tuckaleechee Cove and Weir's Cove. Brownlow remained at Weir's, while Dowell went on to Walden Creek. Wallace further claimed that a young woman working in Dowell's house told another servant that she had listened at the door during one of these meetings and had heard Brownlow and Dowell tell the men that the Union Army was on its way to East Tennessee and that the bridges were going to be burned. The Dowell servant later denied the story.

Brownlow naturally gave a completely different account of his activities. He asserted that he had simply preached at the Methodist church in Sevierville the day after the bridge burnings and had never mentioned political issues. He admitted that he had hidden in Weir's Cove, but only because he feared that Confederate authorities would suspect him of instigating the uprising and arrest him. On December 2 Brownlow, Cummings and Dowell appeared before a Blount County Justice of the Peace, Solomon Farmer, and swore an affidavit that they had possessed no advanced knowledge of the bridge burnings. Brownlow would later reveal that he remained in Weir's Cove for nearly a month, where Unionists kept him hidden, fed him, and watched for Confederate troops. Finally, in mid-December Brownlow returned to Knoxville and requested permission to leave the Confederacy. Confederate authorities instead arrested and imprisoned him. Brownlow would not leave East Tennessee until March, when Secretary of War Benjamin ordered that he be sent to Union lines near Nashville.[28]

The firestorm in East Tennessee considerably rattled western North Carolina. Governor Henry T. Clark wrote Benjamin that he was besieged with letters from all the border counties begging for protection from Unionists massed in their camps. Robert Meece wrote that "there is a good deal of excitement in Haywood at this time, caused by the rebellion in East Tennessee." Militia musters were being held once a week, and Vance's Twenty-ninth North Carolina Infantry had been sent to Greene County. Another secessionist reported from Asheville that "The traitors of East Tennessee has been burning the railroad bridges they have called on the people of this place for help. The citizens and soldiers held a meeting in town last night. The militia is to be called out in all the countys west and armed with the best arms they can get—they have sent runners to South Carolina and Raleigh for powder some of the people are very excited here." Clark personally minimized the danger of actual attacks, but he expressed his own fears that the dissent raging in East Tennessee might spread across the border and fuel similar dissent in North Carolina. Clark also worried that East Tennessee refugees escaping across the border would create chaos wherever they went. In time, both of Clark's prophecies, and the fears of his constituents, would come to pass.[29]

CHAPTER 4

INNOCENCE ENDS: THE CHAOS OF WAR

ROM EARLY 1862 ON, RESIDENTS OF THE SMOKIES SUFFERED INCREASINGLY FROM UNPREDICTABLE VIOLENCE, A GNAWING SENSE of insecurity, and the disintegration of ordinary life. In both East Tennessee and western North Carolina, Unionists and secessionists fought a bloody war against each other and against enemy troops to control territory, to achieve local political control, to take revenge, and to frustrate the operations of enemy forces. Both sides committed numerous atrocities in this war, and both preyed on the population at large, breaking into houses, taking food and valuables, and terrorizing inhabitants. Western North Carolina, and to a lesser extent East Tennessee, also suffered from a huge influx of Confederate deserters who lived off the area, banded together for protection, and defied all attempts to return them to their commands. Partisan and deserter violence overwhelmed local attempts to keep order, and state and Confederate officials lacked the resources, and sometimes the willingness, to intervene effectively. Though the knowledge would have offered little comfort, Smokies residents were not alone in their suffering, for the entire southern Appalachians were caught in an epidemic of violence and disorder that left behind an appalling toll of destruction.

While the swift Confederate response to the bridge burnings in East Tennessee intimidated Unionists for a time, the effects were short lived. In March 1862 Major General Edmund Kirby Smith, who had just taken command of East Tennessee, reported that Unionists controlled all but six counties in the region: "No one can conceive the actual condition of East Tennessee, disloyal to the core, it is more dangerous and difficult to operate in than the country of an acknowledged enemy.... East Tennessee is an enemy's country, its people beyond the influence and control of our troops and in open rebellion." Other evidence reveals that Blount, Cocke, and Sevier all remained intensely opposed to the Confederacy. Alonzo Shahan, one of few Sevier County men who had volunteered for Confederate service, complained that his neighbors "look[ed] at me as a disgrace almost like they could tear me all to pieces." Colonel William Gibbs Allen, commander of the Fifth Tennessee Cavalry (Confederate), asserted that Blount was "the most uncompromising Union county in East Tennessee or Kentucky." And in October 1862 William McCampbell informed T. A. R. Nelson that even a year of war and occupation had not changed the loyalties of Cocke, Sevier, and Jefferson Counties: "You have given up all hope of preserving the Union, but it will be hard to persuade the masses to give up a cause to which they have become so ardently attached."[1]

Confederate authorities therefore made continued, though sporadic, attempts to suppress Unionist activity in the Tennessee Smokies. Four companies of the Fifth Tennessee Cavalry under Colonel spent nearly all of August and September 1862 operating against Unionist bushwhackers in Blount and Sevier Counties. On one patrol Allen's men rode "deep into the mountains," surprised a large Unionist band in their remote hideaway, and killed or captured most of them. Allen claimed that several of the guerrillas had federal commissions authorizing them to recruit men into Northern service. Allen also sent several patrols into Sevier County to arrest suspected Unionist leaders and confiscate weapons. Then in early 1863 Allen brought the entire Fifth Tennessee Cavalry to Blount, where they remained for most of January and February. On this visit Allen's men were particularly plagued by one band of Unionists based on the Little Tennessee River about ten miles southwest of Maryville. These partisans would hide in the brush along nearby roads, fire on Confederate patrols every time they rode by, and run before the troopers could engage them. Finally one officer, whose intake of alcohol had supposedly made him particularly belligerent, ordered his men immediately to charge the woods if they were fired on. The loyalists ambushed the troops as usual, but this time the Confederates rushed the woods as soon as they heard shots. They caught the Unionists by surprise, killed seven, and wounded many more. Allen claimed that his men suffered no more harassment from that particular band.[2]

Cocke and Sevier Counties also remained particularly troublesome to Confederate authorities. Sometime in the summer of 1862 Unionists ambushed a company of Confederate soldiers marching down the Newport Road and shot one man in the arm. Shortly thereafter the troops came to the home of Mark Bird, who was known to be a loyalist. Apparently in retaliation for the ambush, the Confederates shot Bird and burned his house. A little further on they met a second Unionist, Mark Fox, and cursed him for being a Tory. When Fox rashly cursed them back, the troops killed him as well. That same summer the Templer Lewis Scouts were attempting to capture a loyalist named McMahan and force him into the Confederate Army. McMahan ran into the Newport post office to escape, and the postmaster, who apparently opposed the Scouts' activities, locked the front door and let McMahan out the back. The Scouts fired several shots into the front door, but McMahan escaped unharmed. McMahan, however, had the very bad sense to return to his home that night. Learning of this presence, the Scouts surrounded his house and killed him. At times the violence went the other way, however. Sometime in 1862 James Harley, a conscript officer in Cocke County, captured Halcomb Lowell, a Unionist who had been avoiding service. Harley locked Lowell in a cabin, intending to bring him to the enrolling officer the next morning, but that night Lowell managed to escape his confinement and the Confederate Army. Lowell did not forget his treatment, however, for months later he ambushed Harley and his oldest son on the road and killed them both.[3]

The open rebellion in East Tennessee remained an embarrassment to Confederate authorities, and when Major General Sam Jones temporarily replaced Kirby Smith as department commander he was determined to stamp out resistance permanently. Soon after his appointment, Jones sent a full infantry regiment, the Thirty-first Alabama, to Newport to "thoroughly scour the country in the vicinity, and break up and destroy all parties banded together in opposition to the laws of the Confederate Government and in defiance of its authority." Shortly thereafter Jones sent another 250 infantry and 75 cavalry to Sevier County to break up a large Unionist band reported near Bluff Mountain and to arrest anyone found aiding them. Jones instructed the expedition commander, Colonel Lawrence M. Allen, that "should resistance be offered you will of course use any force necessary to accomplish your object." After eliminating the partisan band, Allen was to leave the cavalry in Sevier to assist the provost marshal in enforcing conscription and confiscating weapons. Given the small number of Confederate troops available in East Tennessee, the size of the forces Jones sent to the Smokies reveals the seriousness of the loyalist threat there. At the same time, these intermittent, heavy-handed operations, which foraged heavily off the population and frequently harassed the families of suspected guerrillas, had little effect beyond temporarily sending the bushwhackers into hiding and further alienating the Unionist population. Only cavalry had much chance of catching bushwhackers in the Smokies, and only troops who remained in an area long enough to gain a thorough knowledge of the terrain and the population enjoyed much success in combating partisan bands. But commanders in East Tennessee had far too few troops to blanket every disloyal county, so the guerrilla war went on.[4]

Despite the region's early enthusiasm for the war, substantial dissent quickly emerged in the North Carolina Smokies as well. In both Haywood and Jackson Counties a disturbing number of men refused to join the volunteer Confederate companies, banded together for protection, and in some cases threatened and attacked their secessionist neighbors. In July 1861 J. C. Bradley mentioned that there were a significant number of "Lincoln men" in Haywood and concluded "I fear no damage from them as regards myself. I think if some of the leaders were hanged the balance would see the error of their ways and return home." Similarly, in March 1862 W. B. Ferguson, a volunteer from Haywood County, wrote home "We the Haywood boys have heard that a certain 'clan' have wished that we all might be taken prisoner. We say to them, 'sin no more.'"[5]

A number of men in Macon County were also less than enthusiastic about the war. While some avoided service altogether, others who had volunteered in the first flush of enthusiasm refused to report to camps when their time came. Alfred Bell repeatedly complained that many volunteers not only stayed home but did so openly and without shame. When first entreaties and then threats had no effect, Bell sent a detachment to Macon County to bring back the recruits. Even that show of force did not have the desired result, however, for on January 30 Bell wrote "I suppose my boys is having some difficulty in arresting those traitors and deserters. The Maj will write Lt Bird this evening & if those Torys resist their arrests he will send force enough to wipe out the whole lot.... If they do resist he will show them braggart Torys that they should behave themselves and not interfere with his orders." Those resisting service apparently enjoyed considerable support, however, and the issue divided the community. Alfred's wife Mary reported that "Every man on Sugar Fork is mad at him [Bird] for going to help take them to Camp Henrietta and I think some of them have made some threats he carries a pistol that shoots seven times and I look for him some time when he is drunk to kill some one or some one to kill him." The following month Mary wrote Alfred that one of their nephews, Tom McDowell, would not enlist in Alfred's company: "Uncle Silas had sent him off South until he found out what he had to do. Mary said she would rather die than see him go in your compa-ny...they thought you did wrong in helping to arrest him...." But Alfred was adamant: "We all wish that Bird had proceeded to have obeyed his orders & those Torys had resisted we would have been ordered there forthwith & I hope & trust that we may be ordered there yet. There is application made by proper authority to let us go back & chasten those tories. My camp & the Battalion generally is powerfully enraged at such an insult."[6]

By the fall of 1862 loyalists and dis-senters had become a serious threat in the Smokies. In September Lizzie Lenoir wrote from Haywood that "the Tories have been cutting up considerably in this county" and described the difficulties Confederate authorities had dealing with them. Three of her father's neighbors had recently gone out to capture three bushwhackers who had robbed several homes and who were rumored to be hiding nearby. When the posse approached the reported hideout, however, they found at least eight partisans waiting. The bushwhackers fired first and immediately killed one of the Haywood men. The posse fired back, wounding one of the partisans, and then ran. The fallen man left behind a wife and eight children, and his sudden death aroused the whole community. The following day a much larg-er group went out after the bushwhackers, but the trail was cold and they found no signs of their prey. County authorities then called out the militia, but while these troops spent four full days scouring the area, they also came up empty. Lenoir and others believed that immediately after the first encounter the bushwhackers had fled to Tennessee, out of reach of Haywood authorities.[7]

Similarly, one night in November 1862 a band of 30-40 loyalists brazenly marched into Waynesville, battered their way into the county jail, and freed J. H. Franklin, a Unionist who had been jailed for murder-ing a man named Nolan. The loyalists threatened to burn the town then disappeared into the mountains beyond Jonathan's Creek. A large band of volun-teers, including several Cherokee, pursued the bushwhackers to the border, but once again they met so much partisan resistance that they were forced to halt. Reporting that "there are supposed to be several hundred deserters, Tories and rascals collected in there," the posse called for help from the militia, while Governor Zebulon Vance telegraphed Kirby Smith and asked him to seal off the border. Again, however, the pursuit was far too slow, and the bushwhackers escaped.[8]

These incidents reveal three critical factors that shaped the partisan war in the Smokies. The first was the terrain itself, which proved a huge advantage to bushwhackers and a huge liability for authorities attempting to combat them. Explaining Confederate difficulties in the region, J. B. Fitzgerald noted that "perhaps no section affords such advantages for concealment and evading law as this… such as get in there go with impunity, it gives encouragement to deserters from the army, Tories and outlaws in the surrounding county." The second constant was that the border itself hampered efforts to contain the resistance. When pursued, bands operating in one state could simply cross over to the other, and since Tennessee and North Carolina never achieved any kind of effective coordination, partisans used the border to their advantage to the war's end. And the third critical factor was the absolute inability of local officials either to respond effectively to the partisan threat themselves or to secure substantial help from state or Confederate officials. The main antebellum institutions for law and order, the county court, the county sheriff, and the posse, were wholly overwhelmed early in the war. The militia was supposed to be available to quell disturbances beyond the means of local officials, but by 1862 so many men were serving in the regular armies that the county militias barely continued to function. In East Tennessee the militias were also, with good reason, considered disloyal and therefore seldom employed. Confederate commanders in East Tennessee and western North Carolina were always hard pressed for men, and rarely could they spare regular troops for police duty. The decision to commit troops to the battlefield rather than behind the lines was wholly logical, yet the cruel result was that disorder in the Smokies, and in many other parts of the South, continued to increase. That disorder ate away at the morale of Confederate soldiers and citizens, denied the Confederacy resources it desperately needed, and added to the misery of Smokies families. It also cost the Confederacy additional troops, for as the suffering at home increased, more and more men from the Smokies determined that their responsibility to protect and provide for their families outweighed their duty to the new nation, and they deserted.[9]

Partisan violence therefore continued unabated until the end of the war. In January 1863, following a loyalist attack on the town of Marshall, Colonel William Holland Thomas took 200 white and Cherokee soldiers to Haywood, Jackson, and Cherokee Counties to "arrest all deserters and recusant conscripts and all Tories who have been engaging in unlawful practices on the Tennessee line of the mountains." At about the same time, A. S. Merriman wrote that "crime and violence" were "fearfully on the increase in this section of the state. A report might be made that would astonish you." C. D. Smith reported from Franklin that W. W. Holden had aroused all the loyalist sentiment in the area. Unionists had become more bold and outspoken, and many had banded together with deserters. Recently loyalists had helped a partisan band from Tennessee steal ten horses and a slave. And Captain Stephen Whitaker, a Cherokee County native commanding a

Harper's Weekly

War in the heavily-forested Southern mountains was intrinsically guerilla in nature.

company of the Sixty-ninth North Carolina Infantry, wrote despairingly that he had received dozens of complaints of bushwhacker depredations in Cherokee County. Whitaker warned that if nothing were done to protect soldiers' families, many of the volunteers from Cherokee would desert and return home.[10]

Partisan violence even reached a prominent Confederate officer. In September 1863 Lieutenant Colonel William C. Walker, who commanded the battalion attached to Thomas's command, fell seriously ill and went home to recover. Loyalists soon learned of his presence, and one night bushwhackers came to Walker's home, knocked on the door, and shot Walker as soon as he appeared. Walker's son, Columbus, was also ill with typhoid

fever, but the bushwhackers took him prisoner, rode eight miles away, and then let him loose. Remarkably, Columbus made his way home and survived. The killing shocked Confederate troops from Cherokee and considerably increased the fears they had for their families.[11]

By this time loyalists from both sides of the border were apparently cooperating. In February 1863 Stephen Thomas, a secessionist from Haywood, complained that East Tennessee Unionists had crossed the border at numerous points and were "robbing stealing and plundering almost all the time and shooting at Southern men when ever they can....They have taken nearly all the guns in the neighborhood.... They take bacon clothing thread and even the women's clothing." Thomas reported that the bushwhackers had become bold enough even to challenge regular troops. When a squad of infantry went out to capture one particularly troublesome band, they found four bushwhackers barricaded inside a house. The troops broke down the door and rushed in, but rather than surrendering the bushwhackers immediately began firing. The captain grappled with one of the loyalists, and in the struggle the man shot himself with his own pistol. The other bushwhackers had better aim, however, and they managed to kill one soldier and wound several others. Eventually the squad retreated from the house, and the bushwhackers escaped. Thomas, outraged at the bushwhackers' boldness, hoped that more forces would be sent and that Confederate troops would "shoot and hang them as fast as they can get hold of them."[12]

Thomas's wish came partially true. Confederate troops had been watching the homes of several suspected bushwhackers and conscript evaders in the Big Bear section of Haywood County, and eventually they captured three men, Henry Grooms, George Grooms, Jr., and Michael Caldwell. The Guardsmen marched the men several miles before stopping at a crossroads. There they demanded that George Grooms, Jr. play a popular song, *Bonaparte's Retreat*, on his fiddle. When the song ended the Guardsmen shot all three men and left the bodies on the road. Eliza Grooms would later find her dead relatives and bring the bodies home. Another brother, John Grooms, may have eventually killed one of the soldiers in revenge. Confederate troops also shot two 12-year-old boys in Cocke County, though whether the shootings were deliberate or accidental is unclear. By

Library of Congress

Lieutenant General James Longstreet attempted to retake Knoxville for the Confederacy.

this time even young boys were seen as threats, and troops sometimes fired on anyone who ran from them.[13]

Unionists continued to fight back, however. In January 1864, 27 men came to the home of William D. Walker, a prominent Cherokee County secessionist who operated a store, an inn, and a tavern, and who at various times had also served as postmaster, justice of the peace, and judge. The men destroyed all of Walker's clothing and furniture, dragged him from his house, and took him to Union authorities in Knoxville. His wife tried to follow to see where he was being taken, but she could not keep up and had to return home. Walker was then moved from prison to prison until he eventually ended up at Camp Douglas, Illinois. Unable to

Confederate Major General John C. Breckinridge was called upon to suppress the actions of Unionists in East Tennessee and western North Carolina.

withstand prison conditions, Walker died in November 1864. That same month Lieutenant General James Longstreet ordered Brigadier General John C. Vaughn to send a detachment to Chimney Top Mountain "to drive away the bushwhackers that are reported to be there. They ought to be severely punished, and if driven away a good foraging country will be opened to us."

In mid-April W. H. Porter notified Colonel William Holland Thomas that bushwhackers from the Yellow Creek area had ambushed part of a Confederate company and killed two men. Porter had sent a scout after them, with no success. On August 10 Captain James Taylor wrote Thomas that a band of bushwhackers from Tennessee had announced that they intended to ambush two Confederate Home Guard units in Cherokee. Taylor had

a detachment out watching for them. And in April 1865, at the very end of the war, 50 bushwhackers under Timothy Lyons, a deserter from the First Wisconsin Cavalry, burned the courthouse in Murphy.[14]

The deteriorating conditions in western North Carolina also came to the attention of Governor Zebulon Vance, and in October 1864 Vance wrote to Major General John C. Breckinridge, the new commander of the Department of East Tennessee and Southwest Virginia, for help. Vance claimed that in Cherokee County and the surrounding area "the warfare between scattering bands and insurgent troops is conducted on both sides without any regard whatever to the rule of civilized war or the dictates of humanity." Vance was particularly concerned about several men from the Cherokee Home Guard who had been captured by loyalist partisans and threatened with execution. Vance blamed much of the violence on "tory renegades from both North Carolina and Tennessee pretend[ing] to be acting under regular federal authority." Vance urged Breckinridge to write to the federal commander in East Tennessee and insist that he bring Unionists under control. If federal officers refused, Vance proposed that Breckinridge institute a system of retaliatory measures for loyalist depredations. Vance further stated that if the Cherokee Home Guardsmen were killed he would order retaliations against captured Federal troops.[15]

Union authorities did make some attempts to limit the activities of Unionist partisans. In June 1864 Union Provost Marshal Samuel P. Carter informed Wade Newman, captain of the Home Guards in Cocke County, that he had received reliable information that the Guards were "engaged in horse stealing and plundering citizens indiscriminately, Union as well as secession sympathizers." Carter ordered Newman to disband and threatened that if he refused Newman and his men would be punished "as robbers and outlaws." Newman apparently ignored the threat, for Carter subsequently ordered a deputy provost marshal to investigate charges that Newman and John Shields had stolen horses and property and to arrest them if necessary. In May 1864 Carter also ordered Captain S. T. Bryan to arrest Major Dunn, the head of the Maryville Home Guards, for similar offenses.[16]

But Union officials also contributed significantly to the partisan war on the border. In Cherokee County Goldman Bryson had organized a loyalist partisan band early in the war and had become notorious for his attacks on secessionists, particularly his burning of the jail in Murphy in February 1863. Bryson had farmed land in Monroe County, Tennessee before the war, and he easily operated on both sides of the border. When Union forces entered East Tennessee in September 1863, Bryson received a commission from Major General Ambrose Burnside to return to Cherokee County for two weeks to recruit. But Bryson's mission was short lived. Secessionists reported Bryson's presence to Confederate officers, and Major General C. L. Stevenson, who believed that Bryson "had been sent with his command by Burnside to get in my rear and obtain information as to our movements and intentions," sent 100 Confederate cavalry under Colonel John C. Vaughn "to intercept, and, if possible, destroy the party." On October 27 Vaughn's men came across Bryson's band in

Union Major General John M. Schofield authorized the notorious George W. Kirk to recruit Union loyalists from East Tennessee and western North Carolina to fight the Confederates.

Cherokee County. They killed two men, captured 17, scattered the rest, and took 30 horses. The following day Lieutenant C. H. Taylor, part of a company stationed at Murphy, took 19 men and picked up Bryson's trail. They had marched 25 miles "when I came upon [Bryson] and fired on him, killing him and capturing one man with him. I found on his possession his orders from General Burnside and his roll and other papers."[17]

Bryson's failure did not discourage Union authorities, and in February 1864 Major General John M. Schofield authorized George Kirk to recruit one or more regiments from among loyalists in the border counties of East Tennessee and North Carolina. Kirk, who was from Greene

Library of Congress

Union Lieutenant Colonel Robert Klein (seated, in uniform) attacked a camp of Confederate deserters and other guerillas at Chilhowee. Others in the photo include (standing, left to right) James Doughty, unknown, unknown, Henry W. Dodd, unknown, unknown. Seated from left to right: John Irving, Klein, Dan Cole. On ground: Dan Plue, Klein's son, W. J. Lee, unknown, Wood, Sanford McGee, John W. Langford.

County, Tennessee, had made a name for himself guiding Unionists to Kentucky. He was charismatic, ruthless, and a skilled partisan leader, and he soon had enough recruits to make up two regiments, the Second and Third North Carolina Mounted Infantries. In April 1864 Kirk raided into North Carolina and attempted to destroy the Yadkin Bridge near Salisbury. He did not reach the bridge, but he surprised a conscript camp at Salisbury, killed one officer and ten men, and took 279 prisoners. He also destroyed one locomotive, three train cars, a train depot, and a commissary. Schofield then instructed Kirk to concentrate on organizing loyalists in the mountains. Kirk claimed that he was conducting legitimate military operations, but Confederates accused Kirk's men of robbing and terrorizing secessionists and enriching themselves. Kirk, in fact, became an object of terror to secessionists in the Smokies. On July 24, 1864 L. Cowles wrote his sister "You speak of the Kirk raiders and say again you are not afraid of them—surely you do not believe all the stories that are told on them desperate fellows or you would be frightened to death." Similarly, Colonel William Gibbs described Kirk as "the notorious robber and murderer... who had made up a command from East Tennessee and western North Carolina, and comprised of deserters and the scum of the country generally.... men of bad standing and of extremely disreputable characters who, before the war, were regularly before the courts for nearly every species of crime." Kirk would play a leading role in Union operations in the Smokies until the end of the war.[18]

Other Union troops also entered the fray in the North Carolina Smokies. In mid-January Lieutenant Colonel Robert Klein of the Third Indiana Cavalry learned that a band of "absentees, deserters, and paroled soldiers of the rebel army, and rebel citizens" had established a camp at Chilhowee. They were taking livestock and other property from Unionists in Blount and Monroe Counties and selling the goods in North Carolina. Klein took 100 men from his regiment and rode up the Little Tennessee River to within about eight miles from the bushwhacker camp. He then sent 28 men across the river. The current was swift and the river full of ice, so the crossing was difficult, but only one man was lost. Klein's men then scattered the Confederate pickets and charged into camp without warning. They captured 23 guerrillas, along with horses, weapons, and equipment, and routed the rest.[19]

In the North Carolina Smokies deserters proved to be as great a threat as loyalists. In 1863 Colonel John S. Preston, head of the Confederate Conscript Bureau, sent Lieutenant Colonel George Lay to investigate numerous complaints of conscript evasion and desertion in western North Carolina. After inspecting the entire area Lay concluded that conditions were even worse than reported. Men were openly deserting and taking their muskets and ammunition with them. Upon reaching western North Carolina they took refuge in the mountains and organized into bands of 50-100 men. The rough terrain offered so many hiding places that Confederate patrols had managed to capture only a handful of deserters, and Lay attributed those captures to luck rather than skill. These patrols were always outnumbered, and they faced the constant threat of ambush. In Cherokee County deserters had "assumed a sort of military occupation," terrorizing the population and particularly targeting the families of Confederate soldiers. Lay believed it would take two to three full regiments to clear the region of deserters and restore order.[20]

Other officers agreed with Lay. Captain J. C. McCrea reported that every border county in western North Carolina was overrun with "deserters, renegade conscripts, and tories" who were robbing residents, particularly the "unprotected wives of soldiers," and threatening violence against anyone who moved against them. McCrea asserted that enrolling officers could not travel about the border counties without substantial escorts, and recommended that regular troops be sent to suppress the resistance. As McCrea astutely noted, desertion and conscript evasion fed on each other: "The impunity with which deserters remain at home has produced the worst effect upon the conscripts, who generally run and join the deserters in the mountains upon any attempt made to arrest them."[21]

Similarly, First Lieutenant J. N. Bryson, who had been sent to Cherokee County to bring back deserters, reported that none would return. Worse, they had become "a terror to the citizens, and especially the soldiers' wives who are alone. They are killing cattle, sheep, and hogs; also stealing bee-gums, breaking into smoke-houses,

Confederate Major William W. Stringfield was sent to western North Carolina in 1864 to restore order to a place chaotic with deserters, Unionists, militias, renegade soldiers and rampant thievery.

"largely in the ascendancy, and are augmenting their number every day. They are killing stock, disarming the citizens." The militias in both counties were outnumbered and intimidated, and Pearson asserted that he could not carry out his duties without a large force.[22]

Major W. W. Stringfield left a particularly vivid account of the disorderly conditions in the North Carolina Smokies. In September 1864 Thomas was ordered to Raleigh to answer charges, and Stringfield was sent to take over Thomas's command. Stringfield was determined to restore order, but he faced a daunting task. Cherokee County, along with Clay and Graham Counties, was not only "much infested by Union element," but also troubled by "some very indiscreet and very unwise men and soldiers on our side in this section.... This was a sort of half-way ground between Tennessee and South Carolina and Georgia. Negroes, horses, and other property were stolen in Tennessee, carried to Georgia and South Carolina and sold. My soldiers from the Valley of Virginia did not like this and I had plenty of help to put it down. Several bands of 'scouts' caused much of this trouble. I ordered these to their commands, took horses, cattle and other property from them, several times at the muzzles of their pistols." This was a rather startling admission for a Confederate officer, but other evidence supports Stringfield's claim. In February 1865 Confederate Colonel John C. Vaughn reported that officers from Major General Joseph Wheeler's command had established a camp of about 100 men in Cherokee County. They were raiding into East Tennessee, stealing property, and selling it in Georgia. More men from Wheeler's and

etc." Deserters had also killed one officer, Lieutenant Robert, while he was home on leave, and had shot at a second officer, Captain Berry, when he attempted to collect absentees. They had then announced that no other officer who came into the county to enforce conscription or round up deserters would get out alive. Bryson agreed with Lay that only a large force could restore order, but he urged that no soldiers from Cherokee be used, for if all deserters were not driven out those who remained would burn the houses of those soldiers' families. Yet another enrolling officer, Captain D. C. Pearson, reported in August 1863 that deserters in Cherokee were

Vaughn's commands were deserting every day to join the camp, and Vaughn urged that troops be sent immediately to break it up. Stringfield also remembered that "Cherokee County was the scene of many small raids by night riders who rode back and forth across the mountains till the end of the war.... In this time of danger and distress, many citizens were moving away to Tennessee or to South Carolina, or wherever they could find protection from the scouts and raiders."[23]

Stringfield faced other difficulties as well. In Murphy, Stringfield gave papers to a number of families exempting them from foraging, but a band of deserters soon stole a horse from a man named Pleasant Henry. When Henry complained, Stringfield, apparently outraged, rode off after them alone. He overtook the band of nine men, ordered them to stop, and seized the bridle of the stolen horse. Stringfield claimed that six or seven of the men then aimed their pistols at him, but that he insisted that he was taking the horse and that they would have to shoot him. The deserters backed down, and Stringfield returned the horse to Henry. Stringfield also asserted that several times he had to prevent Confederate troops from executing Federal prisoners. On one of these occasions J. A. P. Edwards was with a detachment of Confederate troops in Haywood and Madison Counties hunting deserters and bushwhackers. They had captured two men, "either Federal soldiers or bushwhackers," and the detachment commander had just directed three men to take the prisoners into a laurel thicket and execute them. At that moment Stringfield rode up, realized what was about to happen, and ordered the Confederates to untie the men. "When no one moved or obeyed his order, he at once dismounted and cut the ropes loosening the arms of the men himself. Meanwhile our lieutenant expostulated and was very indignant. He drew his pistol and brought it in front of his person, whereupon Major Stringfield drew his sword over our lieutenant's head, and ordered him to put up his pistol." The other troops then separated the officers, but "Stringfield's sudden and timely appearance certainly saved the life of Mitchell Rixby and the other man whose name I do not know."[24]

Conditions also steadily worsened in the Tennessee Smokies. Longstreet's attempt to retake Knoxville in late 1863 emboldened secessionists, and Confederate partisans from Tennessee, North Carolina, and Georgia became more active in East Tennessee. In November 1863, just after Confederate cavalry had occupied Blount County, a secessionist band rode into the Nine Mile Creek region. Who they were, or where they came from, is unknown, but it is clear that they knew the area and the population. Unionist scouts gave warning of their approach, and most loyalist men managed to hide. But two Unionist Home Guard members, Lark Anderson and Love Fields, did not move quickly enough, and they were captured. The Confederate partisans then rode to the home of John S. Crye, another Home Guard member. Pretending that they were Crye's friends and that they had come to warn him about the bushwhackers, they tricked a younger sister into revealing that Crye was hiding at the home of George Best. Best was not only Crye's father-in-law, he was also an outspoken Unionist with three sons in the Union Army. The

Confederate partisans captured Crye and Best and rode away with the four prisoners. Eventually they stopped at a spring near Best's grist mill. The Confederates sent their prisoners to the spring, but while the loyalists were lying on the ground drinking the partisan band shot three of them and left their bodies where they fell. For reasons unknown they took Best on to Monroe County before killing him.[25]

Cades Cove also suffered considerably in this war. Some time in 1863 secessionist partisans from North Carolina began raiding into the Cove, killing men, robbing houses, and driving livestock back to North Carolina. Men began hiding out in the wooded areas of the Cove, and the Primitive Baptist Church, one of the central institutions in the Cove, was forced to close. Russell Gregory, the pastor of the church, then organized loyalist men into a Home Guard and the women and children into a warning network. Major Charles G. Davis, who escaped from Libby Prison in Virginia and made his way to Knoxville, passed through the Cove in December 1863 and left a vivid account of this system's workings: "We entered the Cove about 3 P.M. and very unexpectedly caused quite an alarm. A girl was on duty as a sentinel. She gave the alarm with a horn. When she blew the horn we were looking down into the Cove. In an instant it was alive. The men were driving their cattle before them, and every man had a gun over his shoulder....We marched in and went to Mrs. Rowan's home. She was very much frightened when she saw us, but we soon satisfied her that we were friends....We had not more than gotten seated when a woman came running up the road to Mrs. R. and informed her that the

Rebs were coming. We jumped up ready to run, but we soon found out that the woman had taken us for the Rebels....We were resting very comfortably at Mr. Spark's telling our story when a horseman came riding up from the lower end the of the Cove and said the Rebels are coming sure, that one of the citizens had seen them.... After waiting for an hour, we found that it was another false alarm. The report had gone down one side of the Cove and up the other."

This system would be put to the test in the spring of 1864, when Unionists learned that a major raid was imminent. They felled trees across the road that the raiders would have to use for an exit, and the Home Guard set an ambush along the road. When the bushwhackers passed through with their plunder, the loyalists began firing, and the two sides fought a chaotic skirmish for nearly an hour. The loyalists wounded two secessionists, and eventually the raiders abandoned their plunder and left. From that point on, Confederate bushwhackers raided only at night, with far less success. Gregory had won a significant victory, but he would pay for his activities. Two weeks after the ambush Confederates came back into the Cove and killed Gregory in his house.[26]

The violence in the Tennessee Smokies continued after Longstreet gave up the attempt on Knoxville and retreated toward Bulls Gap. In late November two Texas soldiers retreating from Knoxville came to Rockford Cotton Mills. They asked why the workers were not in the army and demanded that they give up any firearms. The owner of the Mills, Charles Coffin, asserted that the War Department had assigned men to the work, but the soldiers persisted, and an argument ensued. One of the soldiers shot and killed Coffin, but the mill workers retaliated by killing one soldier and wounding the other. In December one Union officer reported that Confederate guerrillas had threatened grist mills at Maryville, and the following month another complained that the mountains near Maryville were "infested" with "brigands."[27]

Confederate partisans were active in Cocke County as well. In January 1864 the Reverend Henry M. Sheed, a Methodist minister from Parrottsville, wrote to Union Provost Marshal Samuel P. Carter for help. Sheed claimed that about 100 renegade Confederate cavalry under a Captain Rumbaugh had taken control of the county and were stealing food, clothes, blankets, and other goods from Unionist homes. Worse, they had committed a whole string of atrocities. Sheed claimed that Rumbaugh's men had set fire to homes and strung up men by the neck to force families to reveal where their valuables were hidden. They had cut off the ears of a Methodist Episcopal minister and then beaten him to death with their guns. They had killed two Union soldiers who were home after being captured and paroled. Worst of all, Rumbaugh's men had broken into the home of David Hume, a Unionist with two sons in the Federal Army, stolen every bit of food, clothing, and furniture, and raped his two daughters. They had then gone to the home of a third daughter, found her in bed with her new baby, stripped the coverings from her bed, and left mother and child to die from exposure. It is impossible to tell whether all these charges were true, but Carter had already received several other reports of Confederate depredations in Cocke, as well as charges that two Cocke County secessionists, General Alexander Smith and James Swaggert, were encouraging Rumbaugh's men. Carter forwarded Sheed's letter to the department commander and asked for 500 cavalry to clear Cocke County of enemy units.[28]

Union troops did return to the Tennessee Smokies in January 1864, but their presence provided only limited protection to loyalists. In late March 1864 a company of Confederate cavalry under Captain Thomas Osborn rode into Blount and Sevier Counties to scout Federal positions. Confederate records show that Osborn's company was regularly enrolled, but the unit seems to have operated independently much of the time. On that night they stopped at Louisville and captured a prominent Unionist, Horace Foster, with the intention of holding him as a hostage for John Tish, a secessionist currently imprisoned in Knoxville. What happened then remains in dispute, but it appears that as the Confederates rode on toward Sevierville, Foster broke away from his guards and ran. Several troops fired into the dark and wounded their prisoner. Osborn's men then took Foster back to his house and left him there, but rode off with four horses, a mule, and a wagon. Five days later Osborn's company killed another Blount County loyalist, Elijah Hatcher. A Federal military commission later investigated Osborn's raid into Blount and found substantial cooperation between Confederate troops and Blount County secessionists. The commission alleged that James McGhee, a Confederate supporter who had recently taken an oath of allegiance to the Federal government, "did, in various ways, harass and injure the Union citizens of Blount County, Tenn; that he did point out Union citizens to the rebel soldiers and pilot them to the houses of Union men, for the purpose of arresting them and seizing their property." It also charged that three other Blount County secessionists, Henry Buram, William Henderson, and William T. Johnson, had ridden with Osborn's company and led them to Foster's house. The commission further found that a fifth secessionist, James Nuckles, had participated in the killing of Elijah Hatcher. Another Unionist charged that Osborn's men and Blount County secessionists had "set fire to the dwellings of Union men to force them to tell where their money was, to force them to deliver it; failing in this, they have taken them to trees and hanged them."[29]

Although most Confederate troops left East Tennessee in the spring of 1864, secessionist partisans continued their war on loyalists. In July 1864 Crofton Hall reported from Blount County that "Rebbles" raided into the county one night, killed one Unionist, and shot but did not kill another. Two months later Hall reported that Unionists had suffered so many raids that they were building a brush fence on top of Chilhowee Mountain from the Little Tennessee River to the Tennessee River to keep out raiders. In August officers of the Second Tennessee Cavalry (Union), then based at Decatur, Alabama, informed Tennessee Military Governor Andrew Johnson that Unionist families in Blount, Cocke, Sevier, Jefferson, and Monroe Counties were so menaced by bands of deserters, secessionists, bushwhackers, and

thieves that they had been forced to go deep into the Smokies to hide. Conditions were too dangerous for families to risk working in their fields, so no crops were being raised, and many loyalists faced starvation. The soldiers begged Johnson to send troops to protect their families. Union Provost Marshal Samuel P. Carter also complained that large numbers of men in Blount County were "advancing secessionist principles and intimidating Union men" and ordered the Blount County Provost Marshal to suppress their activities. That same month Osborn's men returned to Sevier County to impress horses. After the Confederates took two loyalists prisoner, however, the Home Guards ambushed Osborn's men, forcing them to abandon the prisoners and leave the county.

In January 1865 Colonel John Shannon, who was gathering forage in Cocke County, complained about harassment from independent scouts or guerrillas "of the most desperate character." They were based near Newport at the intersection of the Pigeon and Cosby rivers: "That is the home of the bushwhackers, and where they keep their stock, and throughout a most damnably secession hole." Shannon complained that he was unable to send forage to Knoxville, for if he left supplies by the river for collection the guerrillas would immediately find and burn them. Shannon claimed that his mounted men had completely worn out their horses chasing bushwhackers. And in February Barbara Hall wrote from Blount County that "The rogs [rogues] and the rebs is taking every thing that they can get their hands on and killing folks every where and a gone." One of their neighbors had shot and wounded one bushwhacker, but they had then captured him and carried him off. Barbara was glad that her husband James was in the Union Army, for "the men that is at home is a feird to stay in the house." Barbara told James to stay in service his full time.[30]

While Unionist partisans fought Confederate troops and secessionists at home, thousands of others from East Tennessee, and hundreds from western North Carolina, left to join the Union Army. These escapes were accomplished through a remarkably well organized network of men and women who guided recruits along safe paths, scouted for Confederate patrols, ferried groups across rivers, operated safe houses, and provided food and other supplies. John Hyde of Cherokee described part of the escape network there. One man would guide escapees 25 miles from his house to N. G. Howell's farm. Howell would then bring them another 15 miles to Hyde's house, and Hyde would take the escapees across the border to Tennessee. Green Burgess claimed that he used his position in a Confederate Home Guard unit to recruit volunteers for the Union Army and guide them to Kentucky. Similarly, Miles Sneed claimed that he went to work in an iron forge in Cherokee to avoid Confederate service. "I was permitted to go about and was thus enabled to hide and feed many men who would otherwise perhaps have been captured or would have starved." And W. Roane of Haywood County proved so effective in guiding loyalist recruits and escaped prisoners to Union lines that Provost Marshal Carter ordered that he be given transportation whenever he needed it.

Similar networks existed in other counties. In Sevier, Unionists maintained a series of signal fires on the higher peaks. When a group of recruits was ready to leave, they would light a fire near their rendezvous. If the way were clear, Unionists at the next station would light their fire, and so on down the line. Dr. Joseph C. Strong, a physician and wealthy farmer in Sevier County, opened his farm to any group attempting to reach Kentucky. He also regularly housed Spencer Deaton, one of East Tennessee's best known pilots. William J. Hackney, a Quaker from Friendsville, Blount County, also determined that he would do whatever he could for anyone who opposed the war. A particularly large cave happened to be located just across the creek from the meeting house where he was a leader. The entrance was hidden in thick brush, and the cave's existence was not widely known. Hackney secretly stocked the cave with provisions and bedding, and quietly offered its use to those avoiding conscription, those traveling to Kentucky, and those who had deserted Confederate service. He also guided a number of groups as far toward Kentucky as he could.[31]

This form of resistance hurt the Confederacy in many ways. It denied the new nation badly needed soldiers while adding to Union manpower. It forced the Confederacy to pull regular soldiers away from the front to patrol the major escape routes, hunt down conscripts, and guard them in camps. And it hurt Confederate morale, for the loyalist success in defying conscription revealed Confederate political and military weaknesses and encouraged other men to evade service. At the same time, this enterprise also carried great risks, for many who attempted to escape to

John H. Ragan, a native of Sevier County, became the Confederate Postmaster.

Library of Congress

Kentucky, and some who helped them escape, were imprisoned or executed for their disloyalty.

A few Smokies Unionists left dramatic accounts of their escapes. Before the war, Robert Allen Ragan worked for a livestock farmer in Cocke County, raising hogs and driving them to market in South Carolina. In 1860, at the age of 20, he was elected lieutenant colonel of the county militia, a position with more political than military significance. When the war began Ragan took up teaching to avoid military service, but in the spring of 1862 Confederate troops marched into his school and arrested him. After being enrolled, Ragan was taken to Knoxville and confined with about 300 other Unionists, many of whom had been captured trying to reach Kentucky. Ragan

was fortunate, however, for his father happened to be a cousin of Confederate Postmaster John H. Ragan, a Sevier County native. Postmaster Ragan arranged for Robert's release, and he returned home. Even so, the county enrolling officer, Henry Kilgore, continued to threaten Ragan, and eventually he was forced to go into hiding. Like hundreds of others avoiding conscription, Ragan spent several months living in the woods near his home, constantly on the move and frequently running from Confederate troops. In April Ragan heard that a large group of Unionists in Greene County had hired a pilot and were preparing to leave for Kentucky. Determined to escape his plight, Ragan went to Greene, taking with him Joseph Smith of Parrottsville. While waiting for the pilot, Ragan and Smith spent most of their time hiding in a large pile of straw and being fed by a loyalist family. Eventually the pilot appeared and the group set out. But the night before their departure Ragan had had a strong premonition of danger, so instead of leaving with the group he went back home to hide. Ragan's premonition, if real, was all too true. Confederate forces intercepted the Unionists before they even made it out of Greene County and captured everyone except the pilot, who escaped by jumping into Lick Creek. Forced into service, the Unionists were sent to Vicksburg, where most were either killed or captured. Joseph Smith, Ragan's companion, had the sad misfortune to be shot in the face. He contracted blood poisoning from the wound, and died.

After this narrow escape Ragan went back to hiding out. He moved back and forth between his uncle's house in Cocke

County and his father-in-law's farm in Greene, and sometimes wore women's clothing to avoid detection. Finally, in May 1863 Ragan learned that another expedition was forming in Greene County, and he went back to his father-in-law's house to await their departure. Apparently his presence was noticed, however, for the night after he arrived a detachment of Confederate soldiers came up the lane toward the house. Ragan was upstairs sleeping, but his father-in-law saw the troops and shouted a warning. Not waiting to dress, Ragan ran out the back door, jumped a fence, and hid in a briar thicket. He then realized that in jumping the fence he had landed on a sharp rock and cut the ball of his foot to the bone. Ragan crawled back to the house for help, but found that 20 soldiers were crowded inside eating. They had stacked their guns against a wall, and Ragan was sorely tempted to grab them and shoot as many soldiers as he could. He knew, however, that the Confederates would likely retaliate by burning the house and perhaps killing his father-in-law, so he remained hidden. Once the Confederate troops left, he bandaged his foot and made his way to the meeting place, where he found 420 loyalists gathered. Ragan, however, found he could not walk well enough to keep up, so once again he gave up a chance to escape.

Finally, in July 1863 Ragan heard that George Kirk was leading an expedition from Greene County. This time Ragan arrived at the rendezvous without incident and left with about 100 other men. They made the trip without serious problems and arrived safely at Camp Dick Robinson. After enlisting, however, Ragan volunteered to return to East Tennessee to

Courtesy Joey Wooldridge, James Kirk Collection

Colonel George W. Kirk (left) poses with his father Alexander (standing) and brother John. Colonel Kirk was originally from Greene County, Tennessee. He led Union loyalists from the southern Appalachians on many raids in the South and became known as a ruthless robber and murderer.

recruit other loyalists. Ragan and four other men slipped back into Greene County and again hid at his father-in-law's house. Ragan then sent a message to his father, who was a deputy sheriff in Cocke County, cautiously to spread the word that he would be taking volunteers back to Kentucky. About 120 men responded, and Ragan led them away.

Their first night out a wicked storm blew up, and the loyalists had to travel single file, each holding onto the man in front, to avoid being separated. When they reached the Nolachucky River, however, they had a stroke of luck. The ferry owner was a Unionist, and he agreed to take the group across. They continued steadily on from there, traveling at night and resting during the day, but the going was dangerous and slow. Confederate cavalry patrolled most roads, so the party had to travel across rough terrain. Even then they sometimes had to cross roads, and though they did so in small groups and quick rushes, more than once they barely avoided Confederate troops. At all times the loyalists feared detection, and they talked in the barest whispers to avoid being overheard. Fortunately they found help along the way. Ragan particularly remembered that slaves "were always loyal, and we could depend on them. They would never 'give us away'." Slaves would bring them whatever food they could, and sometimes show them places to hide during the day. Even so, as often happened, the Unionists' supplies ran low and their shoes and clothes wore out long before they reached Kentucky. Ragan noticed that one volunteer, James H. Randolph, was marching on bruised and bloody feet. When Ragan went to encourage him, Randolph replied that "when we get back to Tennessee we will give them Hell and rub it in."[32]

Two other loyalists, J. A. Andes and Will A. McTeer of Sevier County, found it equally difficult to reach Kentucky. McTeer left Sevier with six other young men in July 1862. They were supposed to join a large party of Unionists in Knox County, but they arrived a day too late. Rather than return home, McTeer and the others chose to wait until the pilot returned. They moved from place to place and eventually settled at a large Unionist farm on the French Broad River. One day when they were down by the river they were nearly discovered by a Confederate soldier and a local secessionist who were out fishing, but they managed to hide in the brush along the bank. Finally the pilot returned to Knox, and McTeer and his companions joined a new expedition. The first few days went by without incident, but then they accidentally came upon a camp of Confederate troops. They could not go around, so they cautiously filed by, moving as silently as they could and fearing detection at any moment. McTeer remembered that they passed so closely that they could hear the Confederate soldiers talking and shoeing their horses. The troops did not hear them, however, and the pilot guided the party safely to Jefferson County. There he passed the volunteers on to Lieutenant W. T. Perham, an officer with the Sixth Tennessee Infantry, who had been sent back to East Tennessee to scout Confederate movements and recruit.

Perham led the loyalists to the Clinch River, but there they found the water too high to ford. There was no ferry, and no others boats were available, for the Confederates had confiscated or destroyed them all. Finally, the Unionists built a makeshift raft out of planks taken from a barn and crossed the river. They had no more adventures for several days, but when they were approaching the Kentucky border they nearly ran into a Confederate patrol. The loyalists scattered and hid in the brush along the road, and then waited, silent and afraid, until the patrol disappeared out of sight. McTeer claimed that his shoes completely wore out before they reached Kentucky and that he finished the journey on blistered, bleeding, and infected feet. In the end, however, the party reached the small Union force then occupying Cumberland Gap, and McTeer joined the Second Tennessee Cavalry.[33]

Andes originally intended to leave Sevier County in September 1862. He changed his plans, however, when Confederate forces drove Union troops out of Cumberland Gap and invaded Kentucky. But the following month, when a pilot came to Sevierville, Andes again changed his mind, and he and about 450 other loyalists set out. Unlike McTeer, Andes had no trouble until he reached Cumberland Gap. There Unionists saw the Confederate Army of Tennessee retreating from Kentucky and had to take great care to avoid any troops, but they crossed the border safely. Upon reaching Kentucky, the Unionists had a nasty surprise. Union forces had moved north to meet the Confederate invasion, and the loyalists had to travel all the way to Lexington to find a camp where they could enlist. The weather turned cold, and they trekked many days in mixed rain and snow. By the time they reached Union lines many were ill, and all were exhausted.[34]

Yet another expedition of Unionists left Blount and Knox Counties in April 1862, shortly after the First Conscription Act was passed. They had made extensive preparations for the trip, including storing up supplies and hiding a large boat to use in crossing the Clinch River. But it stormed the night they were scheduled to leave, and only about 150 men, half the number expected, showed up. Upon gathering, the Unionists learned that two men had been captured on their way to the rendezvous,

raising fears that Confederate troops would be sent in pursuit. The Unionists hiked to the Clinch River as quickly as possible and prepared to cross, but then found that only half the group could fit on the boat. While the first group was crossing someone shouted a warning that Confederate cavalry were coming. At first most of the men prepared to scatter, but a few more determined loyalists proposed to stand and fight, and the rest agreed. When the "cavalry" rode up, however, they turned out to be a small party of Anderson County Unionists who had come to guide the loyalists to the border. In the meantime the group on the boat heard the uproar and chose not to wait after crossing. They soon found a loyalist who was willing to guide them, and after several days hard walking they reached Kentucky without incident.

The second group, conversely, chose to wait until daylight to cross the river. That decision almost proved disastrous, for a local secessionist spotted the gathering and ran to the nearest Confederate post to give warning. However, a nearby loyalist heard the secessionist tell his story. He reached the river before the Confederate troops, and the Unionists scattered and hid. They were not discovered, and the next morning they crossed the river safely. They, too, reached Kentucky safely.[35]

But not all escapes turned out so happily for the loyalists. Shade T. Harris, a Unionist from Dandridge, reached Union lines in 1862. He then went back to Sevier County to recruit. In December 1862, however, a local secessionist reported Harris' presence to Confederate officers, and he was captured. Harris was tried as a Confederate deserter, convicted, and sentenced to die, but President Davis commuted the sentence to imprisonment. Abraham Hopkins of Cataloochee also joined the Union Army and went back home to recruit. But secessionists discovered his activities, waylaid Hopkins at Mount Sterling Bridge, and killed him. Hopkins was the son of Benjamin Parker Hopkins and Ruth Tinker, who had nine sons in the Confederate Army and three in the Union.

Closely related to the partisan war was the grim contest between Confederate conscription officers who were charged with filling Confederate ranks and Smokies men who had no wish to fight in this war. The first Confederate Conscription Act, passed in April 1862, made all men from ages 18-35 liable to service, while providing exemptions for certain professions. The Confederate Congress raised the age of service to 45 in September 1862; then in February 1864 it tapped all men ages 17-50. Although these acts provided wealthier men far too many ways to escape service, they did reflect a realistic assessment of the new nation's military position. The Confederacy lagged considerably behind the North in manpower, and since the volunteer system had failed to fill the Southern armies, conscription was the only alternative.[37]

At the same time, conscription probably created more dissent than any other Confederate policy. Many men in the Smokies who had not opposed secession also did not wish to leave their families and homes to fight in this war, especially as conditions in the region worsened. Even some loyalists probably would have become peaceful citizens if the Confederacy had not pressured them to fight for a cause they opposed. Further, the enforcement of conscription required Confederate officials to reach directly into every community in ways that inevitably aroused resentment. Many residents who fully supported the war still found the sight of Confederate troops entering homes, questioning wives and children about the location of male inhabitants, and chasing down and imprisoning Southern citizens disturbing. Conscription in fact created its own destructive cycle, for as more men attempted to evade or defy Confederate authority, the new government responded with increased force, further alienating its own citizens.

Estil B. Bible of Cocke County vividly described these conditions: "There were a few families that were fortunate enough to own large estates of river bottom along the banks of the French Broad and Nolachuckey rivers that were wealthy enough to own slaves...the price of a slave was far out of reach of a "Hillbilly" family (like my family) who made their home in the mountains, hills and creek valleys of this region. The slave owners were reluctant to giving up their slaves and were loyal to the South or Seceding States, while the common run of the people who were too poor to own slaves (and didn't want them anyway) were loyal to the Union. Under these circumstances it made the entire region a hunting ground for bands of Rebel soldiers who were sent in here to capture and force the young and middle aged men into the Rebel army. They did succeed in forcing a few men into their army, but the most of them banded up in companies and made their way to Kentucky and joined the Union army...these bands of roving, rebel soldiers was the main worry of the wives and children who were left at home while their men were in the Union Army." Another woman remembered that in Cataloochee "soldiers whipped the women of the Caldwell place, trying to make them tell where [the men] were hiding. They would not tell, so they waited till night when the women went to see the men, and took them out and killed them."[37]

Men liable to conscription devised a host of clever means to avoid the enrolling officers. James Webb of Chestnut Hill stationed a boy on a nearby rise to watch for Confederate troops whenever he went to work in his fields. At night Webb slept near a newly-dug grave, hoping that Confederate officers would never search for conscripts in a cemetery. These schemes worked, and Webb was never captured. Aaron Bible, who farmed near Del Rio, Cocke County, spent much of the war hiding deep in a hollow on a neighboring farm. His wife Sarah would bring food to him at night, and when it snowed she would herd sheep or hogs in front of her to obscure her tracks. Three other men chose Blowing Cave near Chestnut Hill as their hideout. The cave was ideal for this purpose, for few knew of its existence, and the entrance was obscured by trees and brush. Though they had many narrow escapes, these men were never found. "Uncle Pikey" John Allen from Cosby, Cocke County also spent over a year in a cave. Allen had volunteered for Confederate service and had been at Vicksburg when it surrendered. He had been confined on the second floor of a stockade, but he escaped by jumping into the Yazoo at night and swimming across. Allen had then walked all the way home. The trip took two months, and Allen had scavenged from deserted homes along the

way. But Allen was stunned when he reached home: "Instead of finding things as they had been, he found life almost unbearable, the scrabble for food and the relentless hunt for young men to bear arms." To avoid being conscripted, Allen spent the rest of the war hiding in a cave on his father's farm, and his sisters carried food to him.[38]

Though often successful, men who hid out from conscription paid a high price. W. H. Younce wrote that he "knew men personally that lay in those mountains during the three years of war after they were conscripted, and were never captured; but they had to lie in the mountains like wild animals, their beard and hair grew down to their shoulders, and they were really like wild men." So those who did not wish to spend all their time hiding employed other tricks. Jesse O'Neill of Cocke County wore a dress and bonnet every time Confederate soldiers were in the area. The soldiers assumed he was mentally unstable and left him alone. Another woman whitened her husband's beard and hair with flour to make him appear too old to serve. And even when captured, some conscripts managed to escape. Joseph Carlisle, a Unionist from the Del Rio area, was taken by Confederate soldiers and marched off to be enrolled. Along the way Carlisle collapsed and told the officer that he had to rest before continuing. The soldiers continued on, and just as the last one passed Carlisle bolted and disappeared into the undergrowth. Carlisle remained in hiding and eventually joined the Union Army. When Confederate troops appeared unexpectedly at the home of William and Matilda Huff one winter night, William ran out the back door to escape. Seeing nowhere else to hide, he jumped into a bed of leaves that one of his sows had made and buried himself. The night was quite cold, but William was afraid to return to his house, so he remained hidden in the leaves the whole night. On the other side, Newt Hayes, a tanner from Cocke County who made shoes for Confederate troops, found himself in trouble when Union forces invaded. Hayes fled to a hideout in the mountains of North Carolina and remained there many months. At intervals his son would put on a set of his father's clean clothes, pack up food, and trek to the hide-out at night. He would leave the food, exchange the clean clothes for his father's dirty ones, and return home.[39]

But even the most clever ploys some-times failed. When John Roberts of Sevier County joined the Confederate army, his brother-in-law came to stay with the family. To avoid being conscripted, the brother-in-law wore women's clothing. But someone in the community reported him to the Confederate authorities, and Confederate troops killed the man. When Southern troops came to the home of Reuben Williamson of Cocke County, Williamson attempted to escape by jumping out a window. But he was not quite quick

enough, and the troops shot him as he jumped. Williamson died in his own yard. Another man who hid out for months had the habit of coming home at night for brief periods to see his family and get food. One night after eating he sat in a chair in the front doorway to watch for troops while he rested. But the Confederates had picked up on his custom, and they had surrounded the house while the loyalist ate. Confederate troops then burst in the back door and killed the man as he sat.[40]

As the war progressed, the Smoky Mountains region increasingly fell into chaos. Bushwhackers, deserters, and renegade troops plundered the region's residents, stealing horses, livestock, and goods and living off the area's production. Regular troops also increasingly resorted to foraging as Confederate supply systems failed, and they became more and more ruthless in their attempts to suppress dissent. Death could come at any time and any place, and the authority of the Confederate, state, and county governments all collapsed in the face of this chaos. Smokies families, therefore, had many enemies and few friends, and increasingly the mere struggle to survive crowded out all other considerations.

CHAPTER 5

The Price of War

HE WAR TRANSFORMED LIFE
IN THE SMOKY MOUNTAINS
IN MANY WAYS, BUT NO-
WHERE WERE ITS EFFECTS
MORE PERVASIVE AND
far-reaching than in the economic sphere.
The rampant inflation that swept the
Confederacy, the reduced imports and production that caused severe shortages of
goods, and the insufficiency of labor all
bore heavily on the Smokies' relatively
fragile economy. Added to this were the
more direct effects of the war, particularly
foraging by soldiers and the burdensome
Confederate policies of conscription and
the tax-in-kind. Many residents faced
privations before 1861 had ended, and
within two years the Smokies economy had
nearly collapsed. Poorer residents were
driven to extreme measures to survive,
while even wealthier residents went without many things.

Confederate leaders recognized at least
some of the worst effects of their policies.
But once it became clear that the war
would not be won quickly, they faced a
cruel dilemma. The North enjoyed huge
advantages in manpower and production,
and if the new Confederate nation were to
survive it would have to strain its resources
to the limit. Thus, in addition to the
Conscription Acts the Confederate
Congress passed the Tax-in-Kind Act,

which allowed agents to collect ten-percent
of every family's agricultural production.
Further, as the war progressed soldiers were
given more and more authority to impress
goods directly from residents. While the
necessity of all these measures seemed
self-evident, they not only increased the
economic difficulties of the population, but
also involved sweeping assertions of the
central government's authority and drastic
intrusions into the lives of ordinary
Confederate citizens. The spectacle of
revenue agents, conscription officers, and
foraging parties entering homes and farms,
forcing men into military service, and
taking food, livestock and other goods
became difficult even for loyal citizens to
accept. Private property and personal liberty both seemed severely threatened, but
citizens had no appeal and no recourse. As
a result, support for the war declined across
all segments of society, and disaffection
ranging from apathy to evasion of
Confederate demands to outright resistance
steadily increased.[1]

Government records from both the
Confederacy and the Union reveal serious
economic difficulties in the Smokies. In
June 1863 the Confederate Assistant
Quartermaster General reported that it was
"impracticable" to collect the tax-in-kind
in Cherokee, Macon, Jackson, and
Haywood Counties (along with nearly

Union Major General John G. Foster grew concerned that the war was forcing the people of Blount County into abject poverty.

every other county in western North Carolina). In East Tennessee, Cocke County was excluded from the tax, though surprisingly Sevier and Blount were not. Similarly, in 1864 the federal tax assessor for the Fourth District of Sevier County concluded that only 17 of 97 families had the means to pay their assessment. Forty families were listed as destitute, while others were waived because the head of household was either a man serving in the Union Army or a widow. In December 1863 Major General John G. Foster, Commander of the Department of East Tennessee, was so concerned about conditions in Blount County that he sent the commander of the Fourth Army Corps to investigate in person: "Brigadier General

Willich has made representation concerning the destitute condition of the loyal people in the vicinity of Maryville which, if true, will require your immediate attention. You had better go to Maryville at once and make such arrangements as will secure the people from suffering. No orders have been given to General Willich, and I direct you to take entire charge of the these matters and see that the loyal people, where your troops are, are not robbed." And in January 1864 Brigadier General Samuel D. Sturgis lamented that "circumstances should compel us entirely to exhaust the country of these loyal people [Sevier and Blount Counties]. If we remain here long they must suffer, and it will be impossible for them to raise anything next year. The necessity for pressing supplies leads so immediately to plundering that soldiers find no difficulty taking the step from one to the other, and in spite of all I can do to the contrary. It is distressing to witness the sufferings of these people at the hands of their friends for whom they have been so long and so anxiously looking. You cannot help it; neither can I, and I only refer to it because my heart is full of it."[2]

Other evidence shows that the Smokies economy was severely strained. As early as October 1861, Alfred Wilson wrote from Jackson County that "Times in our country is hard for the poor class of people for everything is giting so deer that tha cant by hardly anought to go on salt is from nine to ten dollars a sack her and every other thing in proportion....I think corn can be bought at 50 cts....I dont now how wee will git our nessaryes for money is scarce here." In March 1862 Wilson reported that prices had nearly doubled from pre-war standards. Corn was now $0.75 cents a bushel, bacon

$0.12 a pound, and salt $20 a sack. Similarly, in July 1862 Mary Bell wrote from Macon County "I fear that many a poor family will suffer next winter for the very necessities of life; people are just beginning to lay by their corn, and very many will have to leave with their crops unfinished, some of them probably without seeing any way to have them finished." Business in the region declined accordingly. Judging from the transactions recorded in the store ledger, business at Joseph Cathey's store in Waynesville decreased nearly 400 percent from 1860 to 1862, and had nearly disappeared by 1863. In January 1864 Montgomery McTeer informed Governor Andrew Johnson that dozens of families in Blount County had claims against the Union Army for supplies taken. All were destitute and desperate, and McTeer asked Johnson to use his influence to get their claims settled as quickly as possible. And in March 1864 Robert Ragan, a Greene County Unionist, wrote that dozens of both Unionist and secessionist families from Cocke County (as well as Greene) were coming into Union lines looking for food and protection.[3]

For many families in the Smokies, the issues that had brought on the war faded before the more fundamental concern of survival. Families struggled to continue operating farms and businesses, to secure ever more scarce goods, and to protect their dwindling stores of food against soldiers and bushwhackers. As the war progressed and conditions became more desperate, families devised increasingly ingenious ways to survive, while soldiers and bushwhackers became increasingly aggressive and skilled in foraging. The result was an ongoing, dangerous competition with ever growing

Library of Congress

Union Brigadier General Samuel D. Sturgis recognized that Confederate troops seizing supplies from area farmers was having a devastating effect on the people of Blount and Sevier counties.

stakes.

Smokies families left numerous accounts of this struggle. Matilda Jones, a young girl from Del Rio, remembered that time after time bushwhackers came to her parents' home claiming to be looking for deserters. They would search every inch of the house; then carry off food, clothes, and money. Finally her parents sawed a log from the upper part of the house, placed most of their goods in the cavity, and replaced the log. Another young woman, Sarah Faubian Pangle of Cocke County, recorded that her mother employed a similar trick. Sarah's father, Tilghman Alexander H. Faubian, volunteered with the first Confederate company recruited in Cocke, and her mother was left alone with several children.

They, also, were plagued with unwelcome visitors: "Throughout the country roving bands of 'Bushwhackers' who plundered and murdered, caused fear to strike to the heart of every one not in sympathy with them, they never knew which neighbor was in sympathy with the outlaws. They were constantly spied upon by those they considered friends, and reported to the 'bushwhackers.' In this way they were made an easy prey when they were raiding a town." To protect their food and valuables, Sarah's mother had a carpenter make an opening in a bedroom wall. The opening led to an empty space above the front porch, in which a considerable quantity of goods could be hidden. She then had the boards placed back in the wall, and set the bed against the entry, hiding it from view. Bushwhackers still came in the house regularly, but they never found the opening.[4]

Smokies families contrived dozens of other ingenious hiding places. One common method was to pour wheat or corn into the space between the inner and outer walls of the house. Families would then bore a hole into the wall, seal it with a peg, and hide the peg behind a cabinet or other furniture. When residents needed grain, they would simply remove the peg and let the grain run into a container. Other families hid food under floor boards, inside bed ticks, in openings above ceilings, and under porches. The Giles family, residents of the Cosby area of Cocke County, kept their meat hidden by attaching it to the underside of the kitchen table, and secreted other food and valuables under the wooden floor. Residents of Greenlawn, one of the finest houses in Cocke County, stored dry goods and valuables in the house's hidden staircase and in a storage room that had been dug under the house. Meat was concealed in a large hidden space above the dining room. That space could only be reached by going through a transom and then into a secret opening, and the passage was so small that only a small slave boy could get in and out. Perhaps an even more extreme measure was for women to place food in sacks, tie the sacks around their waists, and hide the sacks with their long skirts. This method was more foolproof, for most soldiers and bushwhackers would not go so far as to the search the persons of women they encountered, but it must have been quite uncomfortable.[5]

Other families chose not to keep food in the house at all, but instead used various hiding places outside. They hung meat and sacks of food from trees in the nearby woods, stored it in caves, hollow logs, or trees, or buried it in the ground. Brothers William Click and Jefferson Click, who operated a woodworking and blacksmith shop near Yellow Springs, concealed their meat in a dugout in the orchard under a pile of rocks. These sites were more difficult for raiders to find, but family members had to be careful not to be seen when they retrieved the goods. Often they brought in supplies only at night, and they always attempted to erase any tracks in the area.[6]

Livestock were more difficult to conceal, but families developed many solutions to this problem as well. The Thomas Denton family kept a milk cow and a pony in a cave on English Mountain, along with meat and flour. They hid the cave entrance with freshly cut brush, and family members would bring the livestock out at night to graze. One of the Click families of Cocke

County hid their horses at Yellow Spring Branch. One of the men would climb to Point Lookout to keep watch, and "anyone who attempted to steal the horses was shot." Cows were kept concealed in a nearby hollow. Mary Moland Queen remembered that she and her brother had to stay out two or three days at a time to tend cattle hidden in a cave, while Matilda Jones wrote that their livestock "were taken up to the base of the mountain and tethered separately in clumps of bushes in the area." In Cocke County, one family dug a cellar to house their livestock, while another man supposedly trained his mare to leave the field they were plowing and hide in the laurels as soon as he unhooked her from the plow. Residents of the Fines Creek area of Haywood County had a neighborhood warning system to protect their livestock. The first person to see raiders approaching would blow a cow horn, and anyone else who heard the call would then sound his or her horn. The warning would quickly spread and give families a chance to hide their animals and goods.[7]

But not all possessions could be hidden, and sometimes Smokies families were caught unawares by bushwhackers or foraging parties. Even in those moments, however, some residents were quick-witted, resourceful, or desperate enough to save their property. In Cocke County, Dorcas Smith had been left at home with two small girls when her husband James had gone to Kentucky to join the Union Army. At one point raiders came to her farm, hauled her stores of food out of the house, and piled them in the yard. When the men went to catch the chickens, Dorcas quickly climbed up on the pile and urinated on the food. The raiders left in disgust, and Dorcas

James and Dorcas Smith, seated. Dorcas took drastic measures to save what little food she had from raiders.

cleaned the food and stored it away again. Mary Ann McGaha Williamson, also of Cocke County, remembered coming home from the mill with her mother and finding "raiders" in the house. Though the raiders took everything else, Mary kept the meal safe by hiding it under the porch. Another woman was in the yard butchering a chicken when a party of Confederate troops rode up. Without hesitation she dunked the carcass down into the slop bucket. The frustrated soldiers left it there and rode on, and as soon as they left the woman pulled the chicken back out, cleaned it, and cooked it. A 14-year-old boy, Joe Thornton, was returning from the mill with a sack of meal when he was stopped by Confederate soldiers. When they told him they needed his horse, he replied "just take the damned

This sketch by Winslow Homer depicts Union troops under Major General George Stoneman "impressing" livestock from a Burke County, NC farm.

Library of Congress

and threatened to cut the animals' throats if the soldiers took anything. The bluff worked, and the soldiers left. Another woman stood at the top of her stairs with an ax to keep Union troops from carrying off the wheat stored in the attic. Still another kept bushwhackers from taking food stored in her loft by grabbing their legs and pulling them down every time they tried to climb up. When the raiders abandoned the loft entrance and went outside to take her horses, she grabbed a musket and chased them off. In Cocke County Gipson Woods remained at home with five daughters when his two sons volunteered for Confederate service. When Union troops came to forage, one daughter held the door, another picked up an ax, and a third a pitchfork. When a soldier attempted to enter the smokehouse, one of the daughters slammed the door on his head and pinned him there. The other troops then agreed to leave if they would let the man free. Similarly, one night bushwhackers broke into the house where Greene Inman lived with two of his unmarried sisters. When one bushwhacker grabbed a length of material, one of the sisters grabbed the other end, and the two struggled. "The intruder seemed quite amused at her bravery, but sternly said, 'Turn loose, or I'll shoot.' Polly boldly replied 'Shoot and be damned,' and the conflict ended." And a young woman in Blount fluently cursed a soldier who was attempting to take the family's last horse, shaming him into leaving the animal.[9]

But women could not always be certain that bushwhackers and soldiers would not use violence against them. In Parrottsville one family hid their hams in the bed ticks. Troops apparently learned this trick, for

old bitch. She's no a-count and blind, too." The soldiers apparently believed his story and left Thornton alone. And in Cocke County the Joshua Click family hung bundles of fodder in the loft of their house. When Confederate troops would appear they would cut the bundles and scatter the fodder to make it more difficult for the troops to take.[8]

When wits failed, the only option left was direct confrontation. This course was risky, for families never knew when soldiers and bushwhackers might become violent, but in some cases audacity succeeded. When troops came to forage from Rachel Dawson's farm in Cocke County, she caught up an ax, went out to their horses,

when they came in the house they pulled the tick off the bed to search it. A baby had been lying on the bed and was thrown to the floor. The furious mother started after the soldier, but stopped when the man threw a chair at her. When Confederate troops came to the home of another woman looking for salt, she gave up half of what she had hidden; then sat on the barrel where the rest was stored. But one of the soldiers slapped her, knocked her off the barrel, and took the rest of the salt. And when troops came to the George Mease house in Cocke County and attempted to take the bedding, one woman grabbed the bedclothes and fought with the soldiers for possession. She was seriously injured in the struggle and died soon after. Many men also suffered violence from foraging troops and bushwhackers. When "Raiders" came to the home of Hugh Norris in the Bogard area of Cocke County, they hanged him from a tree before going to plunder the house. His wife, who was pregnant at the time, managed to cut him down before he died. Confederate troops also caught John Murrell and pulled him up and down from a noose to force him to reveal where the horses in the neighborhood were hidden. When Murrell finally convinced the soldiers he knew nothing, they warned him to say nothing about the incident and let him go. And in the Cosby area four Confederate soldiers dressed in federal uniforms came to Robert McGaha's house asking for food. McGaha, a Unionist, fed them a large meal. As they were finishing, McGaha thought he heard horses approaching and told the men to run out the back. When they got outside one man turned, placed the muzzle of his musket in McGaha's mouth, and shot him dead."[10]

Cades Cove resident James McCauley in Civil War uniform, circa 1863.

A few women actually retrieved goods after they had been taken. When a woman from the Hazel Creek area lost two oxen, she made inquiries until she found that they had been taken by some men from Cades Cove. She then walked to the Cove alone, found the men, confronted them, and demanded to have her stock returned. The men complied, and the woman came home unharmed. Matilda Jones of Jones Cove, Sevier County suffered several visits from Confederate troops, who came into her house and took "whatever they found and wanted." But when a soldier stole Matilda's shoes, she could take no more and ran after the troops. One of the soldiers, Mark Hicks, was from that area,

John Walker in his Union uniform. John is the father of the well known Walker Sisters of Little Greenbrier. During the war he was captured and held at the notorious Andersonville prison, where he reportedly lost 100 pounds due to the harsh conditions.

National Park Archives

January 6, 1862 the Blount County Court established a fund for the families of Confederate soldiers by raising the poll tax by $0.25 and property taxes by $0.10 per $100. The two men chosen by the Court to disburse the funds, Circuit Court Clerk William N. Brickell and Dr. Samuel Pride, released $1,000 each month in January, April, and October. The Court also sent Pride to Virginia to buy salt, and in April 1863 it began using funds to procure and distribute other supplies. County authorities in Cherokee also provided corn to some families. On April 30, 1864 N. N. Davidson instructed William Walker to distribute eight of the twelve sacks of corn he had there. "This is more than there proportional part of what is bought though I understand your people are suffering.... Say to the people not to depend entirely on the county corn for support as I cannot get it hauled as fast as they can consume it."[12]

The war had equally devastating effects on the Smokies' schools and churches. Maryville College was one of the region's most prized institutions. It had been founded in 1842 by the Presbyterian Synod to educate young men for the ministry, and though the faculty numbered only four they steadily turned out highly qualified and badly needed ministers and teachers. The school's endowment increased in the 1850s, and it was adding new facilities. But the war changed all that. When Tennessee seceded the faculty split evenly between supporters of the Union and the Confederacy. One faculty member, John S. Craig, left Maryville in September 1861 and moved to Indiana. Craig claimed that he had to bribe a Confederate officer to get a pass and that he had to leave his property unsold. He also asserted that railroad offi-

and when Matilda pointed out the man who had stolen her shoes Hicks had them returned. That act won Hicks little gratitude, however: "The people in the area, even in his own family, did not like Mark Hicks because he joined the Rebel Army. After the war, he left East Tennessee and went to Arkansas, and as far as I know, he never came back.... My brother's brother, Jerome Eldridge Hicks ... once went to visit the folks out west. When asked if he went to see his uncle Mark Hicks, he said, 'No, I didn't want to see the old Rebel.'"[11]

Local authorities made some attempts to provide for families' basic needs. On

cials threw two of his trunks off the train. Craig, understandably, called Maryville "a little contemptible hotbed of secessionists." Most students either joined Confederate companies or went home. Little more than a week after hostilities began the college closed its doors, and it did not reopen until September 1866. In the intervening period the war nearly destroyed the school. First Confederate and then Union troops used the college's main building as a barracks and a stable. Union troops tore down other buildings and used the bricks to build large baking ovens, and troops on both sides burned door and window frames and even books for fuel. Beyond this destruction, the college was forced to sell other holdings to pay its debts. By the time the war finally ended the college was left with one solitary building, which itself was considerably damaged, and a mere $7,000 in funds. A Quaker academy in Friendsville, Blount County also closed early in the war. Both armies used its buildings for barracks, and in 1865 the school claimed that it had lost 76 horses, nearly 5,000 bushels of grain, and $165,000 in funds. The war also forced private academies in Sevierville, Waynesville, and Franklin to close.[13]

The fate of churches in the Smokies varied considerably. Oconaluftee Baptist Church was divided between Unionists and secessionists, but it continued to meet during the first three years of the war. Beginning in fall of 1864, however, meetings became more sporadic, due to "too much confusion in the land, the cold weather and excessive rain." Similarly, the Big Pigeon Baptist Church met until some time in 1863, when "the ware became so troublesome we had no more regular meet-

ings until first April 1872." Union Baptist Church in Bogard held regular services until January 1, 1862. Members then met only twice in 1863, and the church did not reopen until July 1865. Minutes from that meeting referred to "our once prosperous but now decayed church." The Slate Creek Baptist Church had no recorded meetings from 1860 through 1868. The Big Springs Presbyterian Church nearly stopped keeping records during the war, but the conflict had clear effects. At least one member freed his or her slaves during the war and sent them to Liberia, and at least 11 families could no longer endure conditions in the area and moved west to Illinois and Iowa. At the same time, the war sparked revivals in some churches. On January 27, 1865 Barbara Hall wrote from Blount County that she had just been to a revival meeting at Six Mile Church, where 15 persons had professed faith and 12 had joined the church. The Pleasant Grove Church had added 60 converts, and many other churches were also having revivals.[14]

The political divisions of the war also damaged many churches. Members of Bethany Church claimed on August 26, 1865 that they had "been prohibited from meeting by the oppression of the Rebels and our pastor forbid to attend us and many of our members driven off and for that cause we have been deprived of meeting as a Church from August 1862 to July 1865… therefore we as a Church do declare an unfellowship with all Rebels and their works." Similarly, in September 1866 members of the Nolachucky Association of Primitive Baptists "declare[d] non-fellowship to all rebels or any who do advocate the rebel principles and do drop all

Walter Gregory was the son of Russell Gregory for whom Gregory Bald is named. Russell couldn't serve in the Civil War because he had lost a hand, but he did serve in the Home Guard. Unfortunately he was killed by rebel marauders in 1864. Walter Gregory was also killed in the war.

correspondence with all churches, Ministers, Members and Associations that have countenanced the rebellion in any Sense or form unless they repent and turn away from there sins." And the First Baptist Church in Sevierville did not meet from April 1861 until April 1876, for Confederate troops took their original building, used it for a stable, then destroyed it.[15]

The war produced a number of odd legal situations as well. W. A. Walker, treasurer of a private academy in Maryville, found that the academy held notes against a number of persons who were in the Confederate Army or who had gone south after Union forces occupied the region. In 1864 Walker wrote Oliver P. Temple asking whether the debts would still be honored if Union authorities confiscated these persons' property and if he could levy attachments against the property. Walker also wanted to know if it would be possible to pursue executors and administrators of estates if these persons were in the Confederate forces. In January 1865 Walker again wrote Temple to ask if payments previously made to administrators and executors in Confederate money would be considered final, or whether the payments would have to be withdrawn and made again in United States currency. In a similar case, William Burnett of Sevierville wrote Temple to see if he could get satisfaction for his niece, Evelina Moore. In 1861 Evelina's husband, John Moore, had loaned $1,300 in Tennessee state money to two neighbors. When the note came due, the men offered Moore Confederate notes in payment. Moore refused and demanded payment in state notes. When the neighbors threatened to report Moore for refusing to accept Confederate money, Moore disappeared, made his way to Kentucky, and joined the Union Army. He was later killed in battle. Now that the war was over, Burnett wanted to know if Temple could file two suits against the men, one for payment of the debt in state notes, and one for their threats against John Moore.[16]

Sadly, residents in the Smokies often suffered from troops on both sides, and their loyalty to one side or the other seemed to earn them no consideration or gratitude. Matilda Dunlap was a widow in

Blount County. Her husband had died in 1860, and she was struggling to manage the farm and raise eight children ages four to 18. She claimed that early in the war Confederate troops came to the farm looking for weapons. When she insisted that she had sent her gun to Kentucky, the soldiers left, but told her that if she failed to bring in the weapon they would arrest her. The Confederates returned a few nights later, broke down her door, cursed her, and broke her spinning wheel. After that, Confederate troops regularly came to her farm and took corn and forage. When Dunlap complained, the soldiers again threatened to arrest her. Notwithstanding these dangers, Dunlap claimed that she regularly fed Unionist partisans and gave them information, and that the Confederate provost marshal had promised to arrest her for these activities. Despite Dunlap's situation, in January 1864 Union foraging parties came to her farm every day for a week and systematically stripped it of painfully accumulated supplies of corn and hay. Dunlap first protested vehemently, but the soldiers ignored her. She then asked that they leave enough for her and her children to survive, but all she could save was 50 bushels of corn.[17]

Richard Keeble, who owned a farm in Miller's Cove, Blount County, encountered this same attitude. Keeble claimed that in the first two years of the war he had fed Union soldiers, warned his neighbors of the approach of Confederates, and "joined a body of Unionist men in defending the parties who attempted to burn the bridge at Strawberry Plains." One of Keeble's neighbors, Samuel Walker, testified that he and Keeble had hidden out together many nights and that Keeble had generously

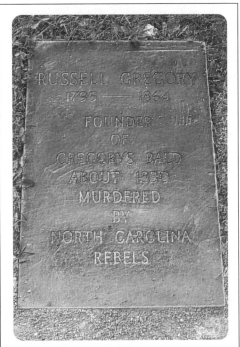

Russell Gregory's tombstone at the Primitive Baptist Cemetery in Cades Cove.

given provisions to the wives of Union soldiers. Keeble claimed that he had suffered much for his loyalty. "Most of the men in my vicinity were gone—time of war. Elijah Hatcher… James Walker… George Amerine… and myself were all old men and left here.…The rebels threatened several times to burn my property on account of my Union sentiments. At one time, I cannot remember the date…a party of rebels came in sight of where I and some black boys were at work. The black boys ran and the rebels shot at us. They then came inquiring, who they were that ran. I told them and then they declared that it was not so—that it was Union men I was harboring, and threatened to burn everything I had. They went off declaring that they would be back the next day at 12:00 and if these men didn't come up they would then burn me out. While they were gone they killed old man Elijah Hatcher, as I was informed. I did not see him killed, but he was killed and they didn't come back anymore." At various times Confederate troops had also taken cattle and hogs from Keeble's farm: "I don't know what officer or soldier took them. I didn't ask them any questions. Sometime before, one of our citizens, a Union man was asking questions and making notes among the rebel soldiers when they arrested him and kept him as a prisoner for some time, so I was afraid to ask too many questions." Despite Keeble's history, sometime in 1864 Union troops camped on his farm for two days and took away corn, oats, two horses, and 1,500 pounds of bacon. When Keeble complained to their commander, the colonel sent a guard to his farm, but foragers evaded the guard and continued to take supplies. Keeble received no payment for anything that was taken.[18]

What Elijah L. Hatcher and his family suffered was even worse. Hatcher left Blount County in September 1862 to join Union forces and served with the Second Tennessee Cavalry until the end of the war. Before going to Kentucky himself he had guided groups of other Unionists out of Tennessee. It was Hatcher's father who, as Keeble stated, was killed when Confederate troops raided Miller's Cove. Even so, in February 1864 40 men from the Fourteenth Illinois Cavalry came to Hatcher's farm and spent three days hauling off corn, oats, hay, and molasses. Hatcher's son asked them to leave enough food for the family to survive, but the soldiers replied that they needed

the supplies more than the family did, and carried on. The soldiers also refused to give receipts for what they took.[19]

Such stories recurred again and again. Thomas Saffell of Sevier County claimed that he used his ferry boat to take Unionists escaping to Kentucky across the French Broad. When Union troops occupied the area, he also helped guide Federal forage wagons. Confederate troops twice arrested him for these activities, shot at him, and took his hat, wallet, and horse. But later Union troops took his ferry boat and used it to haul supplies. They also seized grain, flour, meat, and 14,000 board feet of lumber, and Saffell received no payment for anything. John M. Sutton of the Walden Creek area of Sevier County asserted that he regularly piloted Union troops and wagon trains and was arrested by Confederate troops for carrying messages. Even so, Union troops carried off not only a wheel from his grist mill, but also a new ferry boat which they used to haul grain. Levi Moore of Cherokee County, who had two sons in the Confederate Army and one in a loyalist partisan band, was arrested by the Home Guard in the fall of 1863 and jailed in Murphy. His lawyers were able to have him released, but Confederate troops subsequently burned his grist mill, sawmill, stable, and house. "The rebel soldiers often threatened to kill me for my union sentiments. They cocked their pistols on me perhaps 50 times." But the treatment that Moore received from Union soldiers was little better. In December 1863 Union troops "just busted open the stable door" and took his horse. "I told the man who took the horse not to take it and he said he was walking and had to ride." Union troops came back in April 1865 and took more horses. When Moore complained, the detachment commander "cursed me and said that 'I had steers and to plow them.'" Jared Meade, a merchant in Louisville, claimed that he helped send one company of recruits to Kentucky and ran a safe house for others who were escaping. He also gave several hundred dollars in provisions to the families of Union soldiers, "as I was the only man on that part of the mountain, that had anything to help the needy." In the fall of 1863, however, Union troops entered Meade's warehouse and took the machinery from the Steamer *James Williams*, a boat of which he was part owner, to power another steamer. Troops also used Meade's wagons and teams, without pay, to haul supplies.[20]

The experience of Louisa Styles of Cherokee County was particularly appalling. Her husband Thomas had left North Carolina and joined the Union Army. He came home on leave in December 1864, but while there Confederate troops found him and killed him. One of Louisa's sons had joined the Confederate Army and then deserted. He subsequently volunteered for Union service and was killed in battle. Louisa's neighbors testified that "she was mobbed by the Rebels on several instances, and that she was abused by threats that they would kill her and burn her buildings." Even so, at some point Union troops came to her farm and took a horse. Louisa went to Knoxville and secured a receipt. She gave the receipt to her father for safekeeping, but asserted that the receipt was lost when Confederate troops shot her father in his home. When asked if she had suffered injury because of her loyalty to the Union, Louisa answered

with considerable bitterness: "I do not exactly know how to answer, but if the putting of ropes around the necks of some of my children with the threat that they should be hanged, the murder of a son and a husband, at their hands, in cold blood, was doing an injury then I say yes sir a thousand times."[21]

Many other residents claimed that they suffered particular abuse from Confederate soldiers. John A. Rawlings was hit in the chest with a musket stock. Newton Gray was arrested by Confederate troops and had to pay $48 to be released. He was also "clubbed for being a damned Lincolnite as they said. I would not hurrah for Jeff Davis." Hugh Lambert of Cherokee County received threats both from Confederate troops and from a neighbor: "I asked why he treated me so and he said it was because I was a damn homemade Yankee and threatened my life and swore they would burn me up." And the case of Mary L. T. Wallace of Maryville was particularly sad. Sometime in the summer of 1864 Confederate soldiers burned her house and took all of her furniture, her Southern money, and almost everything else of value. "I should be more or less than human not to feel very bitterly towards the perpetuators of such an outrage committed by a drunken officer and without any provocation or shadow of excuse." She had survived by moving in with her sister, selling her few remaining valuables, and boarding officers. She had about $1,000 in Knoxville bonds that her husband had left her and $2,000 in another state, but she could not retrieve the $2,000 or redeem the bonds. Wallace eventually wrote Oliver P. Temple for help: "I think I have presented to your mind about as gloomy a picture as you often see.... Justice would require that my losses should be made good from some quarter, but I can't see from what source I would hope to obtain it." [22]

A few slaves in the Smokies also left accounts of their experiences. Lee Cannon of Blount County freed himself when the first opportunity came. When Union troops first appeared in the county, Cannon simply picked up and followed them, and they employed him as a wagon driver. "I was a slave at the beginning of the war, I considered myself free after the occupation of East Tennessee by the Union Army in September 1863." In March 1864 Cannon returned home and farmed part of his former master's land for a year. The following year he rented a different farm. Joshua Atchley, a white neighbor, claimed that Cannon "would tell me when the rebels were coming to take horses and property. His master was a rebel, and [Cannon] could keep himself posted as to the movements of the rebel soldiers." Cannon also brought supplies to Unionists traveling to Kentucky. Colonel Robert B. Vance gave similar testimony about his slave Israel Garrison. Vance conceded that "the colored people was as a rule loyal to the United States government," and admitted that Garrison was "in the confidence" of the Federal recruiting officers secretly working in the county. Garrison would bring the officers and their recruits provisions and information, and would arrange meetings between pilots and escapees. Garrison also had a small plot that he used to raise provisions for the families of Union soldiers. Garrison and his wife originally lived on neighboring farms owned by the same family, but at some

point the wife was sent to a different farm 20 miles away, for fear that the two would run away. A third slave, Richard Welch, agreed that "all the black people was Union people," but concluded "none of the black people could do much we all had to be still." [23]

A few families in the Smokies left behind lengthy accounts of their struggles. Alfred Bell, a wealthy farmer in Macon County, recruited a company in 1861 and served until the end of the war, while his wife Mary managed the farm and cared for their children. The difficulties the Bells faced were typical, though since they were relatively well off they were better equipped to meet these strains. One of the first effects of the war was the disappearance of critical items. Mary soon found that she could not get cotton cards, which she needed to make thread. She asked Alfred to find some for her, but in January 1862 Alfred told Mary that he had not been able to locate any in Asheville or Raleigh. He would look in Salisbury if he had the chance. In mid-August Alfred wrote that he had searched Knoxville for gingham and cotton flannel but had found none. He had finally found cotton cards in Knoxville and was sending her a pair, but he had had to pay $16. But Mary expressed a determination to make do: "I do not ask the Yankees any odds if I can get thread and dye stuffs I can make my own dresses." She was also encouraged that a store owner in Franklin, John Need, had agreed to let her have whatever she needed on credit while Alfred was away. But goods were scarce and prices high. Nails were $0.25 cents a pound, while glass was $9 a box. Only one store in the area had any candles to sell, and these were

$0.40 cents a pound.[24]

By the spring of 1862 Alfred was facing the realities of war. In late March Confederate sources reported a Union attack at Jacksborough, and Alfred's regiment was ordered to Clinton to guard the ferry there. As it turned out, the "attack" was simply a raid by either Union cavalry or "Tennessee and Kentucky Torys," but their appearance panicked the Confederate companies at Jacksborough, and the orders were so hasty that Alfred's regiment went with only four days rations and little else. Although weather was quite cold, the troops rode all night in open baggage cars and arrived in Knoxville at 8:00 a.m. They were then left standing "in the mud" until 2:00 p.m., when they finally received orders to march to Clinton. Without blankets or tents, they had to sleep on the ground in "mud & water 6 inches deep or deeper" for four nights. Their only rations were "poor beef and wheat bread made without soda grease or anything but salt & water."[25]

The result of this adventure was a massive wave of sickness that prostrated the regiment. On April 6 Alfred wrote that 25 men in his company were in hospitals in Knoxville, and at least 150 men in the regiment were seriously ill. By April 11 only 210 men out of 600 in the regiment were fit for duty. Somewhere between ten and 15 had died, though none were from his company. Two weeks later Alfred reported that four men in his company had now died of typhoid, diarrhea, and measles. Several others were critically ill, including their friend George Moore: "I cannot keep from shedding tears to think how his family will feel when they hear this mournful news." Moore died four days later, and

Alfred wanted someone to come get the body: "Times are so that we cannot take our dear friends home we think there friends at home ought to come and take their remains home & bury them in their own country among their friends." Finally, on June 6 Alfred wrote that three more of his recruits had died and that only two men in his company were truly fit for duty.[26]

This grim news weighed heavily on Mary: "I catch myself constantly wondering if it can be possible that I will ever be happy again or in other words if you will ever live to get home or will I live to see you get home. Poor miserable wretch that some of us are if the war does not end soon how many more hearts will be broken."

Even so, she insisted that Alfred continue writing everything to her: "I want to know the truth all the time if it is bad." Mary also pleaded with Alfred not to extend his service: "There is one thing that I beg of you not to do, for my sake, that is not to enlist. I can look forward now to the time when if you live you can come home." Alfred agreed that he would leave the regiment when his time was up: "We want some of those fellows at home to have to come and defend their country. We are ready and willing to do our part, even, and if us that joines now saves some scamp at home so we aint going to do it we will serve ower time out & then do as we like about reenlisting." Alfred supported the new conscription act, but he believed that the Confederate Congress should raise the eligible age to 40 and give 60-day furloughs to those who had volunteered early in the war. Mary was not so certain that the Conscription Act would eliminate the inequities of the previous volunteer system. Though it would force some into service who should have gone on their own, it would also take many who deserved to be excused, and detain many who had already served their time.[27]

The war came home to Mary in other ways. On February 9, 1862 she wrote Alfred that one of their neighbors who had volunteered, Leander Ledford, had died: "His father heard that they were bringing him home and they were looking for him every day until he got a letter yesterday evening that they had buried him... they all take it very hard." Then in June she learned that another neighbor, William Mann, had died in a hospital at Petersburg. His brother John had gone to stay with William until he died. Shortly after John came home he broke out in measles and shut himself up to recuperate. But when John found that his father had instructed their slaves to bury William, he got up to attend to the burial himself. That day was rainy and cold, and soon after the interment John relapsed and died. "It is distressing to see the men who are coming home with ruined health, and to think that there is a man living who might with a few words stop this cruel and unholy war. I believe we have a just God, and that sooner or later Abraham Lincoln will meet with his just retribution." That same month five other young men from their neighborhood came home wounded. Mary continued to press Alfred not to reenlist: "I am glad to hear you say that you do not intend to sleep without me another winter. That was my notion but I was afraid to say anything about it yet until I saw you and could talk to you about it. I thought I could persuade you to say that you would come home even if the war does not end. I think you will have done your duty by that time."[28]

Mary had to rely on herself in many ways and perform several unfamiliar tasks. In late 1861 she wrote that she had treated an ill hog herself and believed it would recover: "I was afraid I would have to beg my meat next year and you know I am a poor hand to beg." She was also harassed by bushwhackers, and in late May Alfred wrote that he was sending her a shotgun "for you and Matt to shoot those who dare to scare you at night by beating on your door.... Have Dee to bring my other gun home & you & Matt can have four shots... don't be afraid to shoot." He also offered to send her a revolver if she wanted one. Her responsibilities grew in other ways as well. Alfred had received a short leave in August 1861, and in May 1862 Mary gave birth to a baby girl, whom she named Sallie. Mary admitted that she was "glad she is a girl that if I ever do get my husband home that I do not want any boys for the next war that I will hereafter keep all I have at home." She also admitted "I have had the blues ever since yesterday morning as bad as ever any mortal could. I feel now as if I did not have a friend on earth and that happiness has taken wings and flown away." Having the baby made Alfred's absence even more difficult to bear, for "I have no good old man to light the candle and help me with her when she cries it is Ma's turn every time."[29]

Alfred continued to be discouraged with his military service. In June he noted that, although the regiment had now been organized for nearly a year, only 130 men had proper arms. The muskets that the regiment was supposed to receive had gone to another unit. The regiment had seen no fighting, and it appeared they would remain inactive. The company officers had petitioned Colonel Coleman to let the men with arms go to Chattanooga, which was now threatened by Union forces, but Alfred did not believe authorization would be given. Coleman had been in Knoxville the past two weeks, "drinking whiskey I reckon… he don't want to fight & he would hate for his men to be in a fight unless he was with them."[30]

The company's fortunes then took a brief rise before plummeting again. By mid-June Alfred's men were healthy again, and they were assigned to escort prisoners to Atlanta. Shortly thereafter Alfred's company and two others were sent to Charleston, Tennessee to guard the bridge there. Their camp was in a pleasant grove and there were two clean springs of water nearby. "My company is in better health now than it has been for three months." But the conflict between the company officers and Coleman worsened. In early June Alfred had circulated a petition to have Coleman removed, and 13 officers had signed. Coleman had then ordered Alfred and four others arrested. But Alfred was defiant: "I am for Co Bs rights if it costs my commission & all that I am worth."[31]

Two weeks later Alfred was still under arrest and still ready to fight: "If the right of petition is [denied] from us as a free people and fighting for our rights I want to be cashiered.…I won't fight for such freedom or such a government." Alfred was also furious that Major General Edmund Kirby Smith, commander of the Department of East Tennessee, had stated that the company officers' petition was mutinous and seditious and that they were not fit to be officers: "A man of his grade has no right or power to express an opinion that would have any influence on a court martial.…I will not serve with such a man.…I would rather be an equal of a negro & be allowed to ask for what was my right as free people than to be deprived of this liberty. I will never fight for any government that excludes the right of petition." Alfred was also beginning to have doubts about the Confederacy's future. He asked Mary to tell his father to invest all the money they had to spare in land, explaining "I fear there is too much money for it to be good long after the war closes. I had rather have it invested in property— say nothing about this."[32]

Alfred had other problems as well. The plague of desertion had now hit the regiment, and only 16 men remained in his company. "The most of my boys has skidaddled & gone home all on account of our staff officers… the men say they will not serve under them…we are of no servis to the Confederacy and a disgrace to North Carolina." Colonel Coleman had stated that if those who were absent returned on their own there would be no punishment, and Alfred asked Mary to tell the men that if they returned and said nothing about being gone no notice would be taken. But Mary did not believe they would listen: "As to your boys going back or at least some of them, I think they are quite easy on the subject."[33]

At some point Mary's unhappiness with her situation turned to resentment and suspicion. On July 1, 1862 she wrote "You will probably think me selfish, but I would be so glad if you could find time to write oftener.…" She faithfully wrote to him every Tuesday, but she did not know if he received all her letters, since he did not always mention them. The new baby, along with all of her other responsibilities, was wearing on her: "If I was not stouter than I always am when my babes are young I could not stand it—and even now sometimes it almost lays me up.... I tell them all I wish they would cashier you as I have a use for you at home." She could not understand why Alfred could not get a furlough, and pressed him to try harder: "I think you might offer to beg your Col a little for the sake of getting to see your wife and children especially the one you have never seen." [34]

By this time Mary had also heard rumors that Alfred had not been faithful to her, and she wanted the truth. Alfred first denied the rumors emphatically, then attempted to defuse the issue by joking: "Tell Matt that I think I could have traded your pin off to several Gals for a nights bedding up together but not being able to find a Made I did not." But Mary would not be placated, and in August she exploded: "You seem to think that I doubt your coming home I do not know why I should, unless all reports be true." She had heard stories of Alfred drinking, playing cards, and "bedding as many women as any man in camps.... I am afraid that you are so far off that I will never hear of it and that it will make no difference, if such is your thoughts, let me beseech you by all you hold sacred on earth do not think so." Apparently attempting to provoke him, she implied that she had her own admirers: "I recon you wold be a little jealous if you could see the men come to see me, and sit and chat with me an hour at a time." Mary took another shot on September 5: "I expect if I knew it you will have several boys scattered about against

the war ends from the word you send Matt. I know I ought not to doubt but I am afraid man is not to be trusted." At some point Mary apparently sent Alfred an even angrier letter, and then a retraction, for on December 3 Alfred wrote "Your apologies for slandering me was expected and I doe hope never to get another such a raking knowing that I was inosent... I hope henceforth that I will not be condemned before I commit the crime. [35]

Mary had ample reasons for her black mood. She was now dealing with declining food supplies, and she had been "drying all the fruit I can so that if I get out of everything else I can live on dried fruit." She would have had sufficient corn, but she needed to let his father have "what he uses now." Alfred's father had asked her and the children to stay with him over the winter, and she was considering it, primarily because it would ease her concerns about wood for the winter. Some families had given up and were leaving the state. Even more grim was the situation with Sallie. In August Mary and the baby both became ill, and Sallie kept Mary up three nights in a row: "She is pitiful and coughs pretty hard." Though Mary took the baby to a doctor and did everything she could, Sallie died the following month, and Mary fell into a severe depression. In November Mary visited Sallie's grave and remembered the funeral: "I was there sitting on a rock with my little Minnie in my arms and Fannie standing by me but my dear husband was not near me. Oh! how can I bear it, how can I do without you? When will this wicked war cease?" [36]

Sallie's death prompted important changes in Alfred. He professed a new interest in Christianity and determined to reform. On December 3 Alfred wrote that he had "abandoned the last bad habbit that I am guilty of that is swearing… this is a bad place to seek religion." He also attempted to regain Mary's trust, writing "I have not repented the tie that has bound us in love probably you have. If so you have kept it to yourself & I too much confidence to believe it. If I did oh what a miserable man I would be." Mary supported these attempts: "When I think that I can never more see that sweet little form nor hear that prattling voice it does my heart good to think that she is now a shining angel in heaven and if we will only live and act right then we can go to her." Alfred also encouraged Mary to make her own decisions. On December 19, 1862 he wrote "as to buying Martha [a female slave] you have got money & doe as you like about that. I want the money layed out. If you fail to buy her you had better pay some on our land debt & try to buy the adjoining land to ours from Jeffery Siler…." In December he repeated that "As to buying Martha or Liza or anything else you & my sweet babes want I want you not to ask me anything about it—its a nough for you to know that I want you to buy it—I am more than willing. I have a wife & I thank god for it who is not extravagent and are always trying to lay up some thing for the future…." Finally, and less convincingly, Alfred once again promised to come home.[37]

In the meantime Alfred's troubles continued. In late August the regiment had moved to Tazewell, and Coleman had again arrested all the officers, this time for not marching the companies in line. Alfred claimed that Coleman had never given the order and accused him of being drunk all the time. By December the regiment had nearly evaporated: "Some furloughed some sick there is but 90 men for duty in the regt now." Coleman had arrested 20 men who had gone home without leave that summer, six in Alfred's company, and was threatening to court martial them all. Alfred believed these men would all be released, but he was worried about those who were absent now: "I fear somebody will be shot for deserting." On December 10 Alfred reported that he had been in charge of the regiment for two weeks, while Coleman was in Knoxville trying to have the 20 men tried. He was getting along well with Brigadier General [Robert] Reynolds: "I suppose on account of me having his son elected Maj of our regt." By December 29 Coleman had released the 20 men, for which Alfred took some credit.[38]

Alfred also became increasingly concerned about Mary's safety, though not enough to resign. In late February 1864 he wrote that a Mobile paper had reported that Union forces had raided into Macon County, attacked Colonel William Holland Thomas's command, and been turned back. Other men had heard reports that Union troops had burned Murphy: "We are all very anxious to hear from home." Alfred later heard better news and professed some relief: "We was glad to hear that the people at home had all escaped by flying to the mountains and staying there until the women and children ran the Yankees back. We think the home guard of Macon should have a flag presented to them for their gallantry." In March the regiment moved to Pollard, Alabama, and Alfred now reported that only one commissioned officer and four men from each company could be

Alfred Bell's correspondence with his wife, Mary, reveals the tedium and suffering on both the front lines and home fronts.

own father would not & my wife loaned money when she needed it." He also blamed his arrest on regimental politics: "It was all caused by my being the Senior Capt & the office of Maj to fill by others more desirous of promotion than I."[40]

In the summer of 1864 the regiment was ordered to Atlanta, and Alfred finally received a full taste of the war. On July 23 he described continuous skirmishing with Union forces and reported that he had had one man killed and two wounded. The Union Army had cut all the railroads around them, and for the first time Alfred expressed doubts about the war. He now believed that if the Confederacy won at Atlanta the war might end, but if not he did not see how the South could survive, for the Union had twice as many troops as the South. In August Alfred wrote that he was "in the ditches with the boys" near Atlanta and that there was "a great deal of grumbling & dissatisfaction" in his company. The men were on short rations, and there was "so much duty to do that they are worn out." The Union forces shelled them constantly, "which keeps the boys close to their brest works. The pickets fight all the time." The last evening he had gone out to see his men, but the shelling was so heavy he had to turn back. "I think there was 40 or 50 struck within 100 yds of me & I thought some came near hitting me." The regiment had lost three or four killed and several wounded. Bell's optimism had returned, however, for he had heard rumors that Wheeler had recaptured Dalton and Ringgold and torn up the railroad in the Union rear. If that were true, Sherman would have to withdraw.[41]

Alfred also continued to mention coming home. Several officers in the regiment

furloughed at a time. His time would not come until September. Again he mentioned resigning but gave the excuse that his men did not want him to. However, the company officers had all sent a petition to Governor Vance to have the regiment posted to western North Carolina.[39]

Shortly thereafter Coleman arrested Alfred a third time, this time for supposedly neglecting his duties while he was in North Carolina recruiting. Some of Alfred's own men had testified against him, based on information their wives had sent. Alfred was particularly bitter about this, complaining that one woman "ought to remember my father hauled wood for her when her

had resigned, and his men planned to leave as soon as their terms were up. "All my boys say they are going they say they only promised to stay as long as I do the boys dont intend to break their promise." In September Alfred wrote that he had asked to resign, but his request had been denied because he was still under arrest. He had then applied for leave but had received no reply. "So I have concluded to let them refuse if they can afford to feed and pay me to do nothing."[42]

Mary also continued to look for Alfred's return. On April 8, 1864 she hopefully wrote that two men who were home on leave claimed that the regiment would soon be sent back to North Carolina "to guard Macon Cherokee Jackson and Haywood." Alfred had also heard a rumor that "Jackson Co has sent the Rev Wm Hicks with a strong petition to Gov Vance to the War Department to have our Regt sent to Western NC." Conditions at home remained difficult: "We are all on foot now and able for our short rations….I have had all the work to do since Patty has been sick." She was weaving cloth to make clothes for the slaves, but they needed shoes. "If you come try to steal her [Patty] a pair on the road if you can find any." She pushed hard for him to come home: "What about your furloughs do you think you will ever get them & cant you get one anyhow & if you can try for one tell them your family is about to starve." On May 8 Mary continued in the same vein: "This is a quiet pleasant Sabbath day and I feel quite lonely O! how happy I would be if you were here today and we could stroll over the farm and tell to each other our plans and hopes for the future." She was "sorry to hear that you were suffering so much unnecessarily on account of me not having any corn. I hated to write you my condition but you always say you want to know all." She had thought he would be coming home soon and could make arrangements for other provisions. A neighbor had sent her 14 bushels of corn, and she was not feeding the horses any grain. She had also taken other innovative measures. A neighbor woman wanted to send her daughter to school in Franklin, and Mary wanted to send Minnie. "I am to house at the old price and she is to let me have provisions at the old price." Alfred's father also recently told her that he could not stand being lonely any more and wanted her to come live with him. By October Mary seemed at the end of her resources: "I am completely out of heart and can't help it I try to raise my spirits but cannot do it to save my life….When you come home and hear me talk I know you will not blame me. I can't begin to write you my trouble."[43]

But Alfred remained in service until the end. After the Confederate defeat at Atlanta the regiment was sent to Jacksonville, Alabama "with about a thousand others barefoots." His rheumatism was now so bad he had difficulty walking, and he had applied for post duty and had been made captain of the provost guard in Jacksonville. "I hope you get your fodder saved & molasses made & will not fret your self so much about starving." He thought he could buy hogs for her from one of the neighbors. "So have patience & dont be alarmed. I think you have passed through a deal of starvation. I think I will be at home in a few weeks & I hope to be able to supply my wife & babes with a plenty to keep body & soul together." But Alfred remained mired in military bureaucracy. On February 6 he had sent in his resignation and Coleman had accepted it. He had also asked for 30 days leave and been denied, so now he had to wait for the papers to return from Richmond. Ten days later Alfred wrote that he had gone before the Medical Board and been promised a certificate of disability. Once he had that he would again apply for leave. Alfred now conceded that the Confederacy could not last much longer. "The seat of war has been moved at the present time to South & North Carolina and it looks gloomy in the extreme—it looks like Sherman goes where he pleases takes Savannah, Charleston, Columbia & will commence on the towns of North Carolina & I fear will take all the principal towns in the state & go take Richmond and then the Confederacy will nearly be whipped."[44]

In this case Alfred was correct, though fortunately for North Carolina Confederate forces surrendered before Sherman's forces could inflict too much damage on the state. Even so, Alfred remained in service until nearly the war's end, leaving Mary to endure on her own.

James and Barbara Hall of Blount County also left a detailed account of their struggles. James had joined a federal regiment in 1863, and struggled to manage everything at home. For several months James continued to give Barbara detailed instructions. By late 1863 feed for livestock was in short supply, and James wrote a neighbor, Isaac Russell, wanting to know what the Halls' three mules were worth and whether Barbara should sell them. He also asked whether one of the other neighbors would feed them in turn for

being able to work them. In January 1864 James advised Barbara to hire help to cut firewood, fix the fences, plow the wheat ground, and clear the corn fields. The following month he instructed her to see Isaac Russell for help with getting a receipt from Federal officers for the forage they had taken and in requesting a guard for the farm. James asked Barbara to let him know how the wheat crop looked, and urged her to rent extra land to plant oats. He had also arranged for her to get 20 pounds of cotton from a merchant in Maryville and to have blacksmith work done.[45]

In May James wanted to know how much land Mary had put in oats and where she had planted corn. In June he again urged her to hire a neighbor to help with the mowing. Barbara replied that she was getting along well. She had had more than enough help cutting clover, and the corn looked promising. Seven old sheep had died, but six lambs had been born, and the cattle were healthy. In the summer James conceded that if the mules proved too much trouble she should sell them, but he would prefer that she wait until he came home. She should feed the oats rather than selling them, for the price was too low, and he could send her whatever money she needed. He had also arranged for her to buy pork from Isaac Russell. James remained concerned about Barbara's health, and repeatedly urged her not to work too hard and to hire as much help as she could. He also regularly asked how many partisans and Confederate troops were in the area.[46]

But James eventually stopped giving so much advice. In September 1864 he said he could not answer Barbara's questions about where to sow wheat, for "I am not the farmer I will leave that to you." Barbara, also, became increasingly confident and proud of her management. In August she insisted that $210 was not enough for the two horses and that they were worth $240. She wished that James could come home and see the fine crop of corn she had raised and the barn full of feed. Barbara also noted that she had her own patch of cotton which would be enough for her if the bolls opened. She would then not have to pay the extravagant prices the stores were asking for cloth. In February 1865 Barbara wrote that she had purchased 300 pounds of pork and 200 pounds of beef, so she was well supplied. Barbara also received help from neighbors. In January 1864 Henry Simerly, who was in the same company as Hall, wrote his wife, Margaret, to buy two hogs with the money he sent her and divide them with Barbara Hall.[47]

Even good crops could not guarantee security, however, for Blount County was plagued with both bushwhackers and foraging parties. On July 13, 1864 Crawford Hall wrote James that secessionists had killed John Hennel. They had also shot William Yeebrough, but he had survived. Two months later Barbara reported "Times is tolerable hard here yet but I think we can get a long if we are let alone now." She was out of beef and could not buy pork, but she had most of the corn in. She was also sowing wheat and making molasses. Unfortunately the "Rebels" were raiding again. On October 30, 1864 Crawford Hall told James that "The times is hard heare and not likely to get eny better." The corn harvest had been good, but it was not likely

that he would be able to keep it. Similarly, in early 1865 Isaac Russell complained to James that "Mules and horses is worth nothing her for thar stolen but as soon as they get big enuft. I don't know what will become of us."[48]

Like Alfred Bell, James Hall frequently discussed leaving the service, but never did so. In May 1864 he wrote Barbara that if she and his father could find a substitute for him he would come home. He would give $50 and the bounty if necessary, but he wanted her to keep half the bounty if possible. He would send her whatever money was required. If she could not find a substitute, however, he wanted her to stop asking him to come home. On June 23 Barbara replied that it was impossible to find a substitute. She then wrote several times asking if she could come to the camp and see him, but James refused, saying that it was too dangerous. James again raised the possibility of her finding him a substitute in October, but nothing came of this.[49]

Thus Mary Bell, Barbara Hall, and thousands of other Smokies families were left to struggle on while waiting for the war to end. But that end would come with painful slowness. In the fall of 1863 Union forces invaded East Tennessee, and from that time on the Smokies became contested territory. As campaigns in other areas ended, Union forces increased their operations in this area, but the Confederates held on with remarkable tenacity. The result was that suffering among residents of the Smokies increased yet again.

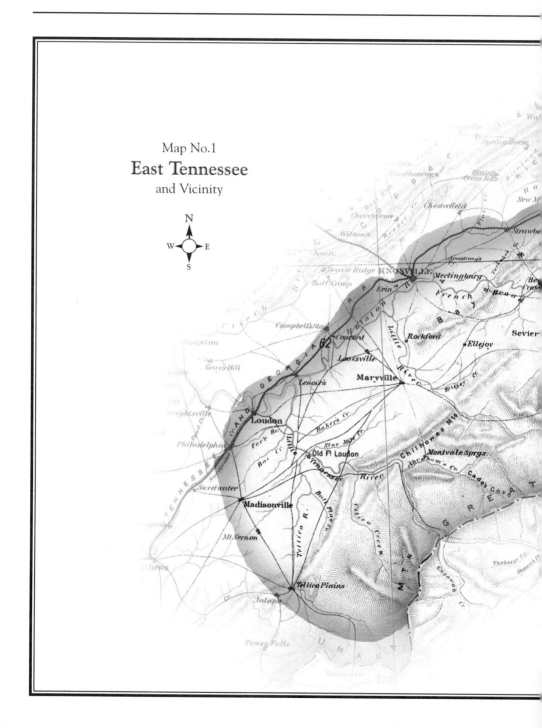

Map No.1
East Tennessee
and Vicinity

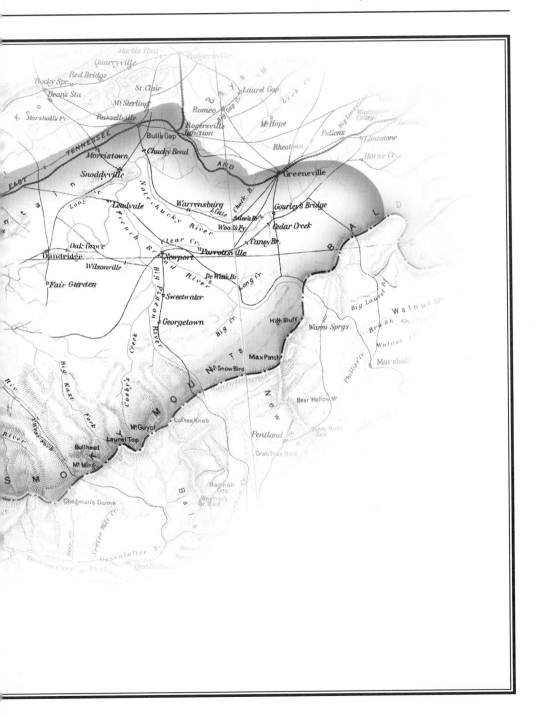

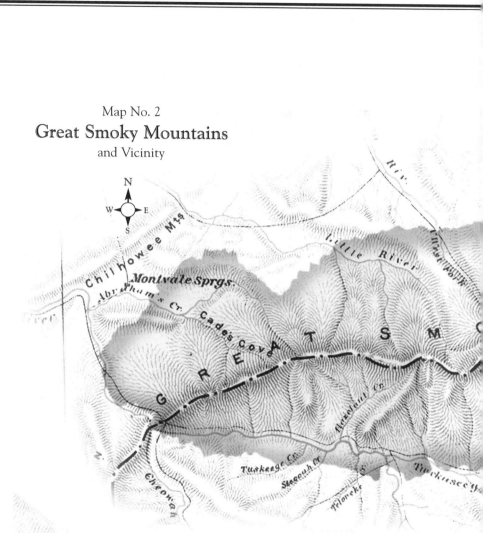

Map No. 2
Great Smoky Mountains
and Vicinity

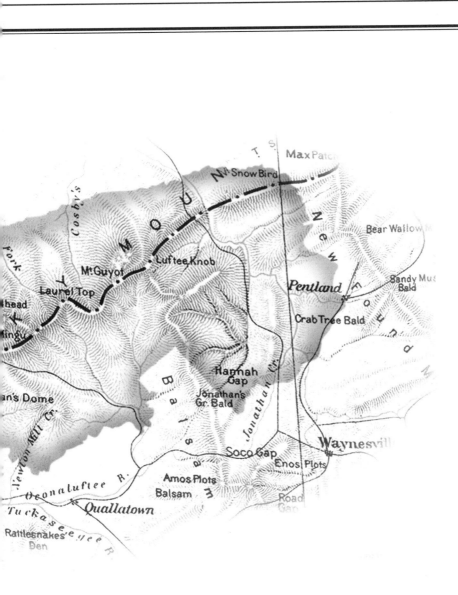

Map No. 3
Western North Carolina
and Vicinity

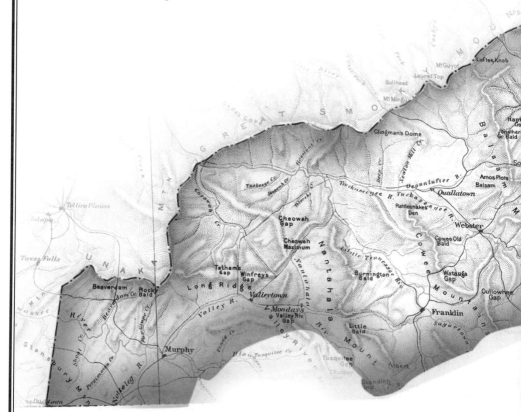

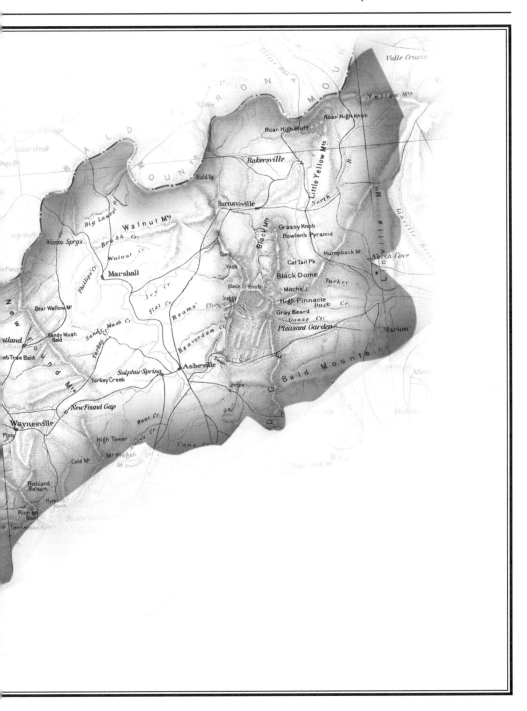

CHAPTER 6

THE LATE WAR: CONFEDERATE DESPERATION

N ONE RESPECT, AT LEAST, GEOGRAPHY, TERRAIN, AND LAGGING ECONOMIC DEVELOPMENT SERVED THE SMOKY MOUNTAINS WELL. The region had little strategic significance in the war, and it remained largely unaffected by most of the major campaigns. The Smoky Mountains held no large cities, no major transportation links, and no large mineral resources that could be exploited for the war, and its agricultural and industrial production was limited. The mountains, therefore, neither invited attack from the Union nor required large garrisons for defense. Despite Confederate fears to the contrary, the North Carolina Smokies were also relatively safe because they offered no effective invasion route to other regions with greater economic and strategic value. Union commanders did not turn their attention to the North Carolina Smokies until the end of the war, and even then the difficult terrain, lack of effective transportation, and limited food resources hampered Northern campaigns.

The Tennessee Smokies were somewhat more threatened than the North Carolina mountains, simply because of East Tennessee's strategic position within the Confederacy. The rail lines running from Chattanooga to Bristol made up part of the most direct route connecting the Deep South with Virginia, while the agricultural production of the East Tennessee Valley and the manufacturing capacity of Knoxville were moderately valuable Confederate assets. The proximity of the Tennessee Smokies both to Knoxville and to the rail lines, and the region's reputation as a haven for Unionist partisans, made the mountains a continued concern. East Tennessee was not considered so crucial as other Confederate territory, however, and the number of troops there in general, and in the Smokies in particular, declined throughout 1862 and 1863. Confederate companies occupied Sevierville and Newport part of the time, but only Maryville was allotted a permanent garrison, and Confederate activities in the region were confined largely to pursuing Unionist bushwhackers and conscript evaders. East Tennessee was also a low priority to the North. Although President Abraham Lincoln took a personal interest in Unionist East Tennessee and frequently exhorted his commanders to liberate the region as soon as possible, Union generals concluded that Middle Tennessee, West Tennessee, and points further south on the Mississippi River were not only more critical but also easier to take and hold. Thus East Tennessee remained in Confederate hands for over two years.[1]

The Smokies' relative isolation from the

main war ended in the fall of 1863, when Union forces finally entered East Tennessee in force. The initial fighting centered around Knoxville, Cumberland Gap, and Chattanooga, and only Blount County was much affected. But in November Confederate forces attempted to retake Knoxville, and both Blount and Sevier Counties, which offered excellent approaches to Knoxville, were drawn into the conflict. After failing to take Knoxville, Confederate forces withdrew into the upper part of the East Tennessee Valley, but the Tennessee Smokies remained contested territory until nearly the end of the war. At the same time, Union forces in East Tennessee and Confederate forces in western North Carolina were increasingly drawn to opportunities for raiding across the border, raids which frequently took them through the Smokies.

It was in late August 1863 when Major General Ambrose Burnside marched the Army of the Ohio south from Kentucky, came through the passes near Jacksborough, Tennessee, and moved straight on to Knoxville. The Confederate commander in East Tennessee, Major General Simon B. Buckner, had only 5,000 men, so rather than attempting to block Burnside he fell back toward Chattanooga to link up with Bragg's Army of Tennessee. Unsure of the scope of the invasion, Buckner ordered Thomas, who was still at Strawberry Plains with his Cherokee companies, to fall back across the border and defend the Smoky Mountain passes. Union cavalry discovered Thomas's movement and pursued him all the way to the border, but the Cherokee troops reached the mountains safely. Colonel F. W. Graham, who led the Union

pursuit, complained that loyalists failed to block Thomas' route and reported that it was impossible to follow the Cherokee troops once they reached the mountains. Thomas then set his men to work fortifying the passes and blockading the roads.[2]

Burnside had no intention of moving on North Carolina at that time, however. Once Union forces had secured Knoxville, he sent one force to hold the rail line and river crossings at Loudon, a second to seize Cumberland Gap, and a third, the One Hundredth Ohio Infantry, up the East Tennessee Valley toward Carter's Depot. The small Confederate force holding the Gap was caught between Burnside's force and the Ninth Army Corps advancing south from Kentucky and forced to surrender.[3]

The Confederate forces holding the upper East Tennessee Valley, which included parts of Thomas' Legion, fared considerably better. Colonel James R. Love had seven companies guarding the railroad bridge at Carter's Depot, while Colonel William C. Walker's battalion was stationed at Zollicoffer. Upon learning of the Union advance up the Valley, Brigadier General Alfred E. Jackson ordered Love to hold Carter's Depot as long as possible. Jackson then led Walker's battalion, a regiment of cavalry, and a battalion of Georgia troops down the valley to join Love. On September 8 Jackson ordered Love to attack Union positions at Telford Station, and Confederate troops broke the Federal line and drove the enemy back to Limestone Bridge on Lick Creek. Elated, Jackson brought up artillery and fresh infantry, launched a second assault, and forced the Union troops to surrender. Jackson took 350 prisoners and claimed another 50 killed or wounded, at the cost

President Abraham Lincoln believed East Tennessee could be used as a base both to encourage loyalist movements elsewhere in the South and to invade other regions of the Confederacy.

General William S. Rosecrans, whose Army of the Tennessee was then facing Bragg's Army of Tennessee at Chickamauga Creek. When Burnside withdrew, Major General Sam Jones sent Brigadier General John Williams's cavalry to join Jackson, and Confederate Major General Robert Ransom brought his small force down from southwest Virginia. Ransom then sent Walker's Battalion back to Carter's Depot and ordered Williams to take all his cavalry and Love's companies to Blue Springs. That proved a mistake, for Brigadier General James Shackelford still had troops at nearby Bull's Gap. On October 10 Shackelford made a night march to Blue Springs, surprised Williams, and drove him back to Greeneville. Walker then brought his battalion down to Greeneville to support Williams, and the Confederates prepared to make an orderly retreat back toward Carter's Depot. But a brigade of Union cavalry circled around during the night and blocked the line of march up the railroad. The next morning Jackson ordered Love to clear the way, and after repeated charges Love's companies drove the Union cavalry off. Over the next two days the Confederates fought a running battle with Union forces, but while Jackson was hard pressed, he held his force together and reached Jonesboro intact. Recognizing that he could do nothing more at that time, Ransom took his men back to Abingdon, Virginia, to watch for another opportunity to raid into Tennessee.[5]

But Burnside's troubles were not over. On September 20 Bragg defeated Rosecrans at the Battle of Chickamauga and shut Union forces up in Chattanooga. Hoping to undo all the gains Northern forces had made in Tennessee in 1863, Bragg then

of 21 Confederate casualties. Walker's battalion led the assault at Telford, and Jackson reported that both Walker's and Love's men fought well.[4]

Control of the upper valley then swayed back and forth. After his victory at Telford Jackson pulled his men back to Carter's Depot and took up strong defensive positions there. A few days later Burnside led a considerably larger force up the rail line from Knoxville, overran Jackson's line, and pushed the Confederates all the way back to Zollicoffer. Burnside had intended to continue advancing to the Virginia border, but he suddenly received orders to bring all his available force to support Major

sent Major General James Longstreet with 15,000 men to retake Knoxville. When Burnside first learned of Longstreet's advance, he considered abandoning Knoxville, taking refuge in the mountains in Blount County where the population was known to be friendly, and living off the country. That decision, if taken, almost certainly would have proven disastrous. Blount County probably could not have supported Burnside's forces for more than two to three weeks, and with no exit route available the army would have had to choose between starvation and surrender. But Burnside's plan was never put to the test. Major General Ulysses S. Grant, who was then bringing forces from Mississippi to rescue Rosecrans, ordered Burnside to fall back on Knoxville, draw Longstreet with him, and defend the city to the last. Deprived of Longstreet's Corps, Bragg would be left vulnerable to the counterstroke Grant was devising. Once he had relieved Rosecrans, Grant could then send troops to rescue Union forces at Knoxville.[6] Burnside, understandably, was not enthusiastic about his army being used as the bait in Grant's scheme, but once set on the course he carried out his orders with considerable energy and skill. Burnside immediately set his engineers to improving the defenses around Knoxville and forced all able-bodied men in the city, both free and slave, to build fortifications. On October 30 Burnside also sent most of his available cavalry and a section of artillery under Brigadier General William P. Sanders to Blount County to guard the crossings of the Little Tennessee River. Union cavalry scoured the roads and fords and constantly skirmished with Confederate cavalry, who were probing the area's defenses. Their

Library of Congress

Major General Ambrose E. Burnside captured Knoxville for the Union and fortified it against a siege by Major General James Longstreet.

mission proved frustrating, for Union commanders were beset with rumors of Confederate advances and found it impossible to separate truth from fancy. On November 2 Blount County Home Guardsmen reported that 1,200 Confederate cavalry had crossed the Little Tennessee near Morganton but had then turned back for fear that the rising water would trap them on the wrong side. The following day Wolford took 12 prisoners at Morganton and sighted a large force on the other side of the river. The prisoners claimed, falsely, that Longstreet intended to cross in force the following morning. On November 4 Sanders found enemy pickets on the Niles Ferry Road and drove them back several miles. Unionists reported that seven Confederate regiments had crossed

Union Major General Ulysses S. Grant ordered General Sherman to Knoxville to break Longstreet's siege of the fortified city.

later Sanders again grumbled about constantly receiving false intelligence and noted "If I even thought of sending scouts out on every report of citizens, I would have no horses left in a few days." Sanders had even received reports that a small Cherokee force had entered Cades Cove, though he did not credit this story. On November 12, however, a small Confederate force supposedly guided by a doctor from Maryville crossed Chilhowee Mountain, attacked Union pickets at Maryville, and escaped by way of Montvale.[7]

As this news came in, Burnside grew increasingly concerned about Union positions in Blount County. On November 5 Colonel Edward Porter, Burnside's chief of staff, instructed Sanders immediately to fall back toward Knoxville if he became convinced that Longstreet intended to attack in force. Porter informed Sanders that Burnside was "frequently anxious in regard to the state of affairs in your front," and ordered him to report every day even if he had no new information. The following day Burnside ordered Sanders to move his main force to the north side of the Little Tennessee, while leaving strong outposts at Maryville and Morganton. Burnside warned that Union cavalry at Rogersville had been "badly whipped" and that the Confederates might attempt to exploit this success. On November 10 the post commander at Maryville promised that he would learn of any Confederate crossing in force within three hours after it had begun, that he would immediately "be amongst them," and that he would send Sanders ample warning. As it turned out, he managed to do none of these things. The following day Colonel Charles D. Pennebaker, whose cavalry brigade had been stationed at Morganton,

the river. The following day Union forces attacked a Confederate regiment crossing the Little Tennessee at Motley's Ford and took another 40 prisoners. Despite these successes, Sanders noted that scouting the area was proving difficult for his small force, for "there is a terrible number of roads leading to this place," and concluded "I am by no means satisfied that [the Confederates] really intend to try to occupy this country." Similarly, on November 10 Sanders complained "It is almost impossible to get a true report from any citizen, even those who are undoubted Union men, as they do not wait to find out the truth, but run on the slightest rumor." A few days

moved his main force back to Rockford and left only two companies at Morganton to continue scouting.[8]

In the meantime Longstreet was in fact moving on Blount. On November 3 Confederate cavalry crossed the Little Tennessee at Porter's Ford and sent one detachment toward Morganton and one toward Maryville. They found the fords at Morganton too high for the army to cross and reported 200 Union troops at Maryville. Another scout noted that "the enemy's pickets are as thick as hops and it is almost impossible to send men over." The following day Confederate forces approached to within five miles of Maryville. They found two regiments of Wolford's brigade near the town and a third on the Knoxville Road. Union scouting parties "were on nearly all the roads leading from Maryville." Colonel G. G. Dibrell noted that loyalist bushwhackers had killed one of his officers, Lieutenant Arthur Henry, and claimed that all the Blount County Home Guards had been sent to Knoxville to help collect supplies. Finally, on November 12 Longstreet ordered Major General Joseph Wheeler's four cavalry brigades to capture the enemy force at Maryville, which he estimated at anywhere from 500 to 4,000 men. If Wheeler were successful at Maryville, he was to create a diversion on Burnside's left flank and secure the approaches to Knoxville. If he failed, he was to rejoin the main army. Rapid movement was crucial, and the Confederate troopers were ordered to take no wagons and only two days rations. Wheeler crossed the Little Tennessee River at Motley's Ford late on November 13 and made an all night march. Early the next morning Confederate cavalry completely

Major General William S. Rosecrans was defeated by Major General Braxton Bragg at the Battle of Chickamauga.

surprised the two companies at Morganton and captured them. Wheeler then pushed on to Maryville and found only the Eleventh Kentucky Cavalry guarding the town. Wheeler attempted to surround Maryville and cut off all retreat, but the attempt failed, "my guides having deceived me in reference to its exact location." Wheeler then charged the Eleventh Kentucky, scattered them, and captured 151 men. Finally alerted, Brigadier General Frank Wolford brought up the rest of his cavalry to block the Confederate advance. Wheeler in turn ordered up two more brigades and pushed the Union cavalry back. Wheeler claimed, probably with some exaggeration, that his men "drove [Wolford] over the Little River in the

Union Brigadier General Frank Wolford repeatedly battled Confederate forces near Sevierville.

wildest confusion."[9]

The next day Sanders reinforced Wolford with additional cavalry and a battery. The Union force attacked Wheeler's men and, after an initial repulse, pushed the lead regiment back. Confederate and Union versions of what happened then differ considerably. Sanders claimed that, having received orders to withdraw, he fought a delaying action all the way back to Knoxville, keeping his force intact and slowing the Confederate advance. Wheeler, conversely, reported that his men easily drove Sanders back three miles to Stock Creek. Finding Sanders's men deployed in a wood on a ridge behind the creek, Wheeler dismounted half his command and sent them across the creek on foot. The remaining troopers went to find a ford. While the

dismounted force drove back Sanders's left, Wheeler's remaining cavalry quickly crossed the river, fell on the Union right, and broke the whole line. "The entire mass of the enemy swept on toward Knoxville in the wildest confusion" and "dashed across their pontoons in their fright into the city." Wheeler claimed another 141 prisoners and dozens killed and wounded, including many who drowned attempting to cross the Holston River. The next day Wheeler attempted to advance again but, finding the fortifications far too strong, rejoined the main army. But Sanders had been killed in the fighting, and Union forces were now shut up in Knoxville. In the meantime Longstreet had crossed his main force at Loudon and advanced rapidly toward the city. [10]

Even so, Longstreet had lost his opportunity for a quick assault and a quick victory. Sanders's men had given Burnside sufficient time to make considerable improvements to Knoxville's fortifications, and Longstreet now had to lay siege to the city. Secure behind their fortifications, the only thing that could threaten Union forces was starvation. Reports concerning the size of Burnside's food stocks and the length of time he could have held out vary widely, but in any case Smoky Mountain loyalists now made a critical contribution to the survival of the Union army. For a number of reasons, including faulty maps and a mistrust of local guides, Longstreet had failed to stop traffic on the south branch of the French Broad River, which flowed from Sevierville into Knoxville. Unionists in Cocke, Blount, and Sevier counties had apparently been stockpiling supplies in anticipation of the Union invasion, and every night while the siege lasted they loaded rafts with provisions and floated them down the river to waiting parties of Northern troops. Burnside sent Colonel James Doughty of the Fourteenth Tennessee Cavalry with a detachment of troops to bring in the supplies, and Union troops constructed a long boom to catch the rafts. After a few days a secessionist woman warned Longstreet about these activities, and Confederates sent a heavy raft down the river to destroy the boom. But a Unionist woman brought the news to Doughty, and Federal troops put out a larger boom to intercept the raft. As Kirby Smith had stated in March 1862, for Confederate troops East Tennessee was, indeed, an enemy's country.[11]

On November 25 Union forces broke Bragg's lines around Chattanooga and sent the Army of Tennessee reeling back into Georgia. Grant then ordered Major General William T. Sherman to take the Fifteenth and Fourth Corps to Knoxville to break Longstreet's siege. In his last communication to Grant, Burnside had stated that his supplies would be exhausted by Thanksgiving, so Sherman prepared to travel light and drive his men hard. Sherman divided his forces into three columns and sent them on different routes through Blount County: the left through Unita and Louisville, the center to Morganton, and the right on the Madisonville and Knoxville Road. The three columns were to converge at Maryville before marching on Knoxville. When the center column reached the Little Tennessee River, however, they found that high water made the fords impassable. But Sherman's engineers thought they could bridge the river using supplies at hand. So while some work parties began felling and shaping trees, others crossed the river in small boats, dismantled every last building in Morganton except a church, and floated the lumber back across the river. Union work parties then erected a makeshift trestle bridge, and the column crossed the river. In the meantime, the left column improvised a second bridge by driving a line of wagons into the river, roping them together, and laying planks across the wagon beds. Union forces then camped just outside Maryville, and Sherman and his staff rode on toward Knoxville to assess the situation.[12]

Once again Longstreet played into Grant's hands. Immediately after Grant had determined to drive Confederate forces away from Knoxville, he had sent five couriers to Burnside notifying him of Sherman's approach, with the intent that at least one be captured. One was, and Longstreet now faced the choice of attacking the city immediately, retreating, or being caught between two Union forces. In the meantime another courier made it as far as Kingston, but he could go no further. No man would volunteer to take his message, so Mary Love, a Unionist from Louisville who happened to be visiting in Kingston, volunteered. She was stopped and questioned by Confederate soldiers along the way, but she told them she was the sister of Dr. John Lewis of Louisville, which was true, and that she was on her way to take care of his ill sister. Love eventually reached the home of her brother-in-law Horace Foster, a Unionist in Louisville, but could go no further. A 13-year-old boy, John T. Brown, then carried the message into Knoxville. Once again Smoky Mountain Unionists had

Confederate Major General Joseph Wheeler routed Union forces in Maryville and drove his cavalry on in an effort to retake Knoxville.

come to Burnside's aid, and the Union commander knew that help was coming.[13]

After considerable debate, Longstreet made the unfortunate decision to assault the fortifications on the southwest side of Knoxville, which had been named Fort Sanders after the recently fallen general. In the early morning hours of November 29, three brigades hidden in the woods rushed the Union defenses and immediately bogged down. Unable to survey the ground thoroughly, Longstreet had not realized that a whole series of obstacles, including a moat, a row of abatis, and a tangle of stumps and telegraph wire, blocked the approaches to Fort Sanders. Line after line of attacking Confederates tumbled into the moat to be shot down by Union troops in perfectly sited firing positions. In six hours of fighting Longstreet lost nearly 800 men, while Union losses were negligible. Having no choice left, Longstreet gave up his mission and marched his force north of Knoxville to Bull's Gap.[14]

Sherman reached the city a day after the fight at Fort Sanders had concluded. There he saw "a large pen of fine cattle" and other stores of supplies, and found Burnside and his staff enjoying a substantial Thanksgiving dinner. After having marched so hard to rescue Burnside's army from starvation, Sherman was considerably provoked. Even so, he offered to join forces with Burnside and drive Longstreet completely out of East Tennessee. Burnside declined the offer, but he did agree to keep Major General Gordon Granger's Fourth Corps. Sherman then marched the rest of his force back out of Blount County and returned to Chattanooga. Though Sherman's men were in Blount only four days, the county suffered considerably from their presence, for Sherman's men had lived entirely off local supplies.[15]

Before leaving Blount County, Sherman sent Colonel Eli Long with three cavalry regiments to Maryville to intercept 300 Confederate wagons that reportedly had been cut off at Loudon by Sherman's advance and were now trying to escape to North Carolina. Long followed the wagon train across the mountains into North Carolina as far as Murphy, but never caught up to it. He did, however, drive a small cavalry force and a company of Home Guards out of Murphy. Returning to Maryville on December 11, Long reported that the road from Maryville to Murphy was "for the most part good. After leaving

Tellico Plains the route lies through a mountainous country, but the road over the mountains is well engineered and practicable for wagons." But the surrounding country was devastated: "The country is very poor, the fields poorly cultivated and grain and forage more scarce than any locality previously visited during my entire trip....Frequent incursions have been made in there by rebel cavalry, and but few cattle of any kind, horse or mules, were found." Long's report offered grim testimony to the effects the war had already had on the Carolina Smokies.[16]

It was at this point that Confederate forces in western North Carolina began to stir. In November 1863 the War Department assigned Brigadier General Robert B. Vance to command the Department of Western North Carolina. Vance, the brother of North Carolina Governor Zebulon B. Vance, and the former commander of the Twenty-ninth North Carolina Infantry, was determined to restore life to what had become a somnolent theater. Bragg, who clearly had no understanding of the conditions in western North Carolina and who still hoped to recapture East Tennessee, encouraged Vance's ambitions.[17]

On November 4, 1863 Vance urged Thomas to shift his perspective from defensive to offensive operations. The new commander predicted that Confederate forces would soon have an opportunity to regain East Tennessee, and warned Thomas to be prepared to move back across the border: "In the meantime you can push up operations in your region...keep in view the operations of our Army in East Tennessee, so that if an effort is made to dislodge the enemy from that important

Library of Congress

Confederate Major General Braxton Bragg defeated Major General Rosecrans at the Battle of Chickamauga and successfully shut Union forces up in Chattanooga.

country we can assist." Vance also urged Thomas to attend to problems at home: "It is very important to arrest every deserter in the country, and you will give especial attention to that....Deserters soon become our worst enemies." Vance promised that he would supply Thomas's men with shoes, clothing, and ammunition and that he would have Love's companies sent back to North Carolina. The following month Vance again ordered Thomas to watch for any opportunity to harass Union forces in East Tennessee. In the meantime Thomas had written to Thomas P. Siler, a farmer and merchant in Macon County, asking about conditions across the border. Siler replied that when he left Loudon on November 27, Longstreet still had Knoxville surrounded and that several hundred Confederate cavalry were based at

Longstreet's forces attacked Knoxville at Fort Sanders on November 29, 1863. The Confederates suffered nearly 800 casualties in the horrific assault.

Maryville and Louisville. Since then he had heard that Burnside was still besieged, but that Union forces had retaken Loudon and that the Confederate cavalry in Blount had retreated toward Nantahala and Cherokee. Siler urged Thomas to send a small force into Blount to guard the border against Federal raids and to "be a terror to the Tories and rogues who have been stealing horses and negroes."[18]

In compliance with Vance's orders, in early December Thomas moved across the mountains to Gatlinburg. Exactly what he intended to accomplish is unclear, for Gatlinburg, while relatively safe, was an unlikely base for threatening anywhere except Sevierville, and Thomas's force was too small for anything but limited raids. Even so, Thomas apparently intended to stay the winter, for his men built a camp of log huts, and some of the soldiers' wives moved to the camp. Thomas then sent out scouting parties. When Sevier County Home Guardsmen captured one of Thomas's men and jailed him in Sevierville, Thomas marched 200 men to Sevierville, captured 60 Home Guardsmen, broke down the jail, and freed his men. He then released the Guardsmen after relieving them of their arms and ammunition, and returned to Gatlinburg. Loyalists claimed that Thomas's men also robbed several homes before leaving.

The Sevier County Guardsmen wasted

no time in reporting Thomas's presence to Union authorities, and Brigadier General Samuel D. Sturgis immediately sent Colonel William Palmer and the Fifteenth Pennsylvania Cavalry to wipe out the Confederate camp. Guided by local loyalists, Palmer took 150 men "by a circuitous and almost impassable trail from Weir's Cove" to a point three miles in the rear of Gatlinburg. A second force of 50 men approached Gatlinburg from the north by the Sevierville Road, while a third picketed all the roads out of Sevierville to prevent local secessionists from warning Thomas of the attack. Palmer planned to trap the Confederates between the two advancing forces and cut off their retreat, but like so many similar schemes, the attempt failed. Although the assaulting forces managed to reach Gatlinburg at nearly the same time, their routes did not bring them to the positions Palmer had expected, the result of operating in steep wooded country with few roads and no maps. Further, Thomas's camp was located on a steep ridge, and he had carefully picketed his position. When Union forces drew near the pickets fired and ran, alerting the whole camp and forcing Palmer's men to dismount and slowly work their way up the ridge. After an hour's skirmishing, Thomas safely drew his forces back into the mountains and then back to Quallatown. Palmer's total catch was one prisoner, a few horses that had been impressed from Sevier County loyalists, a small cache of arms and supplies, and a prized souvenir, Thomas's hat. Again, the mountains had frustrated a carefully planned operation: "The steep wooded ridge on which they had their camp jutted onto the mountain on the east, and it was impracticable to prevent the

rebels on retreating from taking up this mountain when we could not reach them, and when they continued firing from behind that cove for several hours." Disgusted, Palmer returned the horses to the Unionists who came to claim them, burned the entire camp, and returned to Dandridge. On the other side, Thomas praised his men for their resolute exchange of fire with Union troops and claimed that "the enemy have at least been taught that while we hold the Smoky Mountains, western North Carolina and the adjacent portions of East Tennessee are hard to subjugate."[19]

In the meantime Vance was making his own move into Tennessee. In early November he raided into Cocke and Greene Counties, rounded up hundreds of hogs, horses, and cattle, and started back toward the border. Burnside learned of the raid on November 10 and sent the Ninth Michigan Cavalry to investigate. Vance found about 200 Federal troops blocking his route near Newport, but he immediately charged and drove them back. Vance then returned safely to Asheville, bringing all the captured livestock with him. Brigadier General Vance reported his success to Governor Vance and asked for more troops to continue his operations. The governor sent the request on to the War Department, but as always the Confederacy had no troops to spare.[20]

Vance refused to allow either this rejection or Thomas's repulse to alter his plans, however. In early January 1864 Longstreet, who was then camped near Bull's Gap, ordered Vance to occupy Newport. Longstreet intended Vance to protect his left flank, but Vance had other aims as well. Vance left Asheville on

January 8 with 250 infantry, 375 cavalry, and a battery. Thomas brought another 250 infantry from Jackson and Cherokee Counties, and Vance led his little army through Oconaluftee Gap and on to Gatlinburg. The mountain crossing was in itself a notable feat, for the road down into Tennessee was so steep that Vance's men had to dismantle the wagons and artillery caissons and carry them by hand. Upon reaching Gatlinburg Vance, for reasons that remain unclear, split his forces. Taking half the cavalry, he rode on toward Sevierville, while leaving the remaining forces at Gatlinburg under the command of Thomas and Lieutenant Colonel James Henry. On January 13 Vance ran across a Union supply train and scooped up 17 wagons, 23 Federal soldiers, and a load of badly needed medical supplies. Vance then sent orders to Henry to take the remaining cavalry, scout through Weir's Cove, and meet him at Schultz's Mill on Cosby Creek near Newport. Inexplicably, Thomas and the infantry were to fall back into North Carolina.

Union forces were again quick to respond. Unionists reported Vance's raid, and Palmer took the Fifteenth Pennsylvania Cavalry and detachments from the Tenth Ohio and First Tennessee Cavalries and went in pursuit. Again aided by Sevier County Home Guardsmen, Palmer found Vance on the Newport Road 23 miles out of Sevierville, near his expected rendezvous with Henry on Cosby Creek. Vance, who had stopped to rest his horses, had failed to picket his position, and Palmer's assault took him completely by surprise: "I immediately charged them in column of fours routing the entire command, which fled in the utmost disorder,

throwing away their guns, belts, blankets, saddle bags etc. and numbers of them quitting their horses." A subsequent report noted that "the remnants of the rebel party broke and fled to the mountains closely pursued by the Union home guard." Union forces captured Vance, his entire staff, and another 50 prisoners. They also regained the 17 lost wagons, along with 150 horses and Vance's artillery. Immensely satisfied with the victory, Palmer noted that he immediately "sent the Home Guards to scour the mountains for dismounted rebels." The next day Palmer learned that Thomas was still at Gatlinburg and asked for fresh cavalry to capture his force. None was available, however, and once again Thomas would escape.

Vance had botched the entire operation and had only himself to blame for his capture. Rather than occupying Newport as ordered, he had gone off on a fruitless raid. Further, though he was far from home and in enemy territory, he had chosen to divide his already small force, leaving himself vulnerable to attack. Vance's ambitions far exceeded his military experience and abilities, and he and his men paid the price. But Henry and Thomas had also contributed to the disaster. Rather than setting out for Cosby Creek as ordered, Henry had initially chosen to fall back with Thomas's infantry, and Thomas apparently had not objected. On January 15 Henry had finally reversed course and ventured out toward Schultz's Mill, but by that time Vance was a prisoner and his cavalry were scattered. Learning of the defeat, Henry again retreated, and both he and Thomas returned safely to North Carolina.

Vance's disastrous raid proved a considerable embarrassment to the Confederacy, and authorities searched for a scapegoat. Colonel John B. Palmer, who replaced Vance as commander of the District of Western North Carolina, arrested Henry for disobeying orders and for not supporting Vance. Henry in turned blamed Thomas for issuing vague and confusing orders and for "retreating" with his infantry. Palmer wrote a long report on the operation and sent it to Secretary of War James Seddon and Governor Vance. Seddon passed the report on to Davis, but the Secretary of War refused to blame any one person, noting that Vance's capture "seems to have resulted from disobedience to orders by another and lack of due precautions by himself." Davis concluded that, with Vance in enemy hands, nothing more could be done, and there the matter ended.[21]

Following Longstreet's retreat from Knoxville, the focus of the fighting in East Tennessee shifted to the upper Tennessee Valley and to the Smoky Mountains. Having established winter quarters near Bull's Gap, Longstreet began sending out foraging parties to strip the surrounding country of subsistence. In part this was simple necessity, for Longstreet's men were largely cut off from Confederate supply lines. Longstreet reported that he had to depend entirely on the countryside for supplies, forage, and "in some measure for clothing," and conceded that "the general disposition of the troops was made more with a view to gathering supplies, than for active military operations." In part, however, it was also policy, for Longstreet stated that he intended both to deny Federal troops the ability to operate in upper East Tennessee and to make Unionists bear the burdens of the war. Longstreet's foragers reached as far as Blount, Sevier, and Cocke Counties, and thus the Smokies were drawn into this conflict for resources.[22]

Union and Confederate troops soon came to blows in the Smokies. In late December Longstreet sent most of his cavalry to Jefferson and Sevier Counties to protect his forage trains and guard the French Broad River crossings. When Union Major General John G. Foster sent his own cavalry to Sevier to forage, they found a division of infantry at Maryville and large cavalry forces on the north side of the French Broad. They also found few supplies, and withdrew. Then in mid-January Colonel Palmer reported that the Confederates had exhausted nearly all available supplies around Morristown and were now foraging on the south side of the French Broad and Nolachucky Rivers. The foraging parties were lightly guarded, but Morgan's and Armstrong's cavalry divisions were on the north side of the French Broad. Palmer also noted that several companies of Confederate cavalry were taking supplies near Newport and Cosby Creek. Palmer argued that if he were given a brigade of cavalry he could capture a large number of supply wagons and escape before the Confederate cavalry could react: "They can never catch us in these woods and mountains, and we have the whole population to guide and picket for us." No brigade was available, however, and Palmer was denied his chance at another triumph.[23]

By mid-January Union forces had used up their own supplies around Mossy Creek, and Major General John G. Foster, who had replaced Burnside in East Tennessee, determined to contest Confederate control of the prime foraging areas along the

French Broad. Foster left the Ninth Infantry Corps at Strawberry Plains to guard Knoxville and the railroad, and marched the Fourth and Twenty-Third Infantry Corps to Dandridge. Foster intended to cross the river there, collect supplies along the French Broad and Nolachucky, threaten Longstreet's flank, and cut Confederate communications with North Carolina. On January 16 Union cavalry drove Longstreet's troopers back from the French Broad, and the following day Foster threw up a temporary bridge and began crossing his infantry. To their considerable surprise, however, the Union troops found themselves not on the opposite bank but instead on an island. In one of those seemingly bizarre but not uncommon incidents, Foster's maps had been faulty, and his engineers had laid their bridge to an island in the middle of the river. At the same time, Foster received reports that Longstreet was approaching with his whole force. His entire plan ruined, the Union general threw up his hands and sent his Corps back to Strawberry Plains and Knoxville.[24]

The question of supplies could not be ignored, however. In early January Brigadier General Samuel D. Sturgis, commander of the Cavalry Division, Army of the Ohio, reported that his forces had "consumed almost all the forage and supplies on the south side of the French Broad River not absolutely necessary for the support of the Union families during the winter" and had proposed sending part of his force to Blount and Cocke Counties, which reportedly still contained substantial supplies. Foster now agreed to the plan, and by January 19 Sturgis had moved his men to Sevier County. He sent Brigadier

General Edward McCook to scout the fords near Dandridge, ordered Wolford to Fair Garden, and stationed Brigadier General Israel Garrard on the Newport Road. Other forces were sent to the Little Pigeon River and Boyd's Creek to hold the fords and forage in the Dutch and Irish Bottoms. Sturgis initially reported that Longstreet's main forces remained near Morristown and showed no intention of advancing: "The question then with us is one purely of forage." But that optimistic assessment would soon be shattered. On January 21 local Unionists brought word that Confederate cavalry had crossed the French Broad near Dandridge. In the meantime, Sturgis also found that Longstreet's forces had already taken so much forage from the Dutch Bottoms and Irish Bottoms that "a division of cavalry could not subsist longer than three days." The only thing left was to remain near Sevierville until supplies there were exhausted.[25]

Sturgis thus made dispositions to meet the Confederate advance. Having only one brigade, McCook's, near Dandridge, Sturgis sent Brigadier General William Campbell's brigade to join him, and ordered McCook to drive the Confederates back across the river. Sturgis's remaining brigades, Wolford's and Garrard's, took up positions on the Wilsonville and Newport Road four miles from Fair Garden. Sturgis wrote Foster that he intended to concentrate his entire force to meet the enemy advance. He was not optimistic of success, however, for the roads were in terrible condition and his horses were nearly exhausted from four weeks' hard use. Foster replied that if Sturgis found himself overwhelmed he was to fall back toward Maryville, where

Brigadier General August Willich had two infantry brigades and four guns. Willich did not know how long he could remain at Maryville, however, for the deputy provost marshal there had estimated that the county could supply the Federal force for only 30 days. Willich had asked for wagons so he could draw forage from a larger area, and cavalry to escort them, but he had received neither. In the meantime Sturgis sent two small forces to Cocke County, one to destroy a Confederate pontoon bridge that had supposedly been laid over the Nolachucky River, and one to intercept a large Confederate wagon train reported near Newport. Neither force found its intended target. But a third detachment attacked Confederate pickets near Newport, killed three Confederate troops and took 16 prisoners, and captured 3,000 bushels of corn.[26]

In the last week of January the Confederate cavalry finally moved. On January 26, Armstrong's, Martin's, and Morgan's divisions of cavalry, with their attached artillery, left Fair Garden and advanced on the road to Sevierville. They met General Wolford's brigade astride the road six miles outside Sevierville, charged, and drove the smaller Union force back two miles. Sturgis then sent Garrard's brigade to reinforce Wolford, but he was pessimistic about their prospects: "We will do the best we can, but I do not feel like promising much." As Sturgis feared, the Confederate cavalry advanced again, and Wolford and Garrard fell back another two miles.

The next day, however, Sturgis indeed did the best he could. Leaving Wolford's and LaGrange's brigades just outside Sevierville, he sent Campbell's brigade to block the Fair Garden Road, and ordered McCook to attack at daybreak. McCook enjoyed surprising success and drove the Confederates back two miles. Sturgis then sent LaGrange up the road to join McCook, while Campbell was ordered to assault the Confederate left. While Campbell made steady progress and gained about a mile of ground, LaGrange came up unobserved, fell on the Confederate right, and forced it back. Considerably encouraged, Sturgis moved Wolford and Garrard to block Armstrong from joining Martin and Morgan, and at about 4:00 p.m. he sent Garrard to reinforce McCook and LaGrange and ordered a general charge. The Confederates broke and ran, leaving behind 50-60 killed and wounded, two guns, and 150 prisoners, including three regimental commanders. Union cavalry also took Morgan's battle flag and nearly captured Morgan himself. Sturgis was immensely satisfied with the result: "The rout of the enemy was complete, and Morgan's division is entirely destroyed and Generals Martin and Morgan are reported lost by the rebels." Wolford and Garrard reached Fair Garden too late to join the pursuit, and since McCook's and LaGrange's brigades were exhausted, Sturgis called a halt. The Union troopers had not in fact shattered Morgan's division, but they had won a signal victory. Longstreet reported that Martin had been in a "severe cavalry fight," had been driven back four miles, and had lost 200 killed, wounded, and missing.[27]

The Union celebration was short lived, however. On January 29 Sturgis learned that Longstreet had reacted to the defeat at Fair Garden by sending three infantry brigades across the French Broad River near Dandridge. Sturgis reported that he lacked sufficient force to fight infantry while also collecting supplies, and he ordered Willich to ship all the stores he had collected to Knoxville as quickly as possible. But Sturgis still hoped to destroy Armstrong's cavalry division, which was then posted on the Newport Road near Indian Creek, before it could be reinforced. Sturgis left Garrard and McCook to watch for Longstreet's infantry and sent Wolford and LaGrange to attack Armstrong. The Union cavalry found the Confederates strongly posted on the creek bed and reinforced by three regiments of infantry. Wolford and LaGrange dismounted their men and repeatedly assaulted the Confederate position, but they made little progress and suffered heavy casualties. Near sundown Sturgis learned that the remaining Confederate infantry were advancing toward Garrard's and McCook's rear. Conceding defeat, Sturgis pulled his whole force back to Fair Garden, sent his wagons and supplies to Maryville, and forwarded the captured artillery to Knoxville. Sturgis then slowly marched his cavalry through Weir's Cove and Tuckaleechee Cove, giving them plenty of time to rest and forage. Sturgis noted his considerable regret at having to concede the ground: "It is hard to leave these loyal people to the mercies of the enemy, but it can't be helped. If I had had a division of infantry at Sevierville I could have annihilated both those divisions of rebel cavalry, for the rout was complete and men scattered beyond all possible hope of reorganization in Morgan's Division." Sturgis estimated his own losses at around 100 and reported 400 Confederate killed and wounded.[28]

The skirmishing for resources then shifted to Blount County. On January 31 Sturgis reported that Longstreet's main force was now positioned near Sevierville, ready to threaten both Maryville and Knoxville. Sturgis moved his cavalry to Maryville to support Willich, but due to lack of supplies he did not know how long he could remain there. Willich had given him rations, but the infantry commander estimated that he had supplies sufficient for only 20 days without foraging. The following day Major General John G. Foster ordered Willich to patrol the roads between Sevierville and Maryville, scout toward Louisville and Rockford, and guard the fords on the Holston between Louisville and Knoxville. If the Confederates advanced, he was to fall back to Louisville. Foster also directed Granger to be prepared to send reinforcements to Willich "so as to avoid losing more country." On February 2 Union forces reported that both Martin's and Armstrong's cavalry divisions were at Sevierville and that three infantry brigades were 22 miles west of there on the French Broad.[29]

The battle for supplies in the Smokies went on. On February 7 McCook requested and received permission to move to Motley's Ford, 18 miles from Maryville: "I regard the move as absolutely necessary, as the country is entirely exhausted of forage." McCook reported that he was down to ten days rations and that he had been hauling supplies 12 to 15 miles on horseback, entirely exhausting the brigade's mounts. On February 12 Confederate cavalry attacked Federal pickets at Maryville but were repulsed. Lieutenant Colonel R. O. Selfridge boasted "it is idle to think that the enemy's cavalry can whip us here."

Union and Confederate cavalry clashed at Boyd's Creek on February 13 and near Maryville on the following day, with little result. A week later a party of McCook's scouts surprised Confederate foragers in Tuckaleechee Cove, killed one man, captured ten, and burned five wagons.[30]

Control of the Tennessee side of the Smokies continued to swing back and forth. In the summer of 1864 a company of Union troops were finally sent to occupy Maryville permanently. They took the courthouse for their headquarters, forcing county officials to move their records to a vacant store building and into the home of the county entry taker. On August 21, 1864 Wheeler's advanced guard rode into Maryville. Only 23 Union troops were present, but they began firing on the Confederate cavalry and refused to surrender the courthouse. Wheeler's men then brought up artillery to shell the building. When they found that a house blocked their line of sight, the troops set it on fire. Unfortunately, the fire spread to other downtown buildings, and all but three were destroyed. After heavy shelling the Union troops surrendered. In the meantime Polly Toole, a slave in the entry taker's home, carried most of the county records out of the house and store building to safety. The Blount County Court eventually awarded her a pension.[31]

In the meantime, Confederate forces in western North Carolina continued to suffer embarrassments. Attempting to secure supplies and place himself in a better position to intercept Federal raids, Thomas moved his Cherokee companies up the Tuckasegee River to the mouth of Deep Creek in late January. When Sturgis came through Tuckaleechee Cove after the fight

at Fair Garden, loyalists in the cove reported Thomas's move. Sturgis, claiming that Thomas's men "had become a terror to the Union people of East Tennessee and the border of North Carolina from the atrocities they were daily perpetrating," sent the Fourteenth Illinois Cavalry under Major Francis M. Davidson to push them back. This time Thomas was not so careful in selecting and picketing his position, and the Union troopers completely surprised the camp and scattered the Cherokee troops. Davidson boastfully and implausibly claimed that he had captured 22 Cherokee and 32 white troops and killed another 200. Davidson explained the high casualty figure by noting that after one of his officers was wounded his men took no more prisoners. Davidson took the Cherokee prisoners back to Knoxville, where authorities supposedly offered them $5,000 in gold if they would kill Thomas, and then released them. Most of the prisoners immediately returned to Thomas and continued to fight for the Confederacy. But a small number changed sides, joined the Third North Carolina Mounted Infantry, and fought with the Union until the end of the war. When they returned home, they were threatened with execution as traitors, but they apparently escaped this penalty.

Thomas, of course, offered a completely different version of the encounter. He asserted that he had inflicted 12 casualties on the federal force while losing only five killed and wounded. He further insisted that, rather than suffering defeat, he had actually frustrated Davidson's intention to move much further into Cherokee. John B. Palmer was so incensed at this new federal incursion, however, that he went to

Jackson County to investigate the incident personally. Palmer concluded that Thomas had had only two men killed and 20 to 30 captured and attributed Davidson's success to the 50 or so loyalists who had guided Union forces to Thomas's camp.[32]

Encouraged by Davidson's success, Union forces continued to cross the border. On February 11 LaGrange sent a scout from Motley's Ford into Cherokee County. The Union cavalry encountered no resistance and found only six companies of infantry in the county. The roads were not blockaded, and there had been sufficient forage to support a larger cavalry force. Six days later Sturgis ordered the First Wisconsin Cavalry to raid into Cherokee County. The Union troopers impressed a number of horses and mules, took 35 Home Guards prisoner, and returned to East Tennessee unscathed.[33]

These raids demonstrated the Smokies' vulnerability to attack and badly scared Confederate authorities. In late March Love pointed out that Longstreet's return to Virginia would leave western North Carolina wide open to attack. Love concluded that the Confederate command had effectively abandoned both East Tennessee and western North Carolina to the enemy. Major John D. Ashmore, Post Commander at Greeneville, South Carolina, warned that Davidson's attack was actually a probe to test the possibility of future, larger raids. Ashmore pointed out that if Federal forces could move through Cherokee and Macon Counties untouched they could easily cross into South Carolina and strike the Confederate industrial complex at Greenville, Walhalla, Pendleton, Anderson, and Spartanburg.

Ashmore had one company of cavalry out watching the approaches from Haywood, Henderson, and Buncombe Counties, but he asked for a second company to guard the roads from Macon, Jackson, and Cherokee. The governor of South Carolina, M. L. Bonham, likewise believed that this region was vulnerable, and in both March and April he requested additional forces to protect the factories and iron works near Walhalla.[34]

Thomas, also, continued to call attention to the weaknesses of his position. He pointed out that, with Longstreet's withdrawal to Bull's Gap, the only troops available to defend the border were a company of Georgia troops at Hiwassee Pass and Thomas's own. But Thomas asserted that his force was far too small for the task and warned that he was in danger of losing the few men he did have. Thomas's regimental quartermaster was still in East Tennessee, and without his services Thomas was unable to draw the regiment's allotted supplies. He had sent his own agents to South Carolina to purchase supplies and ammunition with his own money, but he could not begin to keep up with the unit's needs. The families of Thomas's troops also suffered serious privations, a situation made worse by the fact that the troops had not been paid regularly for months. Claiming that many of the families of the Cherokee troops were living in the woods and subsisting entirely on roots and bark, Thomas predicted that if they received no help his Cherokee troops would desert. If that occurred, he would have no choice but to abandon the border and fall back across the Blue Ridge. In the most urgent terms Thomas requested not only more men but also help with his supply and pay problems. Thomas ended with this blunt warning: "Two causes have deprived this portion of North Carolina of the means of subsistence. First, having but a few slaves among the whites and none among the Indians deprived the country of the necessary amount of labor, after nearly all the men between 18 and 45 had volunteered; second, it was a bad crop year.... It is this condition of the country that has produced starvation, and if not arrested will produce much disloyalty to the South."[35]

This appeal accomplished nothing, so on April 27 Thomas wrote directly to Major General John C. Breckinridge commander of the Department of East Tennessee, asking that Love's and Walker's companies be returned to him. Thomas explained that he had previously appealed to both Buckner and Bragg for their return but, while Bragg had in fact ordered the companies sent back to North Carolina, Ransom had refused to give them up. Thomas pointed out that he was expected to defend a line more than 100 miles long and that he needed all his men. He also claimed, rather implausibly, that if he had his full command he could not only defend the border but also raid into East Tennessee and keep the Federals off guard. Thomas further asked Breckinridge to send him a quartermaster and transport. Major General P. G. T. Beauregard had been allowing Thomas to draw supplies from South Carolina, but both his men and the population were suffering. "The families of my soldiers have to be subsisted or leave the country."[36]

Though Palmer joined Thomas's pleas for help, the Confederate command had little to offer. On May 2 Bragg told Palmer that he had absolutely no cavalry to spare

and could send him no reinforcements. Bragg then offered a series of suggestions whose utter impracticality revealed how little he understood conditions in this region. Bragg did agree that Thomas's companies should be returned to western North Carolina, but in referring to them as "several hundred men" he considerably overestimated their numbers. Bragg further suggested that Major General Joseph Johnston, whose Army of Tennessee was even then being pressed back by Sherman, could extend his right flank to cover the approaches to North Carolina. Finally, Bragg urged that Brigadier General John Hunt Morgan's small cavalry force in East Tennessee be placed under a new commander and moved as close to Knoxville as possible to shield the border. Morgan's cavalry had, indeed, suffered severe lapses in discipline and leadership, but his force was far too small to defend the border against a determined Union raid. Despite this discouraging reply, Palmer continued to make his case. In June 1864, after Colonel George Kirk's Second and Third North Carolina Mounted Infantry burned the department commander's own house in Mitchell, Palmer sent a stark message to Bragg pointing out that it was impossible for him to defend a front 250 miles long with his few men. Not only could he not keep Union forces out of the region, he also could not pursue them when they appeared, for he had almost no cavalry.[37]

Thomas, also, went on asking for more men. On July 8 he reminded Palmer that Love's and Walker's companies were still in East Tennessee, and claimed that keeping his command divided so long had demoralized it. Thomas again asked Palmer to intervene and have his men returned with their transport, which he sorely lacked. Thomas also asked permission to have the conscripts and reserves in Haywood, Jackson, Macon, and Cherokee Counties sent to him to build up his depleted companies. Thomas claimed that if these things were done he would be able to take a position along the northern base of the Smokies, secure a large quantity of wheat there that would otherwise go to Federal forces, and be in a position to cooperate with Confederate forces in East Tennessee and Georgia in retaking East Tennessee. It is unlikely that Thomas had any intention of doing any of these things, but he was fighting for the survival of his command, and he told Palmer what the department commander wanted to hear.[38]

Thomas made even more fanciful promises in early August, when he passed on information from Union deserters that Federal forces in Knoxville had been reinforced and given orders to destroy the saltworks at Abingdon, Virginia and to seize the border counties of North Carolina. This would "make the Blue Ridge instead of the Smoky Mountains their line, which when added to East Tennessee to constitute a Free State." Thomas asserted that Federal attempts to recruit in East Tennessee and western North Carolina had failed, that "a portion of the North Carolinians and East Tennesseans who had turned copperhead" were hiding in the Smokies to evade Federal authority, and that they would gladly join his command if allowed to do so. Thomas further claimed that many other fugitives in the mountains had already served their time with the Confederate Army or were liable to conscription, and requested permission to

recruit these men into his companies. Thomas claimed that if authorization were not given the fugitives would enter Federal service instead, simply to survive. Not waiting for permission, on August 19 Thomas authorized Lieutenant John Telling, formerly of the Fourth Tennessee Cavalry, to recruit a company of mounted infantry in East Tennessee to operate as scouts. Belying Thomas's claims that men would flock to his command, the company was never completed.[39]

By this time Thomas's command was in crisis, and he was in danger of losing his position. In part this resulted from his repeated command failures. Governor Vance, who had received numerous complaints about Thomas's men, complained that "Col. Thomas is worse than useless, he is a positive injury to the country. His command is a favorite refuge for deserters… he is disobedient of orders and invariably averse to any advance." Vance also insisted that "there are troops enough there to afford ample protection both against the enemy and the Tories and deserters who throng the mountains murdering and robbing the citizens, if under proper control and management." Palmer, likewise, believed that Thomas was incompetent and that any forces put under his command were wasted: "Thomas's Legion, as it is presently organized, is of but little use, either for local defense or aggressive movements." In December 1864 Palmer had attempted to trap two Federal regiments who had occupied Paint Rock, but his forces failed to cut off their retreat, and the Union regiments had escaped. Palmer blamed the failure largely on Thomas: "want of promptness of the part of Thomas's Legion…prevented an earlier movement on my part. I am very anxious to do what I can, but much cannot be expected of me unless I am given control of Thomas's Legion." But in part the crisis also resulted from Thomas' continued efforts to find more men. Sometime in the spring or summer of 1864 Thomas had concluded that it was futile to continue pretending that the great number of deserters in western North Carolina could ever be returned to their units. He not only ceased his own attempts to arrest deserters; he also requested permission to accept them into his regiment. Thomas asserted that if men from western North Carolina were allowed to serve near their homes they would be far less likely to desert. He also argued that it would be better to have deserters under some command, even if it were not their original assignment, rather than running loose as fugitives. The War Department found Thomas's proposal incomprehensible and appalling, and rejected it in the clearest terms. Thomas stubbornly ignored these orders and brought a number of deserters into his unit.[40]

The clash between Thomas and the War Department clearly illustrates the great divide that had grown up between the Confederate government and residents of the Smokies. The War Department, with good reason, viewed desertion as a blight that threatened the survival of the Confederacy and believed that no concessions could be made to deserters. Thomas recognized the demoralizing effects of desertion as well as anyone, but every day he saw around him its main causes, and he refused to be hampered by what he saw as failed national policies. Thomas, in fact, had lost all faith in the Confederate command. He believed that Confederate officials completely failed to understand the desperate conditions in the North Carolina Smokies and the difficulties he faced in trying to hold together some semblance of an organized command, and he concluded that he had to do whatever was necessary to defend the Smokies and preserve his troops. Faced with a choice between loyalty to the Confederacy as a whole, or loyalty to his own region, Thomas chose the latter. His choice was no different from that of soldiers from this region who deserted simply so they could try to keep their families from starvation, or of residents who hid their food stuffs from Confederate tax collectors and foraging parties. These people did not believe that they had turned against the Confederacy. Rather, they believed that the Confederacy had abandoned them, and they chose home over nation.

Thomas had come to view conscription in the same light. In July 1864 he argued that it would be far more beneficial to take the remaining available men from the border counties and put them in his command, where they could remain near home, rather than continue attempts to send them to the front, where they would almost certainly desert. In a realistic appraisal of conditions in the region, Thomas asserted that, with little slave labor available, continuing attempts to enforce conscription would leave no men available to raise crops. The starvation of the past year would then repeat itself, "nearly depopulating a portion of western North Carolina inhabited by the poorer classes." Insisting that "whenever coercion is resorted to in the enforcement of the Conscription Act the result is merely to give to the enemy men," Thomas argued that it would be far more sensible to leave these men near home, where they could not only defend the border region but also be given regular exemptions to work their farms and provide for the population. Echoing sentiments that had become common throughout the southern Appalachians, Thomas asserted that "the difference between a country like this having no slave labor to rely upon and the greater portion of the Confederacy supported with slaves seems not to have been understood or acted upon by the authorities," and complained that the section with the least interest in slavery had been forced to bear far more than its fair share of the war effort. Thomas concluded that while "many may doubt the correctness of my judgment on the subject but few will doubt my loyalty to the South when they remember that myself and a large portion of my men are purely volunteers...we have been in the service more than two years a large portion of the time without payment...." Thomas was not alone in his views on conscription. Major General Sam Jones, who commanded the Department of East Tennessee for part of 1862, had made nearly identical arguments in October 1862, but in this case also Confederate authorities had rejected these ideas out of hand. A new nation struggling to survive and establish its authority could hardly give up badly needed manpower, apply different policies to different regions, or make concessions to a dissenting population. But Thomas's claims that conscription had failed in western North Carolina and that the region was on the verge of collapse were undeniably true.[41]

Thomas's new policies toward deserters were soon discovered, and in September 1864 he was ordered to Goldsboro to be tried by a court martial. Thomas was charged with disobedience to orders, conduct unbecoming an officer, conduct prejudicial to good order, and incompetence. After a short hearing the court martial found Thomas guilty of all charges. Resourceful to the end, Thomas traveled to Richmond to appeal to President Davis, whom he knew from his time spent in Washington, D.C. lobbying for the Cherokee while Davis was Secretary of War. Thomas must have been remarkably persuasive, for Davis overturned the court's ruling, and Secretary of War Seddon sent Thomas back to his command. Thomas's fortunes took another turn when General William T. Martin replaced Palmer as Commander of the District of East Tennessee and Western North Carolina. Martin solved the conflict between Palmer and Thomas by dividing the district between them, giving Thomas responsibility for the border counties and leaving Palmer the rest of western North Carolina. Martin also persuaded Ransom to release Love's companies and Walker's battalion, and authorized Thomas's officers to go home to recruit. Finally, the new district commander attempted to restore discipline by issuing strict orders that soldiers respect civilian property and remain in their camps unless ordered out. In reference to the frequent unauthorized raiding across the border, he specified that "no companies will be permitted to go into Tennessee without orders."[42]

These reforms came barely in time. Federal raids against the North Carolina Smokies resumed in early February 1865, when Kirk led the Second and Third North Carolina Mounted Infantry through Balsam

Gap, swept through Webster, and headed toward Quallatown, probably with the intention of capturing Thomas. Kirk was brought up short at Soco Creek, however, where Stringfield had entrenched 180 white and 150 Cherokee soldiers. After exchanging fire for over an hour Stringfield ran low on ammunition and fell back to Quallatown.[43]

Kirk gave up the raid and withdrew to East Tennessee, but he returned the following month. Riding out of Newport, Kirk led 600 men up the Jonathan Creek, Mount Sterling, and Tennessee Turnpike toward Mount Sterling Gap. Captain R. M. Howell learned of Kirk's approach, sent one company to block the gap, and pulled his remaining force back to Bethel. Kirk brushed aside the blockading force, and Howell then sent a young boy to warn families further up the road. The first house the boy reached was that of Young Bennett, a prominent secessionist. After quickly hiding the family's valuables, Bennett's wife rode on to warn other families. One woman in Cataloochee, Mary Ann Caldwell, buried the family's food under corn shocks and hid their horses in a cave.

Sadly, Kirk's men burned Bennett's house when they came to it. They then captured Levi Caldwell and his son Hiram in Cataloochee and tied them to the porch of a house. When the men went inside to play cards, the two worked their ropes loose, so that when Kirk's men came back out and set the house on fire, the two ran. Kirk's men chased them on horseback, and while Hiram escaped, Levi did not. He was taken to Tennessee and imprisoned, but though he eventually escaped, the long chase and the time in prison ruined his health, and he died soon after. There were also stories that

Major General Sam Jones warned that drafting men from East Tennessee and western North Carolina to fight for the Confederacy was a very unpopular policy in the region.

William Montgomery Hopkins, whose loyalist brother Abraham had been killed near Mount Sterling Bridge, took his revenge by leading Kirk's men to a church that had been converted to a hospital for Confederate troops. Kirk's men supposedly killed three wounded men and shot but did not kill six others. They also reportedly killed a disturbing number of secessionists: Henry Barnes at Big Creek, Morgan Wells and another man near Mount Sterling Gap, Levin Shelton and another man at Caldwell Creek, and two men at Jonathan's Creek.

When Kirk reached Waynesville he opened the county jail and turned the prisoners loose, probably in the belief that they were loyalists. Kirk's men also burned the home of Colonel Robert Love, the county's most prominent secessionist, and apparently looted several other homes before leaving. That night, while Kirk's men were camped near Waynesville, about 100 soldiers and local secessionists crept up and fired several shots. The Union troops drove them away with no loss to either side. Hoping to throw off any pursuit, the next morning Kirk reversed direction and headed toward Soco Gap. But Howell had positioned his men along that road, and Kirk was unable to force his way through. Kirk tried again the next day, but overnight a company of Cherokee and troops from Jackson had reinforced Howell, and they again held the road against the Federals. But Kirk had one more trick left. Once more he reversed course, eluded the Confederate forces closing in on him, came through Balsam Gap, and returned to East Tennessee.[44]

These new raids induced panic among Confederate forces. Captain J. M. Cooper, who commanded a small force at Franklin, wrote Thomas that given his position and lack of men a Federal force could easily come within a few miles of his post undetected and carry off supplies and stock. Cooper further claimed that families in the area were already close to starvation, and if raided again they would have to leave. Despite his success against Kirk, Stringfield was nearly frantic about his continued ability to defend his line: "These frequent raids into Tennessee will have the effect to draw a Yankee force upon me. And then how must I act? I can but run and hide....I hope that the wrath of Yankeedom now being heaped upon Haywood and Buncombe will suffice for the present." This was a remarkable admission for an officer, but Stringfield insisted that the

perennial shortage of men, muskets, and ammunition left him no choice. Stringfield then went on to criticize the lack of discipline in Thomas's command. In response to bushwhacker threats, Stringfield had ordered two companies to Franklin. But one company commander had been able to assemble fewer than half of his 40 men, while the other refused to cross into a neighboring county. Stringfield further charged that one company had recently elected a known deserter as lieutenant, and insisted that if Thomas did not order a new election he would protest "before a higher tribunal." Stringfield was blunt in his censure of his commander: "You will find some day I fear Col. Thomas a fearful and shameful want of discipline on the part of a great many men and not a few officers of the legion. This must be checked or destroyed or our command is worthless when the hour of trial comes."[45]

That hour came soon enough, but Confederate troops met it with surprising firmness and denied Union forces any clear victory. On March 21 Major General George Stoneman led 6,000 cavalry out of Knoxville to begin the Union's last great raid of the war. Stoneman first stormed up the East Tennessee Valley and scattered the few remaining Confederate forces there. He then turned east and moved into North Carolina. After destroying a number of factories at Salisbury, Stoneman pivoted back toward Asheville, forcing Martin to pull troops away from the border. Major General Alvin C. Gillem, now in command in East Tennessee, sent the Second and Third North Carolina Mounted Infantries to Boone to protect Stoneman's communications. He also ordered Colonel Isaac Kirby to move his infantry brigade toward Asheville to investigate the city's defenses and to support Stoneman's operations. Kirby marched his men hard and reached Asheville on April 6. There he met 300 Confederate troops in line of battle and drove them back into the city. But Kirby then became nervous about his position and halted. One deserter claimed that Martin had 2,000 men and 20 guns in Asheville and that Thomas could bring another 600 men from Waynesville. Another report put the number in Asheville at 1,000, with another 500 nearby. One of Kirby's officers, Lieutenant Colonel Greenwood, believed that Martin had only 400 men and six guns in the city, a remarkably close estimate, and urged his superior to attack. But Gillem had ordered Kirby not bring on a general engagement, and Kirby did not believe he could take the city without a major assault. So Kirby marched back to Greeneville, Tennessee, and Asheville remained in Confederate hands.[46]

The Confederate respite would be short-lived. On April 19 Gillem left Knoxville and marched his division toward Asheville. Love had several companies guarding Swannanoa Gap, so Gillem left one brigade there, marched 40 miles south, and came through Howard Gap. He captured a small infantry force and four guns at Hendersonville, and reached Asheville on April 24. By this time word of the Confederate surrender at Appomattox Courthouse had reached the city, so Palmer and Martin met Gillem and negotiated a truce. Gillem promised 48 hours' notice before resuming hostilities, sent one brigade toward Waynesville and Quallatown, and

Library of Congress

Union Major General George Stoneman led his cavalry out of Knoxville and into North Carolina on one of the Union's last major raids of the war. Stoneman would become governor of California in 1882.

ordered the other two back to Greeneville. Martin gave Gillem three days' rations so Union troops would not have to forage on the way back. Inexplicably, on the following evening Brigadier General Simon B. Brown marched his brigade back to Asheville, demanded the surrender of all Confederate forces in the city, and made Martin and his staff prisoners. When Martin complained to Gillem, the Union commander repudiated Brown's actions and ordered the prisoners released, but the episode left the Confederates embittered.[47]

In the meantime Martin had sent Stringfield and 23 men with a flag of truce to Knoxville to determine whether the

Union Major General Alvin C. Gillem marched his troops into Asheville at war's end and negotiated a truce with the Confederate forces in the city.

major Confederate armies had in fact surrendered. They reached Blount County on April 30 and were passing through Chilhowee Valley on their way to Maryville. The sight of Confederate soldiers aroused considerable interest, and crowds lined the roads to watch: "We discovered on all sides of us men, boys and women running in all directions, blowing horns and shouting." Shortly thereafter they found a company of Home Guardsmen blocking the road. The Union troops demanded that Stringfield surrender, and when he refused they insisted on sending an officer to inspect his detachment. After looking Stringfield's men over the officer charged that one of Stringfield's men had killed his father and that two others were known horse thieves. The Home Guard's

commander, Major Dunn, again called on Stringfield to surrender, and the Confederates prepared to fight. A regular federal officer then intervened and sent Stringfield on to Knoxville. But worse was to come. Union troops arrested Stringfield and his men as soon as they reached Knoxville and threw their flag of truce in the mud. When Stringfield protested, an officer threatened to shoot him. The Confederates were then taken to Stoneman, who insisted that the war was over and required them all to take an oath of allegiance to the Federal government. When they refused, he had them jailed. Stringfield's men were not released until Confederate forces in western North Carolina had surrendered.[48]

In late April Gillem terminated the truce in western North Carolina, and on April 30 Brigadier General Davis Tillson occupied Asheville. Secessionists charged that Union troops robbed stores and houses, wrecked the courthouse, threw the county records into the street, tore down the buildings of Green Hill Academy to make breastworks, and used the Methodist church for a hospital. Love refused to surrender, led his companies out of the city on a back road, and headed toward Waynesville. Tillson then sent the Third North Carolina Mounted Infantry under Colonel William T. Bartlett to Waynesville, and ordered Kirk's Second North Carolina Mounted Infantry to scout toward Franklin. On May 1 Kirk reported two Confederate companies at Valleytown, five at Balsam Gap, and five at Soco Gap. He also noted that Confederate guerrillas infested the roads between Asheville and Waynesville, Webster, and Franklin. Tillson ordered Kirk to "exterminate" the bushwhackers and hold Osborne Gap while keeping in contact with Bartlett. On May 5 Tillson wrote, rather prematurely, that the Confederate troops in western North Carolina were "disgusted with the war" and that the secessionist guerrilla bands were disbanding: "The worst men are leaving the country, and the others are returning to their homes."[49]

Bartlett reached Waynesville on May 6, but Confederate forces were not prepared to give up the town. While Love blocked the road to Balsam Gap, Thomas marched his force from Jackson County, camped near Dellwood, and occupied the other roads out of Waynesville. Thomas then ordered Love to move closer to the town, and the Confederates encountered a detachment of Union troops at White Sulphur Springs and drove them into Waynesville. That night Thomas also advanced his forces and exchanged fire with Bartlett's pickets. The next morning Bartlett asked for a two-day truce and immediately sent couriers to find Kirk. But Kirk had exceeded his orders and had ridden all the way to Hendersonville, and he could not reach Waynesville in time. On May 9, when the truce expired, Thomas and Love arrayed their men on the slopes surrounding Waynesville and built hundreds of campfires, giving the impression of a force much larger than Bartlett's. Accompanied by 20 Cherokee soldiers in full battle dress and ten white troops, Thomas and Love rode down to Waynesville the next morning and demanded Bartlett's surrender. Whether this dramatic attempt to intimidate Bartlett actually succeeded is unclear, but certainly Bartlett could see that Confederate troops had cut him off from supplies and rein-

Confederate General Joseph Johnston was called upon to defend the border between Tennessee and North Carolina.

forcements and made his position untenable. By that time both sides also knew that General Joseph Johnston's forces had surrendered and that the war in the western theater was effectively over. Bartlett, therefore, agreed to withdraw from Waynesville and order Kirk to cease his operations. Thomas and Love, in turn, consented to disband their forces. Bartlett then marched his regiment back to Asheville, and Martin formally surrendered the district.[50]

There were two dramas waiting to be played out in the Smokies. On May 9 Gillem ordered Kirk to return to Asheville by way of Franklin, Webster, and Waynesville. He was to give every Confederate unit he found a chance to surrender and to destroy those who refused. When Kirk reached Franklin he encountered the last remnant of Thomas's command, Captain Stephen Whitaker's company. Whitaker was reluctant to surrender, but neither side wanted to initiate hostilities at this point, so the two sides agreed to a two-day truce. On May 12 Whitaker learned that Martin had surrendered the district, while Kirk received specific orders to force Whitaker to disband. Whitaker at first threatened to fight his way out, but after further consideration he realized that continued bloodshed would be futile, and he sent his company home. Then on May 13 Bartlett was informed that one of Thomas's battalions had been exempted from the surrender. Furious, he wrote to Martin demanding an explanation. Martin insisted that all of Thomas's men had formally surrendered. But the Cherokee companies had kept the weapons that they had owned before the war and were using these against the remaining bushwhackers and robber bands. Thomas also claimed that the 20 Cherokee who made up his personal bodyguard had never been enrolled and were thus not required to surrender. Tillson accepted Martin's explanation, and the conventional war in the Smokies was finally over.[51]

CHAPTER 7

AFTER THE END

HE FORMAL END OF THE WAR BROUGHT LITTLE RELIEF TO THE SMOKIES. THE CONFLICT HAD PROSTRATED THE ECONOMY, AND residents faced continued deprivation and years of slow, painful rebuilding. The partisan war went on, and deserter and criminal bands continued to prey on the population. The great issues of Reconstruction, particularly the status of former slaves, the restoration of the Confederate states to full status in the Union, and the political rights of ex-Confederates, divided voters in the region.

Perhaps the only immediate benefits of peace were the exodus of the regular armies and the return of Confederate and Union veterans to their homes. Some families were denied even this happy event, however. Allen Nolan, a secessionist from Cataloochee, served almost the entire war and survived many battles. After the Confederate surrender Nolan was taken to Knoxville to be discharged. Before he left, officers warned him that conditions in the mountains were still uncertain and that he should go home by way of Hot Springs and Asheville. But Nolan was anxious to reach his family, and he chose to travel directly through the Smokies. Nolan was last seen on Mount Sterling before disappearing forever, apparently the victim of one of the bushwhacker bands that continued to roam the area.[1] A number of Union veterans from Blount County who had been detained in southern prisons went on board the steamer *Sultana* at Vicksburg in late April 1865. The steamer was carrying around 2,000 troops, far more than its authorized capacity, and its boilers had recently been repaired. Some time after the steamer passed Memphis its boilers exploded. Seventeen hundred men who survived the war and military prisons never made it home. Less grim, but still frustrating, was the experience of Roland Henry Plott. Plott had been captured at Cumberland Gap and had remained at Camp Douglas until the war's end. He was supposed to be released on June 16 with the rest of his company, but his name was not on the prison roll, so he had to wait until every other prisoner had been sent home. He expected to be sent by train to Greeneville, Tennessee, but would have to walk home from there.

In East Tennessee the war between loyalists and secessionists went on. Radical Unionists, led by William G. Brownlow, boldly announced their intention of expelling secessionists from the region. Brownlow had resumed publishing his paper in September 1863, and he repeatedly declared that, with the Northern victory, secessionists were no longer welcome in

North Carolina Division of Archives and History

By the end of the war, William Holland Thomas tried to return to his "old life" but like many, he found himself deeply in debt with numerous creditors filing suits against him. 1858 photo.

East Tennessee. Unionists, led in many cases by returning Federal veterans, then launched a new wave of attacks against secessionists, particularly Confederate soldiers, conscription officers, provost marshals, and prominent men who had led the fight for secession. This violence quickly came to the Smokies. James Harris of Blount County had volunteered for Confederate service, been captured, and sent to a military prison in Baltimore. But when he returned home he found that his ordeal was by no means over. Unionists told Harris that if he did not leave they would kill him, so Harris hid out in the woods, just as loyalists had done during the war. But 14 Unionists eventually tracked

Harris down, and while one held a cocked pistol to his chest, another gave him "39 licks with a two-handed brush." Similarly, in Cocke County Unionists warned Robert S. Roadman that if he did not leave they would kill him. Roadman had served in the Confederate forces, and Confederate officials had supposedly used his house to administer loyalty oaths to Unionists. Roadman believed that Unionists hoped to win control of his farm and tannery, but he would not risk staying to save his property, so he and his family left the county. Creece Bussell, who had served with Colonel William Gibbs Allen's Fifth Tennessee Cavalry, was also forced to leave Blount County. Many other Confederates chose to leave the Smokies rather than face ongoing harassment and the chance of death. The Reverend Fielding Pope, who had taught at Maryville College, fled to Georgia in the spring of 1865. George McMahan moved from Sevier County to Alabama, while M. D. L. Taylor left Blount County for Illinois. Major James T. Huff, a Confederate veteran, was able to return to Cocke County only because his uncle Andy Huff was an influential Unionist.[2]

Major William W. Stringfield also faced violence from Smokies Unionists. After being threatened in both New Market and his home town of Strawberry Plains, Stringfield and another man went to Haywood County to find if it would be feasible to relocate there. On approaching a small settlement on Cosby Creek, Cocke County, they saw a crowd of men. Fearing trouble, Stringfield and his companion agreed to pretend to be loyalists and members of an East Tennessee regiment. As they came up to the crowd one man grabbed Stringfield's bridle and ordered the two to

North Carolina Division of Archives and History

Veterans of Thomas's Legion gather for a photo in 1901. The bearded W. W. Stringfield stands in the back row on the far left.

dismount. Stringfield refused, claiming that they were from the First Tennessee Cavalry (Union) and were pursuing a man who had stolen a horse. "At first, I was closely and rapidly questioned by numerous ones, sometimes two of them asking questions at the same time. Some of these questions were close and pointed.... After much talk of a serious and lively character I began to get ready to start on.... One man still held to my bridle declaring that I was a rebel for he could tell by the 'bat of my eyes.' At first I appeared to be very indignant.... As he still refused to let go, I grasped my pistol under my blanket and was getting ready to shoot when he slowly let go the bridle." When they reached Waynesville, one man there told them that he had been stopped

near Newport and that a crowd of men had whipped him, robbed his wagon, cut up his harness, and taken his mules.[3]

Unionists also targeted ministers of the Southern Methodist Church. This denomination had given particularly vigorous and aggressive support to the war, and in East Tennessee it had banned anyone who opposed secession from preaching. Brownlow may have also contributed to this campaign, for as a former Methodist minister he was determined to seize control of the region's churches from secessionists. In Sevier County Unionists placed bundles of switches at church doors as a warning, and several Southern Methodist ministers left the area. Ministers in Blount were also targeted. When W. Gibbs Allen was passing through Blount in 1867 he learned that three ministers had recently been assaulted. One had nearly died, and another had been beaten so badly he could barely talk. While Allen was staying at the home of Creece Bussell's father he met yet another minister "by the name of Graves....Next morning as I started to leave he suggested that he had an appointment three miles away and I could save some travel by going with him....I did not know that place was where they whipped preachers. When we got in sight of the log church there was 15 or 20 standing in the yard. All had guns.... Brother Graves stepped onto [the pulpit] and threw his saddle bags across the front board, he reached into his saddle bags with both hands then drew his right hand out with a .44 instead of a bible and drew his left hand out with a .44 instead of a hymn book and commenced to sing...when the first stanza was through the writer and a lady was the only ones for Brother Graves to preach to...." Another Southern Methodist minister, Reverend Rufus M. Hickey of Sevier County, also faced numerous threats, but he braved them all and continued to preach.[4]

Other secessionists chose to fight back. In Sevier and Cocke Counties, Confederate bands from Tennessee and North Carolina continued to attack Unionists. On April 17, 1865 D. W. Howard sent a petition to the Union commander in Knoxville stating "Now on behalf of the loyal citizens of Sevier only 34 miles from your post...we ask some assistance at your hand to put down the Guerrillers warfare which is now being carried on by the reble guerrillas which are harbored Cocke County by Reble citizens We the citizens of Sevier County cannot stay at home let alone make any crop. The most of us has our land ready to put our corn in the ground and now have to leave or lie in the bushes or be shot down when the desparados comes and every day they come if they want they was down last week and killed every man they saw only some aged men and swore they intended to have every jury man and every person who had anything to do toward assisting the U.S. government now we desire you to send about 200 of the Ninth Tenn Cav to Newport Cocke County and station them there."

One Unionist who had been threatened asked another loyalist to help him keep watch. One man slept on the ground floor, while the other took the second story. A Confederate band came to the house one night, and one secessionist stuck his head in a window and struck a match. The Unionist on the ground floor fired a shotgun and hit the Confederate in the head, but the Confederate fired at the same time and killed this loyalist. The second Unionist then began firing from an upstairs window, and after one secessionist was killed the others left. As the violence in Sevier County continued Federal officials sent a company of troops, probably Home Guards, to restore order, but the Confederates scattered and the company found no resistance. Union veterans, who had tired of not being able to sleep in their homes at peace, finally organized their own protective organization and announced that they would whip or kill ten Confederates for every Unionist who was whipped or killed. William Jack, an influential secessionist from Sevier, then approached John Gann, leader of the Unionists, and the two arranged a truce that greatly diminished

Waynesville Mountaineer

Confederate Veterans of Thomas's Legion at the New Orleans Confederate Convention, 1903.
Left to right; front row : Young Deer, unidentified, Pheasant, Chief David Reed, Sevier Skitty. Back row: The
Rev. Bird Saloneta, Dickey Driver, Lt. Colonel W. W. Stringfield, Lt. Suatie Owl, Jim Keg, Wesley Crow,
unidentified and Calvin Cagle. Cagle is often reported as a member of the legion, but no records
have been found to confirm it. However, his presence in the photograph would
seem to connect him with the command.

the violence. Similarly, in late April 1865 Mary Shrader Webb wrote "The rebels are still in Cocke County and occasionally down in our country. It is the Lewis Scouts. Captain Buckman from North Carolina was with them. They had about 60 men. They killed William W. Allen... and William Hurst. The last raid they made down here about two weeks ago they killed several men in Cocke County."[5]

Unionists also attacked secessionists in the courts. In Knoxville grand juries sitting in 1865, 1866, and 1867 indicted over 2,000 secessionists for treason or for giving aid and comfort to the enemy. Few of these cases were ever tried, for the policies of the Johnson Administration discouraged vengeance, and the new District Court Judge, Connelly F. Trigg, doubted the legal basis of the suits and dismissed nearly all. Even so, the indictments took a toll, for secessionists had to answer the charges, appear in court, and pay court costs. Secessionists also faced hundreds of civil suits in the county courts for damages stemming from arrests, conscription, and the impressing or destruction of property. In Sevier County the administrator of

Edward Hodges's estate brought a suit against John Gaut, who they claimed had encouraged Confederate troops to arrest Hodges in November 1861. Gaut's son urged his attorneys, S. A. Rogers and T. A. R. Nelson, to settle the suits as quickly as possible and to sell his father's farm, for "Father cannot live there in safety on account of the robbers and assassins that frequent that part of the country." Gaut insisted that his father had opposed the arrest and conscription of Unionists and had signed numerous petitions for the release of loyalist prisoners. He also claimed that the men who brought the suit had previously "mobbed and shot" his father and were primarily interested in taking his father's farm. Other Unionists in Sevier, including the administrator of Hodges's estate, also brought suit against W. H. Cannon for his supposed involvement in the arrests of Unionists. And in Cocke County Unionists sued Stringfield for supposedly ordering their crops destroyed.[6]

Violence also continued in the North Carolina Smokies, though on a smaller scale. In Haywood County several men wrote Governor Jonathan Worth claiming that Unionists, whom they labeled "some few Extreme Radical men," were "running all over the county swearing men into what they call the Union League to support a certain set of men and measures which a large Majority of the Union loving law abiding citizens of this county are opposed to they threaten all who refuse to support their secret order." This movement soon diminished and failed to win control, but it was serious enough to cause great concern among conservatives in the region. Similarly, in June 1866 the sheriff of

Cherokee County, William Best, complained to Worth that "men of the basest stamp" came into the county at night to rob homes and then disappeared back into Tennessee. He also claimed that numerous criminals from Tennessee were evading justice by hiding in Cherokee, while felons from Cherokee had escaped to Tennessee. Best proposed that the governors of North Carolina, Tennessee, and Georgia make an agreement to apprehend these men and return them to where they could be prosecuted.[7]

The war left the Smokies' economy in shambles. By 1865 many farms were left without draft animals to work the fields, seed to plant, and livestock to breed. The passing armies had taken hundreds of miles of fence rails for fuel, undoing decades of work and leaving the few remaining livestock free to roam. Rampant inflation, shortages, and lack of business had closed many trading stores, and the chaos of the war forced schools, churches, and even county governments to cease functioning. Matilda Jones wrote from Del Rio that "After the war, times were harder than during the fighting. There were almost no horses or mules, many of the men had been killed and there was no money.... Often as long as ten years after the war former southern soldiers were flogged for merely having fought on the losing side." Similarly, in December 1865 N. G. Phillips lamented that "the condition of this [Cherokee] county render it untenable. The Yankees and Bushwhackers have ruined it. I will have to move my family out." In Blount County only one merchant was in business at the end of the war, and the New Providence Presbyterian Church, the East Tennessee Female

Waynesville Mountaineer

Western North Carolina Confederate Veterans, many of whom served Thomas's Legion.
W. W. Stringfield is seated in front.

Masonic Institute, and Maryville College were all nearly destroyed, their buildings having been stripped for firewood and then turned into stables. As late as 1869, conditions were still so dire in Blount that Quaker associations in the North sent money and representatives to provide relief and help with the rebuilding.[8]

Despite these grim conditions, many residents attempted to rebuild farms and businesses, heal the divisions of the war, and resume ordinary lives. James R. Love returned to Haywood County and picked up his political career. He served as a delegate to the 1868 North Carolina Convention, which rewrote the state constitution, and was then elected to the state senate. Stephen Whitaker went home to his farm in Cherokee County, while James Terrell ran a store in Cherokee and served as Colonel William Holland Thomas's agent. After being driven out of Strawberry Plains, Stringfield moved first to Rogersville and then to Waynesville, where he married Maria Love, granddaughter of

Colonel Robert Love. Stringfield then represented the Love family in its land dealings, operated the White Sulphur Springs Hotel, and served in the North Carolina legislature.[9]

Thomas, also, attempted to return to his old life, but with far less success. Anxious to resume his business activities, in October 1865 Thomas wrote an open letter "To the Citizens of Sevier County" calling for a speedy restoration of normal relations. Thomas promised to remove the blockades on the road as far west as Alum Fort, and urged Sevier Countians to do the same on their side. But Thomas's complex business dealings, which had been neglected during the war years, caught up with him. He was deeply in debt, and he soon faced numerous suits from creditors. Worse, he had used Cherokee land as collateral, and in 1869 his largest creditor, William Johnston of Asheville, secured the title to large tracts of Cherokee land, jeopardizing the position of the entire Quallatown Cherokee population. Fortunately, and perhaps ironically, the Federal government would quickly intervene. In 1868 the Federal Commissioner for Indian Affairs assumed supervision of the Quallatown Cherokee, and in 1870 Congress authorized the Commission to file suit against Johnston on their behalf. In 1874 an arbitrator granted the Cherokee 50,000 acres, which were purchased with Federal trust funds. Thomas's empire could not be salvaged, however, and most of his remaining holdings were lost to other creditors. Thomas also suffered a variety of other physical and mental ailments, and on May 10, 1893 he died an unhappy death.[10]

Conversely, the end of slavery brought new opportunities to African-Americans, though many of their hopes were cruelly disappointed. In Blount County African-Americans, led by a remarkable man named William B. Scott, reached political positions previously unimaginable. Scott, a free black, had lived in Friendsville before the war and worked as a saddle and harness maker. During the war Confederate cavalry broke into the Scott house, took much of the family's personal belongings, and carried off the oldest son. The son escaped two days later, but Scott moved his family to Knoxville, where he worked for a printer. In 1865 the family relocated to Nashville, where Scott began publishing *The Colored Tennessean*. In 1867 they moved again to Maryville, and Scott changed the name of his paper to *The Maryville Republican*. Several African-Americans opened businesses in Maryville immediately after the war, and they began to organize politically. In 1868 four blacks, including a barber, a merchant, a brick mason, and a laborer, were elected to the Maryville Board of Aldermen, and Scott

was elected mayor. Both Scott and Allen Gann were also licensed to practice law, and Scott headed the effort to establish the Freedman's Normal Institute, a highly successful trade school. In Jackson County the percentage of African American families owning land increased to 45 percent in 1900 and 89 percent in 1920, though many of these holdings were small and poor, and throughout the Smokies African-Americans built a considerable number of churches and schools. But, as elsewhere, these gains were sharply and deliberately limited, and the promise of continued change faded before the conservative reaction of white voters.[11]

The Civil War threw Smokies residents into a situation for which they were wholly unprepared. This region was composed mostly of small farms, worked largely by family members and designed to meet the family's needs. Thus, when the war came most families had little excess production, labor, food stores, or cash to meet the burgeoning demands of the conflict. When Confederate and Union foraging parties and tax agents began taking supplies for the armies, families inevitably suffered. If the region had retained its full labor force, families might have been able to increase their production somewhat by cultivating more land, but the war took hundreds of men as well as supplies. Though women labored mightily to keep farms and businesses functioning, even the most heroic efforts could not make up the gap, and their efforts were further hampered by the loss of livestock and by harassment from bushwhackers and soldiers. The region simply could not escape the cruel logic of the war, and large-scale suffering was inevitable.

The Smokies were unfitted for the war in other ways. To meet the Federal threat the Confederate mobilization had to be highly centralized and ruthless, and the Confederate government quickly resorted to conscription, long terms of military service, impressment, and the deployment of regiments wherever they were needed most. Politically and philosophically, however, Smokies residents were entirely unprepared for such onerous, impersonal, bureaucratized policies. Though residents had been fully involved in both state and national politics before the war, their primary focus, and their primary loyalties, were local. Faced with immediate war, the Confederate government had little time to nurture the kind of loyalties and bonds needed to sustain the demands of the conflict. Confederate officials thus made few attempts to build those loyalties, apparently trusting that the issues of the war and the threat to Southern territory would supply what was needed. But in the Tennessee Smokies Unionists wholly rejected the Southern cause, and even on the North Carolina side the issues of the war became less and less important as suffering increased. The majority of residents in the North Carolina Smokies may have preferred to live in the Confederacy, everything else being even, but most were not willing to sacrifice all for that cause. Soldiers made this clear by deserting, and citizens by employing every means possible to keep men and goods out of the hands of the government. Indeed, it might be said that by 1863 these residents, while pro-Southern and pro-slavery, were no longer pro-Confederate.

Notes

Chapter 1

1. Max R. Williams, *History of Jackson County* (Sylva: Jackson County Historical Society, 1987), pp. 39-40.

2. Michael Frome, *Strangers in High Places* (Knoxville: University of Tennessee Press, 1966), pp. 58-61.

3. Frome, *Strangers*, pp. 61-69.

4. Emma Dean Trent Smith, *East Tennessee Lore of Yesteryear* (Whitesburg: Emma Dean Trent Smith, 1987), pp. 547-48, 600-03; Williams, *Jackson*, pp. 67-83, 88-93, 103; Frome, *Strangers*, pp. 68-72; W. Clark Medford, *The Early History of Haywood County* (Waynesville: W. Clark Medford, 1961), pp. 3-4, 11-19, 37-48, 81-85; John C. Inscoe, *Mountain Masters, Slavery, and the Sectional Crisis in Western North Carolina* (Knoxville: University of Tennessee Press, 1989), pp. 40-45, 116-26; W. C. Allen, *The Annals of Haywood County North Carolina, Historical, Sociological, Biographical, and Genealogical* (Spartanburg: Reprint Company, 1982), pp. 25-37.

5. Frome, *Strangers*, pp. 83-85.

6. John R. Finger, *The Eastern Band of Cherokees, 1819-1900* (Knoxville: University of Tennessee Press, 1984), pp. 3-19; Frome, *Strangers*, pp. 85-88; Williams, *Jackson*, pp. 40-43.

7. Williams, *Jackson*, pp. 42-43, 46-47, 73-75, 229-33.

8. Finger, *Cherokees*, pp. 20-81; Frome, *Strangers*, pp. 88-93; Williams, *Jackson*, pp. 43-47.

9. Williams, *Jackson*, pp. 12-19, 83-87; Medford, *Annals*, pp. 74-78; J. B. Killebrew, *Introduction to the Resources of Tennessee* (Nashville: Tavel, Eastman and Howell, 1874), pp. 91-139, 423-47, 460-63, 483-87, 603-06; Inscoe, *Mountain Masters*, pp. 22-23; Alberta and Carson Brewer, *Valley So Wild: A Folk History* (Knoxville: East Tennessee Historical Society, 1975), p. 123.

10. Inscoe, *Mountain Masters*, pp. 60-70, 84-85, 265-69; 1860 Slave Schedules, Cherokee County, North Carolina, Haywood County, North Carolina, Jackson County, North Carolina, Macon County, North Carolina, Blount County, Tennessee, Cocke County, Tennessee, Sevier County, Tennessee, 1860 United States Census.

11. United States Census Bureau, *Statistics of the United States in 1860, Compiled from the Original Returns of the Eighth Census* (Washington, D. C.: Government Printing Office, 1866); Williams, *Jackson*, pp. 84-85, 556-61; Inscoe, *Mountain Masters*, pp. 60-67.

12. Inscoe, *Mountain Masters*, pp. 22, 40-45; Allen, *Annals*, pp. 504-05; Medford, *Early History*, pp. 60, 87-88; Brewer, *Valley*, pp. 105-06; John Preston Arthur, *Western North Carolina: A History* (Raleigh: Edwards & Broughton Printing Company, 1914), pp. 171-72.

13. Inscoe, *Mountain Masters*, pp. 45-48; H. Tyler Blethen and Curtis W. Wood, "A Trader on the Western Carolina Frontier," in Robert D. Mitchell, ed., *Appalachian Frontiers: Settlement, Society, and Development in the Pre-Industrial Era* (Lexington: University Press of Kentucky, 1991), pp. 161-64.

14. Williams, *Jackson*, pp. 545-61.

15. Williams, *Jackson*, pp. 93-94, 151-63; Frome, *Strangers*, p. 78-79; Arthur, *Western North Carolina*, p. 549; Gary C. Jenkins, "The Mining of Alum Cave," *East Tennessee Historical Society Publications* 60 (1988), pp. 78-87.

16. Medford, *Early History*, pp. 18-22, 99-101, 105-06, 118-22; Inscoe, *Mountain Masters*, pp. 46, 154-69; H. C. Wilburn, *The Indian Gap Trail* (Washington, D. C.: National Park Service, 1940).

17. Medford, *Early History*, pp. 30-33, 37-38, 70-71, 96-97; Williams, *Jackson*, pp.73, 256-63, 594-95; Brewer, *Valley*, pp. 282-90; Frome, *Strangers*, pp. 72-75; Smith, *Lore*, pp. 548-49.

Chapter 2

1. Joseph Carlyle Sitterson, *The Secession Movement in North Carolina* (Chapel Hill: University of North Carolina Press, 1939), pp. 178-87.

2. Sitterson, *Secession*, pp. 187-206.

3. Sitterson, *Secession*, pp. 206-10.

4. Sitterson, *Secession*, pp. 211-27.

5. Daniel C. Crofts, *Reluctant Confederates: Upper South Unionists in the Secession Crisis* (Chapel Hill: University of North Carolina Press, 1989).

6. Joseph Cathey to L. F. Siler, February 22, 1861, Joseph Cathey Papers, North Carolina State Archives; Elizabeth D. Powers and Mark E. Hannah, *Cataloochee: Lost Settlement of the Smokies* (Charleston: Powers Hannah Publishers, 1982), p. 50.

7. Sitterson, *Secession*, pp. 229-42; John C. Inscoe, *Mountain Masters, Slavery, and the Sectional Crisis in Western North Carolina* (Knoxville: University of Tennessee Press, 1989), pp. 214-15.

8. Sitterson, *Secession*, pp. 263-95; W. C. Allen, *The Annals of Haywood County North Carolina, Historical, Sociological, Biographical, and Genealogical* (Spartanburg: Reprint Company, 1982), p. 346.

9. Jonathan M. Atkins, *Parties, Politics, and the Sectional Conflict in Tennessee, 1832-1861* (Knoxville: University of Tennessee Press, 1997), pp. 228-39; Mary Emily Robertson Campbell, *The Attitude of Tennesseans Toward the Union, 1847-1861* (New York: Vantage, 1961), pp. 158-63.

10. R. H. Hodsden, A. Lawrence, and John T. Harris to Oliver P. Temple, November 22, 1860, Oliver P. Temple Papers, University of Tennessee Special Collections; Oliver P. Temple, *East Tennessee and the Civil War* (Cincinnati: The R. Clark Company, 1899), pp. 173-74; Jeannette S. Greve, *The Story of Gatlinburg* (Maryville: Brazes Printing Company, 1976), pp. 73-78.

11. Atkins, *Parties*, pp. 239-42; Campbell, *Attitude*, pp. 175-79, 288-90; Crofts, *Reluctant*, pp. 146-52.

12. John W. Andes and Will A. McTeer, *Loyal Mountain Troopers: The Second and Third Tennessee Volunteer Cavalry in the Civil War* (Maryville: Blount County Genealogical and Historical Society, 1992), p. 4; Elkenah D. Rader to Andrew Johnson, March 20, 1861, LeRoy P. Graf and Ralph W. Haskins, *The Papers of Andrew Johnson* (Knoxville: University of Tennessee Press, 1967), vol. 4, pp. 418-19.

13. Atkins, *Parties*, pp. 242-47; Campbell, *Attitude*, pp. 194-99.

14. Temple, *East Tennessee*, pp. 192-95; Thomas B. Campbell, *Thomas A. R. Nelson of East*

*Tennesse*e (Nashville: Tennessee Historical Commission, 1956), pp. 76-83; Thomas William Humes, *The Loyal Mountaineers of Tennessee* (Knoxville: Ogden Brothers, 1888), pp. 100-02.

15. Atkins, *Parties*, pp. 247-58; Campbell, *Attitude*, pp. 205-07, 291-94; Crofts, *Reluctant*, pp. 342-44.

16. John C. Inscoe, "Mountain Unionism, Secession, and Regional Self-Image: The Contrasting Cases of Western North Carolina and East Tennessee," in Winifred Moore, Jr. and Joseph E. Tripp, eds., *Looking South: Chapters in the Story of an American Region* (Westport: Greenwood Press, 1989), pp. 115-32; Michael Frome, *Strangers in High Places* (Knoxville: University of Tennessee Press, 1966), p. 123; Charles Faulkner Bryan, "The Civil War in East Tennessee: A Social, Political, and Economic Study," Dissertation, University of Tennessee, 1978; W. Todd Groce, *Mountain Rebels: East Tennessee Confederates and the Civil War, 1860-1870* (Knoxville: University of Tennessee Press, 1999).

17. James W. McKee, Jr., ed., "Reflections of an East Tennessee Unionist," *Tennessee Historical Quarterly* 33 (1974), pp. 429-35.

18. Noel C. Fisher, *War at Every Door: Partisan Politics and Guerrilla Violence in East Tennessee, 1860-1869* (Chapel Hill: University of North Carolina Press, 1997), pp. 30-33.

19. Temple, *East Tennessee*, pp. 343-65, 565-73; Humes, *Mountaineers*, pp. 108-20, 347-55.

20. Reverend J. M. L. Burnett to Reverend Edmund Cody, July 18, 1861, *A Collection of Thirty-Eight Letters Written or Received by The Reverend J. M. L. Burnett*, McClung Collection.

Chapter 3

1. Stephen Whitaker to his parents, June 16, 1861, Stephen Whitaker Papers, North Carolina State Archives.

2. Sister Addie to Dear Sister, June 5, 1861, Thomas I. Lenoir to W. W. Lenoir, July 2, 1861, Robina Norwood to Lizzie Lenoir, June 17, 1861, July 14, 1861, Lenoir Family Papers, North Carolina State Archives; John C. Inscoe, *Mountain Masters, Slavery, and the Sectional Crisis in Western North Carolina* (Knoxville: University of Tennessee Press, 1989), pp. 260-61; W. Clark Medford, *The Early History of Haywood County* (Waynesville: W. Clark Medford, 1961), pp. 129-36, 153-63; W. C. Allen, *The Annals of Haywood County North Carolina, Historical, Sociological, Biographical, and Genealogical* (Spartanburg: Reprint Company, 1982), pp. 66-69, 142-45; Max R. Williams, *History of Jackson County* (Sylva: Jackson County Historical Society, 1987), pp. 433-40.

3. Edward R. Walker III, *Tales from the Civil War* (Cosby: Busy Bee Printing Service, 1983), pp. 17-18; Elmer C. Mize, "Blount County: A Brief History," *The Blount Journal* 14, 1 (Spring 1995); *Sevier County Heritage* (Don Mills Company, Inc. and the Sevier County Heritage Book Committee, 1982), pp. 3-15.

4. John C. Inscoe and Gordon B. McKinney, *The Heart of Confederate Appalachia: Western North Carolina in the Civil War* (Chapel Hill: University of North Carolina Press, 2000), pp. 59-82; Alfred Bell to Mary Bell, January 18, 1862, Bell Family Papers, Special Collections, Duke University.

5. Sister Addie to Dear Sister, June 5, 1861, Lenoir Family Papers, North Carolina State Archives; Alfred Bell to Mary Bell, November 11, 1861, Bell Family Papers, Special Collections, Duke University; John Sutton to his father, May 26, 1861, *Touring Through*

Jackson (Jackson County Genealogical Society, 1998-1999); H. T. Mingus to his brother, August 23, 1861, *The Bone Rattler* 4 (Fall 1987) p. 31; J. D. Bryon to William Estes, September 29, 1861, Estes Family Papers, Hunter Library, Western Carolina University; R. B. Edmonston to his parents, October 7, 1861, Edmonston/ Kelly Family Papers, Hunter Library, Western Carolina University.

6. Robina Norwood to Lizzie Lenoir, June 17, 1861, July 14, 1861, Lenoir Family Papers, North Carolina State Archives; Mary Bell to Alfred Bell, November 7, 1861, Bell Family Papers, Special Collections, Duke University; Sarah Mingus to H. T. Mingus, October 6, 1861, *The Bone Rattler* 4 (Fall 1987), pp. 29-30.

7. Vernon Crowe, *Storm in the Mountains: Thomas's Confederate Legion of Cherokee Indians and Mountaineers* (Cherokee: Press of the Museum of the Cherokee Indian, 1982), pp. 3-35; E. Stanley Godbold and Mattie U. Russell, *Confederate Colonel and Cherokee Chief: The Life of William Holland Thomas* (Knoxville: University of Tennessee Press, 1990), pp. 336-94; Memoirs of William Williams Stringfield, North Carolina State Archives.

8. Crowe, *Storm*, pp. 17-40; Daniel Ellis, *Thrilling Adventures of Daniel Ellis* (New York: Harper, 1867), pp. 147-48; William G. Brownlow, *Sketches of the Rise, Progress, and Decline of Secession* (Philadelphia: J. B. Lippincott, 1862), pp. 150-54.

9. Crowe, *Storm*, pp. 17-40; Pete Prince, "Fort Harry, Tennessee: A Phenomenon in the Great Smoky Mountains National Park," *Smoky Mountain Historical Society Journal* 29, no. 1 (Spring 2003), pp. 2-10.

10. Oliver P. Temple, *East Tennessee and the Civil War* (Cincinnati: The R. Clark Company, 1899), pp. 426-28; Oliver P. Temple, *Notable Men of Tennessee from 1833 to 1875* (New York:

Cosmopolitan Press, 1912), p. 196; Ellis, *Adventures*; Richard Nelson Current, *Lincoln's Loyalists: Union Soldiers from the Confederacy* (New York: Oxford University Press, 1992), pp. 29-60; Edward Maynard to Horace Maynard, September 1, 1861, Horace Maynard Papers, University of Tennessee Special Collections.

11. William G. McAdoo Diary, August 18, 1861, Library of Congress; Temple, *East Tennessee*, pp. 185-187; Will A. McTeer, "Honoring the Stars and Stripes in East Tennessee," *Western Christian Advocate*, December 1936; Inez Burns, "Women Meet Sherman at Brick Mill," *Maryville-Alcoa Times*, February 28, 1961.

12. Edward R. Walker III, *Tales from the Civil War* (Cosby: Busy Bee Printing Service), pp. 17-18, 94-95.

13. Adjutant and Inspector General Samuel Cooper to Felix K. Zollicoffer, September 1, 1861, *The War of the Rebellion: A Compilation of the Official Records of the Union and Confederate Armies* (Washington: Government Printing Office, 1880-1901), vol. 4, p. 377; Felix K. Zollicoffer, "To the People of East Tennessee," July 7, 1861, Orders, East Tennessee Brigade, 1861, Record Group 109, National Archives; James W. McKee, Jr., "Felix K. Zollicoffer: Confederate Defender of East Tennessee," *East Tennessee Historical Society Publications* 43 (1971), pp. 34-58, (1972), pp. 17-40.

14. Mary Emily Robertson Campbell, *The Attitude of Tennesseans Toward the Union, 1847-1861* (New York: Vantage, 1961), pp. 185-89, 210-12; Brownlow, *Secession*, pp. 224-44.

15. Temple, *East Tennessee*, pp. 367-69; Humes, *Mountaineers*, pp. 141-46; Brownlow, *Secession*, pp. 134-40.

16. Thomas B. Campbell, *Thomas A. R. Nelson of East Tennessee* (Nashville: Tennessee

Historical Commission, 1956), pp. 87-93.

17. McTeer, "Honoring the Stars and Stripes."

18. Temple, *East Tennessee*, pp. 370-77; Temple, *Notable Men*, pp. 88-93; "President Lincoln's Plan of Campaign – 1861 – Undated," *Official Records*, vol. 52, part 1, pp. 191-92; David Madden, "Unionist Resistance to Confederate Occupation: The Bridge Burners of East Tennessee," *East Tennessee Historical Society Publications* 52 (1980), pp. 42-53, (1981), pp. 22-39.

19. Temple, *East Tennessee*, pp. 380-85; Colonel William B. Wood to Cooper, November 11, 1861, Zollicoffer to Cooper, November 9, 1861, November 11, 1861, Letter Book of Col. W. B. Wood, Commanding Post at Knoxville, October 14 – November 25, 1861, Record Group 109, National Archives.

20. Temple, *East Tennessee*, pp. 381-84; "Statement Furnished Colonel Wood by Messrs Wiseman and Fain," Letter Book of Col. W. B. Wood, Commanding Post at Knoxville, October 14 – November 25, 1861, Record Group 109, National Archives.

21. Jesse C. Burt, "East Tennessee, Lincoln, and Sherman," *East Tennessee Historical Society Publications* 34 (1962), pp. 3-25, 35 (1963), pp. 56-75; Lloyd Lewis, *Sherman: Fighting Prophet* (New York: Harcourt, Brace, 1932), pp. 195-98; Francis F. McKinney, *Education in Violence* (Detroit: Wayne State University Press, 1961), pp. 117-19; Andrew Johnson to Brigadier General William T. Sherman, October 30, 1861, LeRoy P. Graf and Ralph W. Haskins, *The Papers of Andrew Johnson* (Knoxville: University of Tennessee Press, 1967), vol. 5, pp. 29-30.

22. Secretary of War Judah P. Benjamin to Colonel W. B. Wood, Colonel Danville Leadbetter, and Brigadier General William Carroll, November 25, 1861, Letter Book of Col. W. B. Wood, Commanding Post at Knoxville, October 14 – November 25, 1861, Record Group 109, National Archives.

23. Humes, *Mountaineers*, pp. 135-37, 152-53; Zollicoffer to Cooper, November 14, 1861, Orders and Letters Sent, General Felix K. Zollicoffer, August 1861 – January 1862, Record Group 109, National Archives; Carroll to Benjamin, November 12, 1861, *Official Records*, vol. 45, part 2, p. 206; Captain G. H. Monsarrat to Benjamin, December 29, 1861, *Official Records* II, vol. 1, p. 919.

24. Wood to Cooper, November 11, 1861, Zollicoffer to Cooper, November 14, 1861, Wood to Benjamin, November 20, 1861, "Statement Furnished Colonel Wood by Messrs Wiseman and Fain," Letter Book of Col. W. B. Wood, Commanding Post at Knoxville, October 14 – November 25, 1861, Record Group 109, National Archives.

25. Temple, *East Tennessee*, pp. 403-409; Humes, *Mountaineers*, pp. 148-53; J. Pickens vs John Crozier, R. B. Reynolds, and William Sneed, February, 1865, T. A. R. Nelson Papers, McClung Collection; Wood to Benjamin, November 10, 1861, November 20, 1861, Letter Book of Col. W. B. Wood, Commanding Post at Knoxville, October 14 – November 25, 1861, Record Group 109, National Archives; Claim of William Rogers, General Records of the Department of the Treasury, Southern Claims Commission, Record Group 56, National Archives.

26. Humes, *Mountaineers*, pp. 148-153; Brigadier General William H. Carroll to General Albert Sidney Johnston, December 5, 1861, *Official Records*, vol. 52, part 2, pp. 228-229; Walker, *Tales*, pp. 99-100; Robert A. Ragan, *Escape from East Tennessee to the Federal Lines* (Washington, D. C.: J. H. Doney, 1910), pp. 51-52; Leadbetter to Cooper, November 28, 1861, *Official Records*, vol. 4, pp. 712-13; Duay O'Neil, "The Hanging

of Peter Reece," *Smoky Mountain Historical Society Newsletter* II, (November 1977) pp. 8-9.

27. Carroll to Benjamin, December 7, 1861, Leadbetter to Cooper, December 8, 1861, *Official Records* II, vol. 1, pp. 852-853.

28. Brownlow, *Secession*, pp. 180-207; Temple, *Notable Men*, pp. 308-311; William G. Brownlow to Carroll, November 22, 1861, *Official Records*, vol. 7, pp. 719-20; J. G. M. Ramsey and William H. Tibbs to President Jefferson Davis, December 7, 1861, John Crozier Ramsey to Benjamin, December 7, 1861, December 10, 1861, Jesse G. Wallace to John Crozier Ramsey, December 18, 1861, Statement, James Cumming, W. G. Brownlow, and W. T. Dowell, December 2, 1861, William G. Swan to Davis, December 7, 1861, Ramsey to Benjamin, December 17, 1861, Benjamin to Ramsey, December 22, 1861, Brownlow to Davis, no date, *Official Records* II, vol. 1, pp. 919-21.

29. Governor Henry J. Clark to Benjamin, November 16, 1861, *Official Records*, vol. 52, part 2, pp. 209-210; Robert Meece to Morgan Meece, December 1, 1861, Hattie Caldwell Davis, *Civil War Letters and Memoirs from the Great Smoky Mountains* (Maggie Valley: Hattie Caldwell Davis, 1999), p. 76.

Chapter 4

1. Major General Edmund Kirby Smith to Cassie, March 3, 1862, March 13, 1862, March 26, 1862, Kirby Smith Papers, Southern Historical Collection; Kirby Smith to Colonel William W. Mackall, March 14, 1862, Kirby Smith to Washington Morgan, April 3, 1862, Department of East Tennessee, Letters and Telegrams Sent, March – September 1862, Record Group 109, National Archives; Alonzo Shahan to "his mother," September 11, 1862, Shahan Family Papers, Tennessee State Library and Archives; Memoirs of William Gibbs Allen, pp. 5-6, Tennessee State Library and Archives;

William McCampbell to T. A. R. Nelson, October 8, 1862, T. A. R. Nelson Papers, McClung Collection.

2. Memoirs of William Gibbs Allen, Tennessee State Library and Archives; Alonzo Shahan to "his mother," September 11, 1862, Shahan Family Papers, Tennessee State Library and Archives.

3. Edward R. Walker III, *Tales from the Civil War* (Cosby: Busy Bee Printing Services, 1983), pp. 98, 103-05, 108.

4. Major General Sam Jones to Colonel L. M. Allen, September 30, 1862, Jones to Colonel D. R. Hundley, October 20, 1862, Department of East Tennessee, Letters and Telegrams Sent, September – November 1862, Record Group 109, National Archives.

5. J. C. Bradley to "Miss Jane" July 28, 1861, W. B. Ferguson to Miss R. J. Ferguson, March 27, 1862, Hattie Caldwell Davis, *Civil War Letters and Memoirs from the Great Smoky Mountains* (Maggie Valley: Hattie Caldwell Davis, 1999), pp. 50-51.

6. Alfred Bell to Mary Bell, November 11, 1862, January 10, 1862, January 12, 1862, January 30, 1862, February 4, 1862, Mary Bell to Alfred Bell, January 30, 1862, February 10, 1862, Bell Family Papers, Special Collections, Duke University.

7. Lizzie Lenoir to Brother Rufus, September 21, 1862, Lenoir Family Papers, North Carolina State Archives.

8. J. B. Fitzgerald to Governor Zebulon B. Vance, November 25, 1862, Frontes W. Johnson, ed. *The Papers of Zebulon Baird Vance* (Raleigh: State Department of Archives and History, 1963), vol. 1, pp. 398-400.

9. Ibid.

10. Brigadier General W. G. M. Davis to Governor Zebulon B. Vance, January 11, 1863, A.S. Merriman to Governor Zebulon B. Vance, February 16, 1863, *The War of the Rebellion: A Compilation of the Official Records of the Union and Confederate Armies* (Washington: Government Printing Office, 1880-1901), vol. 18, pp. 810-11, 881; C. D. Smith to Vance, October 21, 1863, Zebulon Baird Vance Papers, North Carolina State Archives; Stephen Whitaker to Colonel W. H. Thomas, August 13, 1863, Stephen Whitaker Letters, North Carolina State Archives.

11. Vernon Crowe, *Storm in the Mountains: Thomas's Confederate Legion of Cherokee Indians and Mountaineers* (Cherokee: Press of the Museum of the Cherokee Indian, 1982), pp. 55-56.

12. Stephen Thomas to Dr. Lillard, February 6, 1863, Lillard Family Papers, Tennessee State Library and Archives.

13. Davis, *Civil War*, p. 131; Elizabeth D. Powers and Mark E. Hannah, *Cataloochee: Lost Settlement of the Smokies* (Charleston: Powers Hannah Publishers, 1982), pp. 53-55.

14. W. H. Porter to Colonel W. H. Thomas, April 17, 1864, William Holland Thomas Papers, Duke University; Captain James Taylor to Thomas, August 10, 1864, James Terrell Papers, Duke University; John Preston Arthur, *Western North Carolina: A History* (Raleigh: Edwards & Broughton Printing Company, 1914), pp. 611-12; "Courthouse Burned, But Big Ike Did It," Asheville *Citizen-Times*, April 1, 1964.

15. Governor Zebulon B. Vance to Major General John C. Breckinridge, October 29, 1864, *Official Records*, vol. 52, part 3, p. 339.

16. Provost Marshall General Samuel P. Carter to Lieutenant Thomas Underdown, June 3, 1864, Provost Marshal General, District of East Tennessee, Press Copies of Letters Sent, September 1863 – 1864, Record Group 393, National Archives; Carter to Wade Newman, June 20, 1864, Provost Marshal General, District of East Tennessee, Press Copies of Letters Sent, 1864 – 1865, Record Group 393, National Archives; Lieutenant Colonel G. W. Bascom to Captain S. T. Bryan, May 4, 1865, District of East Tennessee, Letters Sent, April 1864 – March 1855, Record Group 393, National Archive.

17. Lieutenant C. H. Taylor to Lieutenant Colonel William C. Walker, October 29, 1861, Report of Major General C. L. Stevenson, November 12, 1863, *Official Records* 31, part 1, p. 235.

18. L. Cowles to Mary, July 24, 1864, Cowles Family Papers, North Carolina State Archives; Memoirs of William Gibbs Allen, Tennessee State Library and Archives; Memoirs of William Williams Stringfield, North Carolina State Archives; Davis, *Letters and Memoirs*, pp. 97-103.

19. Lieutenant Colonel Robert Klein to Brigadier General W. L. Elliott, January 14, 1864, *Official Records*, vol. 32, part 1, pp. 70-71.

20. Lieutenant Colonel George W. Lay to Colonel John Preston, September 2, 1863, *Official Records* IV, vol. 2, pp. 783-85.

21. Captain J. C. McRae to Colonel Peter Mallett, August 13, 1863, *Official Records* IV, vol. 2, pp. 732-34.

22. J. N. Bryson to Lieutenant Colonel W. C. Walker, July 16, 1863, *Official Records* IV, vol. 2, pp. 732-34; Captain D. C. Pearson to Captain J. C. McRae, August 10, 1863, *Official Records* IV, vol. 2, p. 734.

23. Memoirs of William Williams Stringfield,

North Carolina State Archives.

24. Ibid.

25. "Edwin Best Tells Tragic Civil War Story," *The Daily Times*, November 2, 1983.

26. Durwood Dunn, *Cades Cove: The Life and Death of a Southern Appalachian Community, 1818-1937* (Knoxville: University of Tennessee Press, 1988), pp. 131-141.

27. Walker, *Tales*, p. 57.

28. Reverend Henry M. Sheed to Carter, January 5, 1864, *Official Records*, vol. 32, part 2, pp. 29-30.

29. General Orders Number 87, October 13, 1864, General Orders Number 93, October 27, 1864, General Orders, Department of the Ohio, 1864, Record Group 393, National Archives; General Orders Number 10, July 12, 1864, General Orders Number 4, January 23, 1865, General Orders, Provost Marshal General, District of East Tennessee, 1864-1865, Record Group 393, National Archives; Statement of James L. Jenkins in case Foster vs Cox et. al., September 6, 1866, F. A. Leno to T. A. R. Nelson, August 21, 1865, T. A. R. Nelson Papers, McClung Collection.

30. "From the Officers of the Seventh Tennessee Cavalry," August 1, 1864, LeRoy P. Graf and Ralph W. Haskins, *The Papers of Andrew Johnson* (Knoxville: University of Tennessee Press, 1967), vol. 7, pp. 65-66; Colonel John Shannon to Brigadier General Davis Tillson, January 14, 1865, *Official Records*, vol. 45, part 2, pp. 592-93; Provost Marshall General Samuel P. Carter to Thomas Sanderson, October 29, 1864, Provost Marshal General, District of East Tennessee, Press Copies of Letters Sent, September 1863-1864, Record Group 393, National Archives; Barbara Hall to James Hall, February 19, 1864, Crofton Hall to James Hall,

July 14, 1864, Hall Family Papers, Tennessee State Library and Archives.

31. John W. Andes and Will A. McTeer, *Loyal Mountain Troopers: The Second and Third Tennessee Volunteer Cavalry in the Civil War* (Maryville: Blount County Genealogical and Historical Society, 1992), pp. 2-3; Claim of John Hyde, Claim of Greene Burgess, Claim of William Roane, Claim of Miles Sneed, Claim of Thomas Runion, General Records of the Department of the Treasury, Southern Claims Commission, Record Group 56, National Archives; Jane Kizer Thomas, "Southern Heroes, or the Friends (Quakers) in War Time," *The Blount Journal* 14 (Fall 1997), pp. 37-40; Temple, *Notable Men*, p. 196; "Statement of Provost Marshall General Samuel P. Carter," December 31, 1864, Provost Marshal General, District of East Tennessee, Press Copies of Letters Sent, 1864-1865, Record Group 393, National Archives.

32. Robert A. Ragan, *Escape from East Tennessee to the Federal Lines* (Washington, D. C.: J. H. Doney, 1910).

33. McTeer and Andes, *Troopers*, pp. 6-7, 13-18.

34. McTeer and Andes, *Troopers*, pp. 10-13.

35. Humes, *Loyal Mountaineers*, pp. 357-363.

36. Walker, *Tales*, pp. 61, 106.

37. Walker, *Tales*, pp. 119-20; Powers and Hannah, *Cataloochee*, pp. 55-56.

38. Walker, *Tales*, pp. 54, 57-58, 61-62.

39. Walker, *Tales*, pp. 55, 63, 66; Ina W. Van Noppen, *Stoneman's Last Raid* (Boone: North Carolina State College, 1961), pp. 15-16; *Cocke County, Tennessee and Its People* (Heritage Book Committee and Don Mills, Inc., 1992), p. 330.

40. Walker, *Tales*, pp. 37-38, 105-06.

Chapter 5

1. Paul D. Escott, *After Secession: Jefferson Davis and the Failure of Confederate Nationalism* (Baton Rouge: Louisiana State University Press, 1978); Ella Lonn, *Desertion During the Civil War* (New York: The Century Company, 1928); Albert Burton Moore, *Conscription and Conflict in the Confederacy* (New York: The Macmillan Company, 1924).

2. Assistant Quartermaster General Larkin Smith to Colonel A. C. Myers, June 4, 1863, *The War of the Rebellion: A Compilation of the Official Records of the Union and Confederate Armies* (Washington: Government Printing Office, 1880-1901) IV, vol. 2, pp. 575-76; "Tax Assessment for Union Families," April 16, 1864, T. A. R. Nelson Papers, McClung Collection; Major General John G. Foster to Major General Gordon Granger, January 29, 1864, Granger to Foster, January 29, 1864, Report of Brigadier General Samuel D. Sturgis, January 24, 1864, *Official Records* 32, part 2, pp. 114, 254.

3. Alfred Wilson to Jonas Watson, October 29, 1861, March 8, 1862, Mary Ann Covington Wilson Papers, Southern Historical Collection; Store Ledger, Joseph Cathey Papers, North Carolina State Archives; Mary Bell to Alfred Bell, July 10, 1862, Bell Family Papers, Special Collections, Duke University; Montgomery McTeer to Andrew Johnson, June 2, 1864, LeRoy P. Graf and Ralph W. Haskins, *The Papers of Andrew Johnson* (Knoxville: University of Tennessee Press, 1967), vol. 6, pp. 713-714; Robert A. Ragan to his wife, March 29, 1864, Robert A. Ragan Letters, University of Tennessee Special Collections.

4. Edward R. Walker III, *Tales from the Civil War* (Cosby: Busy Bee Printing Service, 1983), pp. 25-26, 34-36.

5. Walker, *Tales*, pp. 72, 74-75, 77, 111-12, 119-20; Nancy L. O'Neil, "Greenlawn: At the Darkening of the Day," *Smoky Mountain Historical 6. Society Newsletter* 26 (Spring 2000), pp. 26-29.

6. Walker, *Tales*, pp. 49, 51, 73, 75-76, 78-79.

7. Walker, *Tales*, pp. 78-79; Hattie Caldwell Davis, *Civil War Letters and Memoirs from the Great Smoky Mountains* (Maggie Valley: Hattie Caldwell Davis, 1999), p. 132.

8. Walker, *Tales*, pp. 50-51, 73-74, 77, 79, 87.

9. Walker, *Tales*, pp. 45, 52, 72, 83.

10. Walker, *Tales*, pp. 41, 54-55, 65, 82-84, 94, 96.

11. Duane Oliver, *Hazel Creek From Then til Now* (Maryville: Stinnet Printing Company, 1989) pp. 45-46; Walker, *Tales*, pp. 11, 89.

12. Maryville Bicentennial Commission, "Chronological Bicentennial History of the City of Maryville," *The Blount Journal* 13 (Spring 1997), pp. 12-13; George Best, "Blount County in the Civil War," George Best Files, Blount County Public Library; N. N. Davidson to William Walker, April 30, 1864, William Walker Papers, North Carolina State Archives.

13. Albert W. Dockter, Jr., "Maryville College, 1819-1994," *The Blount Journal* 10 (Spring 1994), pp. 5-7; Samuel Tyndale Wilson, *A Century of Maryville College, 1819-1919* (Maryville: The Directors of Maryville College, 1916), pp. 111-116; Alberta and Carson Brewer, *Valley So Wild: A Folk History* (Knoxville: East Tennessee Historical Society, 1975), pp. 175-176; John S. Craig to Andrew Johnson, February 21, 1862, *Johnson Papers*, vol. 5, pp. 153-55.

14. Edward J. Best, "New Providence

Presbyterian Church: The First Hundred Years," "Historical Sketches of Big Springs Presbyterian Church," Blount County Files, Churches, Blount County Public Library; Big Pigeon Baptist Church Minutes, 1787-1874, Sevier County Public Library; Minutes of Slate Creek Baptist Church, 1812-1876, Minutes of the East Tennessee Association of Baptists, 1841-1872, McClung Collection; *The History of Blount County Tennessee and Its People, 1795-1995* (Maryville: Blount County History Book Commission, 1995), pp. 20-38; Walker, *Tales*, pp. 17, 29; Florence Cope Bush, *Oconaluftee Baptist: Pioneer Church of the Smokies* (Concord: Misty Cove Press, 1990), pp. 2-4; Barbara Hall to James Hall, January 27, 1865, Hall Family Papers, Tennessee State Library and Archives.

15. Walker, *Tales*, pp. 29-30; Harold Owenby, *Forks of Little Pigeon Church* (Gatlinburg: The Buckhorn Press, 1989), pp. 37-39.

16. W. Walker to Oliver P. Temple, January 13, 1864, January 21, 1865, William Burnett to Oliver P. Temple, June 10, 1865, Oliver P. Temple Papers, University of Tennessee Special Collections.

17. Claim of Matilda Dunlap, General Records of the Department of the Treasury, Southern Claims Commission, Record Group 56, National Archives.

18. Claim of Richard Porter Keeble, General Records of the Department of the Treasury, Southern Claims Commission, Record Group 56, National Archives.

19. Claim of Elijah Hatcher, General Records of the Department of the Treasury, Southern Claims Commission, Record Group 56, National Archives.

20. Claim of Thomas H. Saffell, Claim of John Sutton, Claim of Levi Moore, Claim of Jared Meade, General Records of the Department of the Treasury, Southern Claims Commission, Record Group 56, National Archives.

21. Claim of Louisa Styles, General Records of the Department of the Treasury, Southern Claims Commission, Record Group 56, National Archives.

22. Claim of John A. Rawlings, Claim of Hugh Lambert, General Records of the Department of the Treasury, Southern Claims Commission, Record Group 56, National Archives; Mary Walker to Oliver P. Temple, January 23, 1865, Oliver P. Temple Papers, University of Tennessee Special Collections.

23. Claim of Lee Cannon, Claim of Isaac Garrison, General Records of the Department of the Treasury, Southern Claims Commission, Record Group 56, National Archives.

24. Mary Bell to Alfred Bell, November 7, 1861, November 13, 1861, June 20, 1862, June 28, 1862, Alfred Bell to Mary Bell, January 12, 1862, January 18, 1862, April 2, 1862, August 17, 1862, Bell Family Papers, Special Collections, Duke University.

25. Alfred Bell to Mary Bell, March 29, 1862, April 2, 1862, April 6, 1862, April 14, 1862, Bell Family Papers, Special Collections, Duke University.

26. Alfred Bell to Mary Bell, April 11, 1862, April 14, 1862, April 27, 1862, May 3, 1862, June 6, 1862, Bell Family Papers, Special Collections, Duke University.

27. Mary Bell to Alfred Bell, April 4, 1862, April 28, 1862, Alfred Bell to Mary Bell, April 11, 1862, Bell Family Papers, Special Collections, Duke University.

29. Mary Bell to Alfred Bell, May 15, 1862, June 20, 1862, September 13, 1862, Bell Family Papers, Special Collections, Duke University.

30. Mary Bell to Alfred Bell, December 10, 1861, May 15, 1862, Alfred Bell to Mary Bell, May 8, 1862, May 31, 1862, Bell Family Papers, Special Collections, Duke University.

31. Alfred Bell to Mary Bell, June 8, 1862, Bell Family Papers, Special Collections, Duke University.

32. Alfred Bell to Mary Bell, May 31, 1862, June 13, 1862, June 19, 1862, July 6, 1862, Bell Family Papers, Special Collections, Duke University.

33. Alfred Bell to Mary Bell, July 15, 1862, August 17, 1862, Bell Family Papers, Special Collections, Duke University.

34. Alfred Bell to Mary Bell, August 17, 1862, August 27, 1862, Mary Bell to Alfred Bell, September 5, 1862, Bell Family Papers, Special Collections, Duke University.

35. Mary Bell to Alfred Bell, July 20, 1862, August 26, 1862, Alfred Bell to Mary Bell, August 23, 1862, August 27, 1862, Bell Family Papers, Special Collections, Duke University.

36. Mary Bell to Alfred Bell, June 20, 1862, August 26, 1862, September 5, 1862, Alfred Bell to Mary Bell, December 3, 1862, Bell Family Papers, Special Collections, Duke University.

37. Mary Bell to Alfred Bell, August 26, 1862, September 5, 1862, December 2, 1862, Alfred Bell to Mary Bell, November 28, 1862, Bell Family Papers, Special Collections, Duke University.

38. Alfred Bell to Mary Bell, November 28, 1862, December 3, 1862, December 19, 1862, Bell Family Papers, Special Collections, Duke University.

39. Alfred Bell to Mary Bell, December 3, 1862, December 10, 1862, December 22, 1862, Bell Family Papers, Special Collections, Duke University.

40. Alfred Bell to Mary Bell, February 25, 1864, March 17, 1864, March 31, 1864, April 10, 1864, Bell Family Papers, Special Collections, Duke University.

41. Alfred Bell to Mary Bell, March 31, 1864, April 8, 1864, Bell Family Papers, Special Collections, Duke University.

42. Alfred Bell to Mary Bell, July 14, 1864, August 19, 1864, August 23, 1864, Bell Family Papers, Special Collections, Duke University.

43. Mary Bell to Alfred Bell, March 26, 1864, April 8, 1864, May 8, 1864, Alfred Bell to Mary Bell, April 10, 1864, Bell Family Papers, Special Collections, Duke University.

44. Alfred Bell to Mary Bell, October 22, 1864, February 15, 1864, February 25, 1864, Bell Family Papers, Special Collections, Duke University.

45. James Hall to Barbara Hall, January 11, 1864, January 23, 1864, February 16, 1864, February 20, 1864, James Hall to Isaac Russell, November 9, 1863, Hall Family Papers, Tennessee State Library and Archives.

46. James Hall to Barbara Hall, May 1, 1864, May 18, 1864, June 26, 1864, July 24, 1864, August 7, 1864, Barbara Hall to James Hall, May 18, 1864, November 23, 1864, Hall Family Papers, Tennessee State Library and Archives.

47. James Hall to Barbara Hall, September 18, 1864, Barbara Hall to James Hall, August 2, 1864, September 7, 1864, Henry Simerly to Margaret Simerly, January 11, 1864, Hall Family Papers, Tennessee State Library and Archives.

48. Crofton Hall to James Hall, July 13, 1864,

September 4, 1864, October 30, 1864, Barbara Hall to James Hall, January 27, 1865, Hall Family Papers, Tennessee State Library and Archives.

49. Barbara Hall to James Hall, June 23, 1864, James Hall to Barbara Hall, May 26, 1864, June 5, 1864, June 23, 1864, July 9, 1864, August 15, 1864, Hall Family Papers, Tennessee State Library and Archives.

Chapter 6

1. Herman Hattaway and Archer Jones, *How the North Won: A Military History of the Civil War* (Urbana: University of Illinois Press, 1987), pp. 56-63; T. Harry Williams, *Lincoln and His Generals* (New York: Grosset & Dunlap, 1952), pp. 47-59, 182-85, 205-36.

2. Colonel William Holland Thomas to A. T. Davidson, January 29, 1864, William Holland Thomas Papers, Duke University; Report of Colonel F. W. Graham, September 8, 1863, *The War of the Rebellion: A Compilation of the Official Records of the Union and Confederate Armies* (Washington: Government Printing Office, 1880-1901), vol. 30, part 3, p. 474.

3. William Marvel, *Burnside* (Chapel Hill: University of North Carolina Press, 1991), p. 277; E. D. G. Murray to Colonel Joseph Cathey, December 20, 1864, Joseph Cathey Papers, North Carolina State Archives.

4. Vernon Crowe, *Storm in the Mountains: Thomas's Confederate Legion of Cherokee Indians and Mountaineers* (Cherokee: Press of the Museum of the Cherokee Indian, 1982), pp. 39-40.

5. Marvel, *Burnside*, pp. 279-91.

6. Marvel, *Burnside*, pp. 295-308; Jeffrey D. Wert, *General James Longstreet: The Confederacy's Most Controversial Soldier* (New York: Simon and Schuster, 1991), pp. 338-46.

7. Twenty-Third Army Corps, Special Orders 102, October 30, 1863, Itinerary of Third Brigade, Colonel Charles D. Pennebaker, Report of Brigadier General William P. Sanders, November 5, 1863, *Official Records* 31, part 1, pp. 254, 423, 792; Sanders to Major General Ambrose Burnside, November 4, November 5, November 7, November 8, 1863, Sanders to Major General John G. Parke, November 2, November 3, November 5, November 6, November 11, November 12, November 13, 1863, 1863, Brigadier General R. B. Potter to Burnside, November 6, 1863, *Official Records* 31, part 3, pp. 23, 36, 46, 61-62.

8. Parke to Sanders, November 5, November 6, 1863, Sanders to Parke, November 7, November 8, November 10, November 11, 1863, *Official Records* 31, part 3, pp. 77-80.

9. Report of Major General Joseph Wheeler, December 31, 1863, Report of Major General William T. Martin, January 8, 1864, J. J. Morrison to Wheeler, November 3, 1863, Longstreet to Wheeler, November 12, 1863, November 13, 1863, November 14, 1863, Wheeler to Longstreet, November 13, 1863, *Official Records* 31, part 1, pp. 540-43, 548-51, 628, 686, 688; Colonel George W. Dibrell to Wheeler, November 3, 1863, November 4, 1863, Parke to Major General Ambrose Burnside, November 14, 1863, *Official Records* 31, part 3, pp. 627-28.

10. Burnside to President Abraham Lincoln, November 17, 1863, Brigadier General W. P. Sanders to Burnside, November 14, 1863, Colonel R. K. Byrd to Burnside, November 19, 1863, *Official Records* 31, part 1, pp. 268, 420; Report of Major General Joseph Wheeler, December 31, 1863; Report of Major General William T. Martin, January 8, 1864, Major General Braxton Bragg to Major General James Longstreet, November 4, 1863; Longstreet to Wheeler, November 12, November 13, November 14, 1863, *Official Records* 31, part 3,

pp. 540-550.

11. Marvel, *Burnside*, pp. 315-21; Digby Gordon Seymour, *Divided Loyalties: Fort Sanders and the Civil War in East Tennessee* (Knoxville: University of Tennessee Press, 1963); Major General Edmund Kirby Smith to Cassie, March 3, 1862, March 16, 1862, Kirby Smith Papers, Southern Historical Collection.

12. Report of Colonel John M. Loomis, First Brigade, Fourth Division, Fifteen Army Corps, Itinerary of Second Brigade, Second Cavalry Division, Colonel Eli Long, Report of Major General William T. Sherman, *Official Records* 31, part 2, pp. 435, 579; Headquarters, Army of the Tennessee, Field Orders Dated December 4, 1863, *Official Records* 31, part 3, p. 543; Edward J. Best, "General Sherman Comes to Blount County," *The Blount Journal* 7 (Spring 1991), pp. 4-22, (Fall 1991), pp. 1-12; Elmer Mize, "Blount County: A Brief History of Her Settlement, People, Adventures, Trials and Tribulations," *The Blount Journal* 14 (Spring 1998), pp. 35-37.

13. Inez Burns, "Women Meet Sherman at Brick Mill," *Maryville-Alcoa Times*, February 28, 1961.

14. Wert, *Longstreet*, pp. 346-54; Marvel, *Burnside*, pp. 322-30; Seymour, *Fort Sanders*.

15. William T. Sherman, *Memoirs of General William T. Sherman* (Bloomington: Indiana University Press, 1957), pp. 365-68.

16. Itinerary of Second Brigade, Second Cavalry Division, Colonel Eli Long, *Official Records* 31, part 1, p. 435; Report of Colonel Eli Long, Second Brigade, Second Cavalry Division, *Official Records* 31, part 2, pp. 563-64.

17. Crowe, *Storm*, pp. 360-70.

18. Brigadier General Robert B. Vance to Colonel William Holland Thomas, November 4, 1863, Thomas Siler to Thomas, December 10, 1863, William Holland Thomas Papers, Duke University.

19. Crowe, *Storm*, pp. 367-74.

20. Governor Zebulon B. Vance to Secretary of War James Seddon, November 18, 1863, Brigadier General Robert B. Vance to Governor Vance, November 12, 1863, *Official Records* 29, part 2, p. 836; Brigadier General O. B. Wilcox to Burnside, November 10, 1863, *Official Records*, vol. 31, part 3, p. 19.

21. Thomas to A. F. Davidson, January 22, 1864, William Holland Thomas Papers, Duke University; Report of Brigadier General Samuel Sturgis, January 15, 1864, Report of Colonel William J. Palmer, January 15, 1864, Report of Colonel John. B. Palmer, January 19, 1864, *Official Records* 32, part 1, pp. 74-77; Lieutenant General James Longstreet to General Samuel Cooper, January 18, 1864, *Official Records* 52, part 2, p. 603; Crowe, *Storm*, pp. 377-85.

22. Longstreet to Major General William T. Martin, December 28, 1863, *Official Records* 52, part 2, p. 584; Report of Major General John. G. Foster, Department of the Ohio, of Operations January 1 to February 9, Report of Brigadier General Samuel D. Sturgis, February 4, 1864, *Official Records* 32, part 1, pp. 41-47; Longstreet to President Jefferson Davis, March 16, 1864, *Official Records* 32, part 3, pp. 637-42.

23. Longstreet to Martin, December 28, 1863, *Official Records* 52, part 2, p. 584; Colonel William J. Palmer to Brigadier General Washington Elliott, January 8, 1864, January 10, 1864, January 11, 1864, January 13, 1864, Colonel E. M. McCook to Elliott, *Official Records* 32, part 2, pp. 43, 58-59, 68, 80-81, 175; Longstreet to President Jefferson Davis, March 16, 1864, Davis to Longstreet, March 25, 1864, *Official Records* 32, part 3, pp. 637-42.

24. Report of Major General John G. Foster,

January 29, 1864, Report of Major General John G. Foster, February 21, 1864, *Official Records* 32, part 1, pp. 41-44; Foster to Major General Ulysses S. Grant, January 23, 1864, Brigadier General August Willich to Major General Gordon Granger, January 25, 1864, *Official Records* 32, part 2, pp. 183, 211.

25. Report of Major General John G. Foster, February 21, 1864, Report of Brigadier General Washington L. Elliott, Commanding Cavalry, Department of the Cumberland, February 2, 1864, Report of Brigadier General Samuel D. Sturgis, Commanding Cavalry, Department of the Ohio, January 24, 1864, Report of Brigadier General W. L. Elliott February 2, 1864, Colonel O. H. LaGrange to Captain John Pratt, January 23, 1864, *Official Records* 32, part 1, pp. 24-25, 42-44, 114-15.

26. Report of Brigadier General W. L. Elliott, February 2, 1864, Report of Brigadier General Samuel D. Sturgis, Commanding Cavalry, Department of the Ohio, January 24, 1864, Sturgis to Elliott, February 21, 1864, McCook to Sturgis, February 21, 1864, Brigadier General August Willich to Granger, January 25, 1864, Foster to Granger, January 29, 1864, Granger to Foster, January 29, 1864, *Official Records* 32, part 1, pp. 24-25, 42-44.

27. Report of Major General John G. Foster, Commanding Department of the Ohio, of Operations January 1 through February 9, Itinerary, Army of the Ohio, Report of Major General John G. Foster, Commanding Army of the Ohio, January 26-28, 1864, Report of Brigadier General Washington L. Elliott, Commanding Cavalry, Department of the Cumberland, Report of Brigadier General Samuel D. Sturgis, January 26-28, 1864, Report of Captain Eli Lilly, Eighteenth Indiana Battery, January 31, 1864, Report of Major Edward G. Savage, Ninth Pennsylvania Cavalry, January 29, 1864, Report of Colonel Edward M. McCook, Commanding First Cavalry Division,

Noah Abbott, a Civil War veteran.

Department of the Cumberland, February 2, 1864, Report of Lieutenant Colonel James P. Brownlow, February 2, 1864, Elliott to Sturgis, January 23, 1864, Sturgis to Elliott, February 4, 1864, Colonel William Palmer to Elliott, January 13, 1864, Foster to Major General Ulysses S. Grant, January 23, 1864, Report of Lieutenant General James Longstreet, January 26-28, 1864, *Official Records* 32, part 1, pp. 131-36, 139-40, 146-50, 161.

28. Report of Brigadier General Samuel D. Sturgis, January 26-28, 1864, Report of Major General John G. Foster, January 26-28, 1864, Report of Lieutenant General James Longstreet, January 26-28, 1864, Report of Brigadier General Samuel Beatty, Report of Lieutenant Colonel James D. Brule, Report of Major General Gordon Granger, February 1, 1864, Colonel Israel Garrard to Elliott, February 1,

National Park Archives

Graves of two men killed during the Civil War at Caldwell Fork, just above the Jesse McGee place.

1864, *Official Records* 32, part 1, pp. 131-36; Sturgis to Foster, January 31, 1864, *Official Records* 32, part 2, pp. 273, 653; Longstreet to Davis, March 16, 1864, *Official Records* 32, part 3, pp. 637-42.

29. Foster to Granger, January 30, 1864, January 31, 1864, February 1, 1864, Sturgis to McCook, January 30, 1864, Sturgis to Foster, January 31, 1864, Sturgis to Granger, January 31, 1864, McCook to Foster, February 7, 1864, Lieutenant Colonel R. O. Selfridge to Granger, January 31, 1864, Garrard to Brigadier General E. E. Potter, February 1, 1864, *Official Records* 32, part 2, pp. 273-275, 306, 308; Longstreet to Davis, March 16, 1864, Davis to Longstreet, March 25, 1864, *Official Records* 32, part 3, pp. 637-42.

30. Report of Major General Gordon Granger,

February 19, 1864, *Official Records* 32, part 1, p. 406; McCook to Major General John Schofield, February 7, 1864, McCook to Potter, February 9, 1864, Colonel Daniel Cameron to Captain E. R. Kerstetter, February 10, 1864, February 12, 1864, Potter to Granger, February 11, 1864, Brigadier General Samuel Beatty to Colonel Fullerton, February 11, 1864, Colonel R. O. Selfridge to Lieutenant Colonel J. S. Fullerton, February 12, 1864, Schofield to Granger, February 17, 1864, McCook to Fullerton, February 17, 1864, February 21, 1864, *Official Records* 32, part 2, pp. 348, 356, 360, 368, 381, 416, 417, 441, 484.

31. Edwin J. Best, "Polly O'Toole and the Records of Blount County," Edwin J. Best Records, Blount County Public Library.

32. Report of Brigadier General Samuel D. Sturgis, January 26-28, 1864, Sturgis to Foster, January 31, February 4, 1864, Itinerary of Army of the Cumberland, January 1 through April 30, 1864, Report of Major General John G. Foster, February 7, 1864, *Official Records* 32, part 1, pp. 131-36; Colonel John B. Palmer to Major James Ashmore, February 12, 1864, Sturgis to Foster, *Official Records* 32, part 2, p. 273; Major Davidson to Colonel H. Capon, February 7, 1864, Capon Papers, Library of Congress.

33. Major James Ashmore to General Thomas Jordon, February 15, 1864, Brigadier General John B. Palmer to Ashmore, February 12, 1864, *Official Records* 32, part 2, pp. 746-49; Governor M. L. Bonham to Secretary of War James Seddon, March 4, 1864, *Official Records* 53, pp. 313-15.

34. Governor M. L. Bonham to Secretary of War James Seddon, March 4, 1864, April 22, 1864, Major General Braxton Bragg to Seddon, May 2, 1864, J. K. Sass to Bonham, April 20, 1864, *Official Records* 53, pp. 313-15; Major John D. Ashmore to General Thomas Jordon, February 15, 1864, *Official Records* 32, part 2, pp. 746-49; Itinerary of Army of the Cumberland, January 1-April 30, 1864, *Official Records* 32, part 1, p. 37.

35. Colonel William Holland Thomas to Governor M. L. Bonham, February 28, 1864, *Official Records* 53, pp. 313-15.

36. Thomas to Major General John C. Breckinridge, April 27, 1864, William Holland Thomas Papers, Duke University.

37. Report of Colonel John B. Palmer, July 4, 1864, *Official Records* 39, part 1, pp. 235-36.

38. Colonel William Holland Thomas to Brigadier General John B. Palmer, July 8, 1864, William Holland Thomas Papers, Duke University.

Gravestone of Robert Collins, famous Smokies guide, killed during the Civil War.

39. Colonel William Holland Thomas to Brigadier General John B. Palmer, August 2, 1864, Thomas to Lieutenant John Telling, August 19, 1864, William Holland Thomas Papers, Duke University.

40. J. Keenan to Governor Zebulon B. Vance, June 1, 1863, Zebulon Vance Papers, North Carolina State Archives; Crowe, *Storm*, pp. 98-100.

41. Colonel William Holland Thomas to Brigadier General John B. Palmer, July 8, 1864, William Holland Thomas Papers, Duke University; Secretary of War James Seddon to Governor Robert B. Vance, April 23, 1864, *Official Records* 53, p. 315.

42. "Charges and Specifications Against Colonel William Holland Thomas of Thomas's

North Carolina Legion," Thomas to Sergeant Harmon Brown, August 26, 1864, William Holland Thomas Papers, Duke University; Crowe, *Storm*, pp. 98-100.

43. William Williams Stringfield Memoirs, North Carolina State Archives.

44. William Williams Stringfield Memoirs, North Carolina State Archives; Allen, *Haywood*, pp. 79-83; Davis, *Memoirs and Letters*, pp. 97-103; Elizabeth D. Powers and Mark E. Hannah, *Cataloochee: Lost Settlement of the Smokies* (Charleston: Powers-Hannah Publishers, 1982), pp. 67-72; Hattie Caldwell Davis, *Cataloochee Valley: Vanished Settlement of the Great Smoky Mountains* (Alexander: WorldComm, 1997), pp. 62-69.

45. Captain J. M. Cooper to Colonel William Holland Thomas, February 22, 1864, Major William W. Stringfield to Thomas, February 21, February 22, 1865, William Holland Thomas Papers, Duke University.

46. Ina W. Van Noppen, *Stoneman's Last Raid* Boone: North Carolina State College, 1961; Report of Colonel Isaac Kirby, One Hundred and First Ohio Infantry, April 13, 1865, *Official Records* 49, part 1, pp. 31-33.

47. Report of Brigadier General Alvin C. Gillem, April 25, 1865, Report of Brigadier General Davis Tillson, May 18, 1865, Gillem to Major General George Thomas, April 26, 1865, *Official Records* 49, part 1, pp. 330-39.

48. Memoirs of William Williams Stringfield, North Carolina State Archives.

49. Report of Brigadier General Alvin C. Gillem, April 25, 1865, Report of Brigadier General Davis Tillson of Operations March 22 – May 7, 1865, *Official Records* 49, part 1, pp. 330-339; Tillson to Major G. M. Bascom, May 1, 1865, May 5, 1865, Tillson to Colonel G. G.

Hawley, May 9, 1865, *Official Records* 49, part 2, pp. 475, 556, 622, 690.

50. Allen, *Haywood*, pp. 83-92.

51. William Williams Stringfield Memoirs, North Carolina State Archives.

Chapter 7

1. Hattie Caldwell Davis, *Civil War Letters and Memoirs from the Great Smoky Mountains* (Maggie Valley: Hattie Caldwell Davis, 1999), p. 138; Jerry O. Potter, *The Sultana Tragedy* (Gretna: Pelican Publishing Company, 1962).

2. Charles Faulkner Bryan, "The Civil War in East Tennessee: A Social, Political and Economic Study," Dissertation, University of Tennessee, 1978, pp. 221-230; Fred Arthur Bailey, *Class and Tennessee's Confederate Generation* (Chapel Hill: University of North Carolina Press, 1987), p. 17; Memoirs of William Gibbs Allen, Tennessee Historical Society; Thomas B. Alexander, *Thomas A. R. Nelson of East Tennessee* (Nashville: Tennessee Historical Commission, 1956), p. 46.

3. Memoirs of William Williams Stringfield, North Carolina State Archives.

4. Memoirs of William Gibbs Allen, Tennessee Historical Society; Edward R. Walker III, *Tales from the Civil War* (Cosby: Busy Bee Printing Service, 1983), p. 21.

5. Bailey, *Class*, p. 117; Walker, *Tales*, pp. 8-9, 33-34; "Reconstruction and Radicalism in Blount County, 1863-1870," Edwin James Best Collection, Blount County Public Library.

6. Bryan, "Civil War," pp. 236-240; S. P. Gaut to S. A. Rogers, September 10, 1865, S. P. Gaut to Oliver P. Temple, January 25, 1866, W. H. Cannon to S. A. Rogers and Oliver P. Temple, October 4, 1865, Oliver P. Temple Papers,

University of Tennessee Special Collections; Memoirs of William Williams Stringfield, North Carolina State Archives.

7. T. D. Bryson to Governor Jonathan Worth, October 1, 1866, "Many Citizens" to Worth, July 3, 1867, William Best to Worth, June 26, 1866, Jonathan Worth Papers, North Carolina State Archives.

8. W. Clark Medford, *The Early History of Haywood County* (Waynesville: W. Clark Medford, 1961), pp. 164-69; Walker, *Tales*, pp. 25-26; N. G. Phillips to Col. Cathey, December 24, 1868, Joseph Cathey Papers, Hunter Library, Western Carolina University; John H. Bremmer to Oliver P. Temple, July 9, 1867, Oliver P. Temple Papers, University of Tennessee Special Collections; J. Scott Knight, "John Collins 1814-

1902: Quaker Artist, Minister and Educator," *The Blount Journal* (Spring 2000), pp. 5-8.

9. Vernon Crowe, *Storm in the Mountains* (Cherokee: Press of the Museum of the Cherokee Indian, 1982), pp. 142-44; W. W. Stringfield to His Excellency Andrew Johnson, William W. Stringfield Papers, North Carolina State Archives.

10. William Holland Thomas "To the Citizens of Sevier County," October 4, 1865, William Holland Thomas, Oath of Allegiance, William Holland Thomas Papers, Duke University.

11. Max R. Williams, *History of Jackson County* (Sylva: Jackson County Historical Society, 1987), pp. 413-14; George R. Best Collection, Blount County Public Library.

Bibliography

Archival Sources

BLOUNT COUNTY PUBLIC LIBRARY, MARYVILLE, TENNESSEE
Edwin James Best, Sr. Collection.

SPECIAL COLLECTIONS, DUKE UNIVERSITY, DURHAM, NORTH CAROLINA
Bell Family Papers
Kirby Smith Family Papers
Thomas Lenoir Papers
William Holland Thomas Papers

HUNTER LIBRARY, WESTERN CAROLINA UNIVERSITY, CULLOWHEE, NORTH CAROLINA
Joseph Cathey and Cathey Family Papers
Edmonston/Kelly Family Papers
William Estes Papers
William Walker Papers
James W. Terrell Papers
William Williams Stringfield Papers

MCCLUNG COLLECTION, KNOXVILLE, TENNESSEE
Inez Burns Collection
Joseph Sharp Collection
Records of Cocke County, Tennessee, Minutes of the East Tennessee Association of Baptists, 1841-1872

NATIONAL ARCHIVES, WASHINGTON, D.C.
Record Group 56
Record Group 109
Record Group 393

NORTH CAROLINA STATE ARCHIVES, RALEIGH, NORTH CAROLINA
Joseph Cathey Papers
Mary Gash Papers
Evelyn McIntosh Hyatt Collection
William Williams Stringfield Papers
Thomas Wells Papers

Stephen Whitaker Papers
Jonathan Worth Papers
Zebulon Baird Vance Papers

SOUTHERN HISTORICAL COLLECTION, CHAPEL HILL, NORTH CAROLINA
David Campbell Papers
Mrs. Evelyn McIntosh Hyatt Book
Lenoir Family Papers
Lyle and Siler Family Papers
Theodore Davidson Morrison Collection
David Schenk Books
William and Jeremiah Sloe Papers
Mary Ann Covington Wilson Papers

TENNESSEE STATE LIBRARY AND ARCHIVES, NASHVILLE, TENNESSEE
Memoirs of William Gibbs Allen

UNIVERSITY OF TENNESSEE SPECIAL COLLECTIONS, KNOXVILLE, TENNESSEE
Brownlow Family Papers
Horace Maynard Papers
Robert A. Ragan Letters
Oliver P. Temple Papers

Printed Sources

Brownlow, William G. *Sketches of the Rise, Progress, and Decline of Secession*. Philadelphia: J. B. Lippincott, 1862.

Davis, Hattie Caldwell. *Civil War Letters and Memoirs from the Great Smoky Mountains*. Maggie Valley: Hattie Caldwell Davis, 1999.

Humes, Thomas William. *The Loyal Mountaineers of Tennessee*. Knoxville: Ogden Brothers, 1888.

Johnson, Frontis W., ed. *The Papers of Zebulon Baird Vance*. Raleigh: State Department of Archives and History, 1963.

Sherman, William T. *Memoirs of General William T. Sherman*. Bloomington: Indiana University Press, 1957.

Temple, Oliver P. *East Tennessee and the Civil War*. Cincinnati: The R. Clark Company, 1899.

Temple, Oliver P. *Notable Men of Tennessee from 1833 to 1875*. New York: Cosmopolitan Press, 1912).

Tennesseans in the Civil War. 2 vols. Nashville: Civil War Centennial Commission, 1864.

Walker, Edward R. III. *Tales from the Civil War*. Cosby: Busy Bee Printing Service, 1983.

The War of the Rebellion: A Compilation of the Official Records of the Union and Confederate Armies. 130 vols. Washington: Government Printing Office, 1880-1901.

Published Sources

Allen, W. C. *The Annals of Haywood County North Carolina, Historical, Sociological, Biographical, and Genealogical*. Spartanburg: Reprint Company, 1982.

Andes, John W. and McTeer, Will. A. *Loyal Mountain Troopers: The Second and Third Tennessee Volunteer Cavalry in the Civil War*. Maryville: Blount County Genealogical and Historical Society, 1992.

Arthur, John Preston. *Western North Carolina: A History*. Raleigh: Edwards & Broughton Printing Company, 1914.

Atkins, Jonathan M. *Parties, Politics, and the Sectional Conflict in Tennessee, 1832-1861*. Knoxville: University of Tennessee Press, 1997.

Bailey, Fred Arthur. "Tennessee Antebellum Common Folk." *Tennessee Historical Quarterly* 55 (1996), pp. 40-55.

Barrett, John G. *The Civil War in North Carolina*. Chapel Hill: University of North Carolina Press, 1963.

Blackmum, Ora. *Western North Carolina: Its Mountains and Its People to 1880*. Boone: Appalachian Consortium Press, 1977.

Blair, Carolyn L., and Walker, Ardas. *By Faith Endowed: The Story of Maryville College, 1819-1994*. Maryville: Maryville College Press, 1994.

Bryan, Charles Faulkner. "The Civil War in East Tennessee: A Social, Political and Economic Study." Dissertation, University of Tennessee, 1978.

Brewer, Alberta and Carson. *Valley So Wild: A Folk History*. Knoxville: East Tennessee Historical Society, 1975.

Burns, Inez. *History of Blount County, Tennessee: From War Trail to Landing Strip*. Nashville: Tennessee Historical Commission, 1957.

Burt, Jesse C. "East Tennessee, Lincoln, and Sherman." *East Tennessee Historical Society Publications* 34 (1962), pp. 3-25, 35 (1963), pp. 56-75.

Callahan, Gertrude E. *Montvale: A Narrative of the People Who Lived in the Foothills of the Smoky Mountains*. —, 1978. Chattanooga: Great American Publishing Co., 1974.

Callahan, North. *Smoky Mountain Country*. Sevierville: Smoky Mountains Historical Society, 1952.

Campbell, Mary Emily Robertson. *The Attitude of Tennesseans Toward the Union, 1847-1861*. New York: Vantage, 1961.

Cannon, Robert K. *Volunteers for Union and Liberty: History of the Fifth Tennessee Infantry, USA, 1862-1865*. Knoxville: Bohemian Brigade Publishers, 1995.

Cimprich, John. *Slavery's End in Tennessee, 1861-1865*. Tuscaloosa: University of Alabama Press, 1985.

Crofts, Daniel C. *Reluctant Confederates: Upper South Unionists in the Secession Crisis*. Chapel Hill: University of North Carolina Press, 1989.

Crowe, Vernon. *Storm in the Mountains*. Cherokee: Press of the Museum of the Cherokee Indians, 1982.

Current, Richard Nelson. *Lincoln's Loyalists: Union Soldiers from the Confederacy*. New York: Oxford University Press, 1992.

Davis, Hattie Caldwell. *Cataloochee Valley: Vanished Settlements of the Great Smoky Mountains*. Alexander: WorldComm, 1997.

Dunn, Durwood. *Cades Cove: The Life and Death of a Southern Appalachian Community, 1818-1937*. Knoxville: University of Tennessee Press, 1988.

Escott, Paul D. *After Secession: Jefferson Davis and the Failure of Confederate Nationalism*. Baton Rouge: Louisiana State University Press, 1978.

Finger, John R. *The Eastern Band of the Cherokees, 1819-1900*. Knoxville: University of Tennessee Press, 1984.

Frome, Michael. *Strangers in High Places*. New York: Doubleday and Company, 1966.

Godbold, E. Stanley and Russell, Mattie U. *Confederate Colonel and Cherokee Chief: The Life of William Holland Thomas*. Knoxville: University of Tennessee Press, 1990.

Gray, Lewis Cecil. *History of Agriculture in the Southern United States to 1860*. 2 vols. Gloucester: Peter Smith, 1958.

Greve, Jeannette S. *The Story of Gatlinburg*. Maryville: Brazo Printing Company, 1976.

Groce, W. Todd. *Mountain Rebels: East Tennessee Confederates and the Civil War, 1860-1870*. Knoxville: University of Tennessee Press, 1999.

Harris, William C. "East Tennessee Civil War Refugees and the Impact of the War on Civilians." *East Tennessee Historical Society Publications* 64 (1992), pp. 3-19.

Haywood County Heritage. Don Mills, Inc. and the Haywood County Heritage Book Committee, 1994.

The History of Cherokee County, North Carolina. Cherokee County History Museum and Hunter Publishing Company, 1987.

Inscoe, John C. *Mountain Masters, Slavery, and the Sectional Crisis in North Carolina*. Knoxville: University of Tennessee Press, 1989.

Inscoe, John C., ed. *Appalachians and Race: The Mountain South from Slavery to Segregation*. Lexington: University Press of Kentucky, 2001.

Inscoe, John C., and Kenzer, Robert C., eds. *Enemies of the Country: New Perspectives on Unionists in the Civil War South*. Athens: University of Georgia Press, 2001.

Inscoe, John C., and McKinney, Gordon B. *The Heart of Confederate Appalachia: Western North Carolina in the Civil War*. Chapel Hill: University of North Carolina Press, 2000.

Jackson County Heritage. Walsworth Publishing Company and the Jackson County Genealogical Society, 1992.

Killebrew, J. B. *Introduction to the Resources of Tennessee*. Nashville: Tavel, Eastman and Howell, 1874.

Kirk, Charles, ed. *History of the First Pennsylvania Cavalry*. Philadelphia: Charles H. Kirk, 1906.

Lloyd, Ralph Waldo. *Maryville College: A History of 150 Years, 1819-1969*. Maryville: Maryville College Press, 1969.

Lonn, Ella. *Desertion During the Civil War*. New York: The Century Company, 1928.

Madden, David. "Unionist Resistance to Confederate Occupation: The Bridge Burners of East Tennessee." *East Tennessee Historical Society Publications* 52 (1980), pp. 42-53, (1981), pp. 22-39.

Marvel, William. *Burnside*. Chapel Hill: University of North Carolina Press, 1991.

Medford, W. Clark. *The Early History of Haywood County*. Waynesville: W. Clark Medford, 1961.

——— *Middle History of Haywood County*. Waynesville: W. Clark Medford, 1968.

Mitchell, Robert D., ed. *Appalachian Frontiers: Settlement, Society, and Development in the Pre-Industrial Era*. Lexington: University Press of Kentucky, 1991.

Moore, Albert Burton. *Conscription and Conflict in the Confederacy*. New York: The Macmillan Company, 1924.

Moore, Winifred B., and Tripp, Joseph. *Looking South: Chapters in the Story of an American Region*. New York: Greenwood Press, 1989.

Noe, Kenneth W., and Wilson, Shannon H. *The Civil War in Appalachia: Collected Essays*.
Knoxville: University of Tennessee Press, 1997.

North Carolina State Board of Agriculture. *North Carolina and Its Resources*. Raleigh: M. I. and J. C. Stewart, 1896.

O'Dell, Ruth Webb. *Over the Misty Blue Hills: The Story of Cocke County, Tennessee*. Easley: Southern Historical Press, 1982.

Oliver, Duane. *Hazel Creek From Then til Now*. Maryville: Stinnet Printing Company, 1989.

Owenby, Harold. *Forks of Little Pigeon Church*. Gatlinburg: The Buckhorn Press, 1989.

Peattie, Roderick. *The Great Smoky Mountains and the Blue Ridge*. New York: Vanguard Press, 1943.

Powers, Elizabeth, and Hannah, Mark. *Cataloochee: Lost Settlement of the Smokies*. Charleston: Powers-Hannah Publishers, 1982.

Ragan, Robert A. *Escape from East Tennessee to the Federal Lines*. Washington, D. C.: J. H. Doney, 1910.

Sevier County Heritage. Don Mills Company, Inc. and the Sevier County Heritage Book Committee, 1982.

Seymour, Digby Gordon. *Divided Loyalties: Fort Sanders and the Civil War in East Tennessee*. Knoxville: University of Tennessee Press, 1963.

Shapiro, David. *Appalachia on our Mind: The Southern Mountains and Mountaineers in the American Consciousness*. Chapel Hill: University of North Carolina Press, 1978.

Shields, A. Randolph. *The Cades Cove Story*. Gatlinburg: Great Smoky Mountains Association, 1977.

Sitterson, Joseph Carlyle. *The Secession*

Movement in North Carolina. Chapel Hill: University of North Carolina Press, 1939.

Sutherland, Daniel E. *Guerrillas, Unionists, and Violence on the Home Front*. Fayetteville: University of Arkansas Press, 1999.

Trent, Emma Dean Smith. *East Tennessee's Lore of Yesteryear*. Whitesburg: Emma Dean Smith Trent, 1987.

Trent, Emma Dean Smith. *Faces, Places and Things of Early East Tennessee*. Whitesburg: Emma Dean Smith Trent, 1989.

William, Max, ed. *The History of Jackson County*. Sylva: Jackson County Historical Society, 1987.

Wilson, Samuel Tyndale. *A Century of Maryville College, 1819-1919*. Maryville: The Directors of Maryville College, 1916.

Baird Vance. 1 vols. Raleigh: State Department of Archives and History, 1963.

Sherman, William T. *Memoirs of General William T. Sherman*. Bloomington: Indiana University Press, 1957.

Temple, Oliver P. *East Tennessee and the Civil War*. Cincinnati: The R. Clark Company, 1899.

Temple, Oliver P. *Notable Men of Tennessee from 1833 to 1875*. New York: Cosmopolitan Press, 1912.

Tennesseans in the Civil War. 2 vols. Nashville: Civil War Centennial Commission, 1864.

Walker, Edward R. III. *Tales from the Civil War*. Cosby: Busy Bee Printing Service, 1983.

The War of the Rebellion: A Compilation of the Official Records of the Union and Confederate Armies. 130 vols. Washington: Government Printing Office, 1880-1901.

Glossary

Abatis – A defensive obstacle made by laying felled trees on top of each other with branches, sometimes sharpened, facing the enemy.

Bald – An area on the upper elevation of a mountain that is devoid of trees. Balds are common in the Great Smoky Mountains and were favored areas for grazing. Different theories exist as to their origin.

Battalion – An imprecise term in the Civil War, battalion referred to a number of companies, usually fewer than ten, grouped together for operational and administrative purposes. Battalions were commanded by a colonel or a major.

Brigade – Two or more regiments grouped together under a single commander for operational and administrative purposes. In theory a brigade was commanded by a brigadier general, but in practice brigades were often led by colonels.

Bushwhacker – A term of contempt that soldiers and civilians sometimes applied to enemy guerrillas. The term referred to the guerrillas' supposedly cowardly practice of firing from the brush along a road.

Company – A unit which, when complete, was made up of 100 men, though after the first year of the Civil War few companies had this number. The company was commanded by a captain and was the building block of Civil War armies.

Conscript – Any male subject to conscription (the draft).

Foraging – The practice of soldiers systematically taking food and other supplies from farms and homes. This practice became increasingly common as the Civil War went on, both because supply systems were inadequate for the large armies and because foraging was a means of punishing the enemy civilian population.

Guerrilla – The official term for a combatant who was not formally enrolled in a military unit and who fought without a uniform or other means of identification. In the Civil War, the terms guerrilla, bushwhacker, and partisan were used interchangeably and without much precision.

Home Guard – A unit of men from a small area organized to defend their home region. Home Guard units were based on the same concept as the militia. In the Civil War, some Home Guard units were organized by the state, while others were self-constituted. In the Southern Appalachians it was not unusual early in the war to find two sets of home guards in a particular county—one Union and one Confederate.

Loyalist – Confederates used this as a derogatory term to describe Southern Unionists. Similar terms were "Lincolnite" and "Tory." All these terms were derived from the American Revolution and emphasized the supposed disloyalty of Unionists to their own region.

Outlier – A man hiding away from his home in order to avoid conscription.

Partisan – A member of a military group operating against enemy supply lines, facilities, and isolated troops. In the Civil War, the term partisan was applied both to self-organized groups and to officially enrolled units. The

Confederacy, for example, created a number of Partisan Ranger units early in the war to operate independently against Union lines of communication and supply.

Provost Marshal – A military officer exercising administrative and police powers over a given region.

Regiment – A regiment was made up of ten or more companies and was led by a colonel. Most regiments had state designations (Sixty-ninth North Carolina Infantry, Tenth Michigan Cavalry) and were the primary units of identification.

Sappers and Miners – Terms originally applied to military engineers who built trenches, undermined fortifications, and planted or disarmed mines. In the Civil War the term was sometimes applied to units who performed construction duties of any kind.

Scout – An odd term with multiple meanings, scout could refer to cavalry operating behind enemy lines, cavalry fighting enemy guerrillas, men who were avoiding conscription, and men fighting as guerrillas. Also used to describe a person who guided deserters and former prisoners of war across enemy lines to safety.

Tax in Kind – The Confederate tax of ten percent on a farm's production each year.

Unionist – A person who favored the preservation of the Union. Unionism took different forms. Radical Unionists supported any measures to restore the country, including the abolition of slavery, the confiscation of Confederate property, and eventually the disfranchisement of Confederates. Conservative Unionists also wished to preserve the Union, but opposed measures they considered illegal or unconstitutional, including the suspension of the Writ of Habeas Corpus, the declaration of martial law, and abolition.

Yeoman – A land holder who farmed his own land, i.e. a non-slaveholder.

Index

A

Abingdon, Virginia, 116, 134
Abbott, Noah, **165**
African-Americans, 23, 150
Agricultural Society, 33
Allen, Colonel Lawrence M., 63
Allen, Colonel William Gibbs, 61, 62, 144, 145
Allen, "Uncle Pikey" John, 83
Allen, William, 49
Allen, William W., 147
Alum Cave, Tennessee, 26, 48
Alum Fort, 149
Amerine, George, 95
Anderson, South Carolina, 132
Anderson County, Tennessee, 81
Anderson, Lark, 73
Andersonville prison, 57
Andes, J. A., 80, 81
Appomattox Courthouse, 139
Armstrong, 127, 129, 130
Army of Northern Virginia, 42, 47
Army of Tennessee, 115, 116, 121, 133
Army of the Tennessee, 116
Asheville, North Carolina, 27, 28, 44, 60, 98, 125, 138, 139, 140, 141, 143, 149
Ashmore, Major John D., 132
Atakullakulla, 14
Atchley, Joshua, 98
Athens, Georgia, 24
Atlanta, Georgia, 35, 101, 104, 105
Augusta, Georgia, 22, 24, 27

B

Balsam Gap, North Carolina, 14, 136, 138, 140, 141
Baltimore, Maryland, 24, 144
Barnes, Henry, 137
Bartlett, Colonel William T., 140, 141, 142
Battle of Antietam, 42
Battle of Horseshoe Bend, 17, 18, 45

Battle of Murfreesboro, 43
Battle of Chickamauga, 43, 116, 119, 123
Battle of Seven Pines, 42
Baxter, John, 35
Beauregard, Major General P. G. T., 133
Bell, Alfred, 44, 63, 98, 99, 100, 101, 102, 103, **104**, 105, 106, 107
Bell, Mary, 45, 87, 98, 99, 100, 101, 102, 103, 104, 105, 106, 107
Bell, Senator John, 35
Benjamin, Secretary of War Judah P., 46, 55, 60
Bennett, Young, 137
Berry, Captain, 72
Best, William, 148
Bethel, North Carolina, 137
Bible, Aaron, 83
Bible, Estil B., 82
Big Bear, North Carolina, 67
Big Creek, North Carolina, 27, 137
Bird, Lt., 64
Bird, Mark, 62, 64
Black Republicans, 35
Blount County, Tennessee, 16, 17, 22, 26, 35, 36, 37, 38, 39, 43, 47, 48, 49, 52, 55, 56, 57, 59, 61, 62, 71, 73, 75, 76, 77, 81, 86, 87, 90, 92, 93, 94, 95, 96, 98, 106, 107, 115, 117, 118, 119, 120, 121, 122, 124, 127, 128, 130, 131, 140, 143, 144, 148, 149
Blount County Court, 92, 131
Blowing Cave, Tennessee, 83
Blue Ridge Mountains, 14, 132, 134
Blue Springs, Tennessee, 116
Bluff Mountain, Tennessee, 63
Bogard, Tennessee, 91, 93
Bonaparte's Retreat, 67
Bonham, Govenor M. L., 132
Boone, North Carolina, 138
Boyd's Creek, 15, 128, 131
Bradley County, Tennessee, 53
Bradley, J. C., 63
Bragg, Major General Braxton, 115, 116, 117, 121, **123**, 133

Breckinridge, Major General John C., **68**, 133
Brickell, Circuit Court Clerk William N., 92
Bridges, George, 50, 51
Bristol, Tennessee, 28, 114
British, 14, 16, 17, 26
Brown, Brigadier General Simon B., 139
Brown, John T., 121
Brownlow, William G., **39**, 47, 51, 55, 56, 58, 59, 60, 143, 145
Bryan, Captain S. T., 69
Bryon, Captain J. D., 44
Bryson City, North Carolina, 18
Bryson, First Lieutenant J. N., 71, 72
Bryson, Goldman, 69
Bryson, Sam C., 42
Buckman, Captain, 146
Buckner, Major General Simon B., 115, 133
Bull's Gap, Tennessee, 74, 116, 122, 125
Buncombe County, North Carolina, 132, 138
Buncombe Turnpike, 25, 27
Buram, Henry, 76
Burgess, Green, 77
Burnett, Reverend J. M. L., 40, 41
Burnett, William, 94
Burnside, Major General Ambrose, 69, 115, 116, **117**, 118, 119, 120, 121, 122, 124, 125, 127
Bussell, Creece, 144, 146

C

Cades Cove, 16, 25, 26, 74, 91, 118
Caldwell, 83
Caldwell Creek, 137
Caldwell, Levi, 21, 137
Caldwell, Mary Ann Nailand, 137
Caldwell, Michael, 67
Cameron, Secretary of War Simon, 52
Camp Dick Nelson, 48, 52
Camp Dick Robinson, 79
Camp Douglas, Illinois, 68
Camp Henrietta, 64
Campbell, Brigadier General William, 128, 129
Campbell, Colonel Arthur, 15
Cannon, Lee, 98
Cannon, W. H., 148
Carlisle, Joseph, 83

Carroll, Brigadier General William, 58
Carter County, Tennessee, 47
Carter's Depot, 115, 116
Carter, Union Provost Marshall Samuel P., 68, 69, 75, 76, 77
Cataloochee, Big and Little, 16, 21, 27, 82, 83, 137, 143
Catawba Indians, 11
Cathey, Joseph, 24, 32, 87
Charleston, North Carolina, 22, 24, 25, 27, 28, 101, 106
Chattanooga, Tennessee, 14, 28, 43, 52, 101, 114, 115, 116, 121, 122
Cherokee, North Carolina, 85, 92, 96, 97, 105, 124
Cherokee County, North Carolina, 30, 32, 66, 67, 68, 69, 71, 72, 73, 96, 97, 126, 132, 134, 148, 149
Chestnut Hill, Tennessee, 83
Chickamauga Creek, 116
Chickamauga River, 14
Chilhowee Mountain, 49, 76, 118
Chilhowee Valley, 140
Chimney Top Mountain, 68
Chote, North Carolina, 13, 14, 15
Christian, Colonel William, 14
Cincinnati, Ohio, 27, 28
Clark, Governor Henry T., 46, 59, 60
Clay County, North Carolina, 47, 72
Click family, 88
Click, Jefferson, 88
Click, Joshua, 90
Click, William, 88
Clinch River, 15, 80, 81
Clingman, Georgia, 27
Clingman, Thomas L., 31, **37**, 38, 42
Clingmans Dome, 37
Clinton, Tennessee, 99
Clyde, North Carolina, 28
Cocke County, Tennessee, 17, 22, 26, 35, 36, 37, 39, 43, 49, 57, 58, 61, 62, 67, 69, 75, 76, 78, 79, 82, 83, 84, 86, 87, 88, 89, 90, 91, 120, 125, 127, 128, 129, 144, 146, 147
Coffin, Charles, 74, 75
Coleman, Colonel, 100, 101, 103, 104, 106
Collins, Robert, 48

Collins, Robert, gravestone of, **167**
Columbia, South Carolina, 24, 105
Commander of the District of East Tennessee and Western North Carolina, 136
Committee on Federal Relations, The, 31
Companies A and L of the Sixteenth North Carolina Infantry, 46
Company A, 42, 43, 47
Company B, 43
Company C, 43
Company E, 42
company F, 42
Company I, 43
Company L, 43
Confederate Army of Tennessee, 81
Confederate Assistant Quartermaster General, 85
Confederate Congress, 36, 82, 85, 99
Confederate Conscript Bureau, 71
Confederate Conscription Act, 82, 85, 99, 136
Confederate District Attorney, 51
Confederate District Court, 50
Confederate House of Representatives, 33
Congressional Republicans, 33
Cooper, Captain J. M., 138
Coosa River, 14
Cosby, Tennessee, 49, 76, 83, 88, 91
Cosby Creek, 126, 127, 144
Cowles, L., 70
Craig, John S., 92, 93
Creek Indians, 17
Crittenden Resolutions, 32
Crofts, Daniel, 32
Crye, John S., 73, 74
Cullowhee Mountains, 26
Cumberland Gap, 43, 81, 115
Cummings, Reverend James, 58, 59

D

Dalton, Georgia, 104
Dandridge, Tennessee, 81, 125, 128, 129
Davidson, Colonel Allen T., 33, 46, 47
Davidson, Major Francis M., 131, 132
Davidson, N. N., 92
Davis, Daniel David, 26
Davis, Major Charles G., 74

Davis, Confederate President Jefferson, **45**, 47, 50, 82, 97, 127, 136
Dawson, Rachel, 90
Deaton, Spencer, 77
Decatur, Alabama, 76
Deep Creek, 131
Del Rio, Tennessee, 83, 148
Delaware Indians, 11, 12, 13
Dellwood, North Carolina, 141
Denton, Thomas, 88
Department of East Tennessee, 86, 101, 133, 136
Department of East Tennessee and Southwest Virginia, 68
Dibrell, Colonel G. G., 119
Doughty, Colonel James, 121
Dowell, Reverend W. T., 59
Dowell, W. T., 39
Drowning Bear, 18
Dudley, Governor Edwin B., 21
Duggan, William H. H., 51
Dunlap, Matilda, 94, 95
Dunn, Cynthia, 49
Dunn, Major, 69, 140
Dutch and Irish Bottoms, 128

E

East Tennessee Female Masonic Institute, 148
Easterly, P. H., 39
Echota, North Carolina, 11
Edmonston, R. B., 44
Edwards, J. A. P., 73
Eighth Tennessee Cavalry, 43
Eleventh Kentucky Cavalry, 119
Ellis, Daniel, 47, 48
Ellis, Governor John Willis, 30, 34
Ellis, James, 54
England, 13, 26
English, 11, 12, 13
English Mountain, 88
English Proclamation Line of, 1763, 13
Epsom Salts Manufacturing Company, 26
European, 11, 12, 13, 14

F

Fair Garden, Tennessee, 34, 128, 129, 130, 131
Farmer, Solomon, 59
Faubian, Tilghman Alexander H., 87
Federal Commissioner for Indian Affairs, 150
Ferguson, Colonel Patrick, 15
Ferguson, W. B., 63
Fifteenth and Fourth Corps, 121
Fifteenth Pennsylvania Cavalry, 125, 126
Fifth Tennessee Cavalry, 43, 61, 62, 144
Fines Creek, 89
First Conscription Act, 81
First Tennessee Cavalry, 43, 126, 145
First Wisconsin Cavalry, 68, 132
Fitzgerald, J. B., 65
Fleming, Andrew, 48
Foote, Governor Henry S., 35
Forks of Pigeon, Tennessee, 24
Fort Harry, 48
Fort Loudon, 12
Fort Sanders, 122, **124**
Fort Sumter, 33, 36
Foster, Horace, 75, 76, 121
Foster, Major General John G., **86**, 127, 128, 130
Fourteenth Tennessee Cavalry, 121
Fourteenth Illinois Cavalry, 96, 131
Fourth Army Corps, 86, 121, 122
Fourth District of Sevier County, 86
Fourth Tennessee Cavalry, 134
Foute, Daniel D., 25, **26**
Fowler, Major John Henry, 38
Fox, Mark, 62
Franklin, North Carolina, 15, 25, 27, 93, 98, 105, 138, 140, 142
Franklin, J. H., 64,
Fredericksburg, Virginia, 42
Freedman's Normal Institute, 150
French, 12
French Broad River, 15, 16, 53, 80, 82, 96, 120, 127, 128, 130
French Huguenots, 13
Friendsville, Tennessee, 77, 93, 150
Fultonville, Georgia, 35

G

Gann, Allen, 150
Gann, John, 146
Garrard, Brigadier General Israel, 128, 129, 130
Garrett, Justice of the Peace William Green Berry, 34
Garrison, Israel, 98
Gatlin, Radford, 35
Gatlinburg, Tennessee, 35, 124, 125, 126
Gaut, John, 148
German(s), 13
Gibbs, Colonel William, 61, 70
Giles, family, 88
Gillem, Major General Alvin C., 138, 139, **140**, 141
Goldsboro, North Carolina, 33, 136
Gorman, Thomas, 43
Graham County, North Carolina, 72
Graham, Colonel F. W., 115
Granger, Major General Gordon, 122, 130
Grant, Major General Ulysses S., 117, **118**, 121
Graves, Brother, 146
Graves of Civil War Casualties, **166**
Gray, John D. and Company, 26
Gray, Newton, 97
Great Britain, 12,
Great Island, 12
Great Valley of East Tennessee, 28
Green Hill Academy, 140
Greene County, Tennessee, 17, 36, 53, 58, 60, 78, 79, 87
Greenville, South Carolina, 132, 139
Greeneville Convention, 48, 52
Greeneville, Tennessee, 27, 39, 40, 116
Greenlawn, Tennessee, 88
Greenwood, Lieutenant Colonel, 139
Gregory, Russell, 74, **95**
Gregory, Walter, **94**
Grooms, Eliza, 67
Grooms, George Jr., 67
Grooms, Henry, 67
Grooms, John, 67
Guyot, Arnold, 48

H

Hackney, William J., 77
Hall, Barbara, 77, 93, 106, 107
Hall, Crawford, 107
Hall, Crofton, 76
Hall, James, 77, 106, 107
Hamilton County, Tennessee, 53
Harley, James, 62, 63
Harmon, Jacob, **56**
Harper's Ferry, Virginia, 42
Harris, Governor Isham G., 34, 35, 36, 50
Harris, James, 144
Harris, Shade T., 81, 82
Hatcher, Elijah, 75, 76
Hatcher, Elijah L., 95, 96
Hayes, Newt, 84
Haywood County, North Carolina, 16, 17, 19, 21, 22, 24, 27, 28, 30, 32, 33, 34, 42, 44, 46, 60, 63, 64, 65, 66, 67, 73, 77, 85, 89, 105, 132, 134, 138, 144, 148, 149
Haywood County Court, 27
Haywood Sharpshooters, 44
Hazel Creek, 91
Henderson County, North Carolina, 27, 132
Henderson, William, 76
Hendersonville, North Carolina, 139, 141
Hennel, John, 107
Henry, Lieutenant Arthur, 119
Henry, Lieutenant Colonel James, 126, 127
Henry, Pleasant, 73
Hickey, Reverend Rufus M., 146
Hicks, Jerome Eldridge, 92
Hicks, Mark, 91, 92
Hicks, Rev. Wm., 105
Hiwassee, River, 11, 12
Hiwassee, North Carolina, 15
Hiwassee Pass, 132
Hodges, Edward, 57, 148
Hodges, William, 57
Hodgson, R. H., 56, 57
Holden, W. W., 65
Holden, William C., 43
Holland, Will, 43
Holston River, 12, 13, 14, 46, 53, 130
Holston River Bridge, 46
Home Guards(men), 40, 48, 49, 50, 52, 67, 68,
69, 76, 96, 103, 117, 124, 126, 132, 140, 146
Homer, Willie, 48
Hopkins, Abraham, 82
Hopkins, Benjamin Parker, 82
Hopkins, William Montgomery, 137
Hot Springs, North Carolina, 143
Howard Gap, 139
Howard, D. W., 146
Howell, Captain R. M., 137, 138
Howell, N. G., 77
Huff, Andy, 144
Huff, Major James T., 144
Huff, William and Matilda, 84
Hume, David, 75
Humphreys, District Court Judge William H., 51
Hurst, William, 147
Hyde, John, 77

I

Indian Creek, 130
Indian Gap, 27
Indiana, 26, 43
Inman, Greene, 90
Inscoe, John C., 37, 38
Irish Bottoms, 128
Iroquois Indians, 11, 12, 13

J

Jack, William, 146
Jacksborough, Tennessee, 53, 99, 115
Jackson County, North Carolina, 17, 19, 23, 25, 26, 30, 33, 43, 46, 48, 63, 65, 85, 86, 105, 126, 132, 134, 141, 150
Jackson, Brigadier General Alfred E., 115, 116, 138
Jackson, Eva and Dora, 49
Jackson, General Andrew, **17**, 18, 20, 21
Jacksonville, Alabama, 105
Jefferson County, Tennessee, 17, 36, 61, 76, 80, 127
Johnson, Andrew, 35, 38, 51, 52, 55, 58, 76, 87
Johnson, Elijah, 46
Johnson, William T., 76
Johnston, General Joseph, **141**
Johnston, William, 149, 150

Jonathan Creek, 16, 27, 34, 64, 137,
Jones Cove, 16, 49, 91
Jones, Major General Sam, 63, 116, 136, **137**
Jones, Matilda, 87, 89, 91, 148
Jonesboro, Tennessee, 116
Jonesville, North Carolina, 40
Junaluska, 17

K

Keeble, Richard, 95, 96
Keelin, James, 54
Kilgore, Henry, 78
King's Mountain, North Carolina, 15
Kingston, Tennessee, 12, 40, 121
Kirby, Colonel Isaac, 139
Kirk, George, 69, 70, 71, **79**, 133, 136, 137, 138, 140, 141, 142
Klein, Lieutenant Colonel Robert, **70**, 71
Knox County, Tennessee, 36, 56, 80, 81
Knoxville, Tennessee, 15, 27, 34, 35, 48, 51, 52, 53, 54, 55, 56, 57, 58, 59, 67, 73, 74, 75, 76, 78, 97, 98, 99, 101, 103, 114, 115, 116, 117, 118, 119, 120, 121, 122, 123, 127, 128, 130, 131, 133, 134, 138, 139, 140, 143, 146, 147, 150
Knoxville Road, 119, 121
Knoxville Whig, 39

L

LaGrange, 129, 130, 132
Lambert, Hugh, 97
Lay, Lieutenant Colonel George, 71, 72
Leadbetter, Colonel Daniel, 55, 58
Ledford, Leander, 100
Lenoir, Lizzie, 64
Lenoir, Thomas I., 42
Lewis, Dr. John, 121
Lexington, Kentucky, 81
Libby Prison, 74
Liberia, North Carolina, 93
Lick Creek, **56**, 78, 115
Lillard, Colonel John M., 43
Limestone Bridge, 115
Lincoln, President Abraham, 30, 33, 34, 37, 38, 44, 51, 52, 100, 114, **116**
Lincolnite, 97
Little Pigeon River, 25, 128

Little River Gap, 49
Little Tennessee River, 11, 14, 15, 16, 62, 71, 76, 117, 118, 119, 121
Long Island, South Carolina, 14, 15
Long, Colonel Eli, 122
Longstreet's Corps, 117
Longstreet, Lieutenant General James, **67**, 68, 73, 74, 117, 118, 119, 120, 121, 122, 123, 124, 125, 127, 128, 129, 130, 132
Loudon, Tennessee, 12, 115, 120, 122, 123, 124
Louisville, Kentucky, 27,
Louisville, Tennessee, 38, 75, 97, 121, 124, 130
Love Fields, 73
Love Tract, 16
Love, Colonel James R., 19, 23, 47, **48**, 115, 116, 123, 132, 133, 136, 149
Love, Colonel Robert, 16, 19, 23, 47, 137, 139, 140, 141, 149
Love, Dillard, 23
Love, John B., 23
Love, Maria, 149
Love, Mary, 121
Love, Robert A., 42
Love, Sarah Jane Burney, 19
Lowell, Halcomb, 62
Lower Creek Indians, 17
Lyons, Timothy, 68

M

Macon County, North Carolina, 17, 22, 23, 28, 30, 32, 33, 44, 63, 85, 87, 98, 103, 105, 123, 132, 134
Madison County, North Carolina, 27, 73
Madisonville, Tennessee, 121
Malvern Hill, Virginia, 42
Mann, John, 100
Mann, William, 100
Marshall, North Carolina, 65
Martin, General William T., 129, 130, 136, 139, 141, 142
Maryville, Tennessee, 52, 59, 62, 69, 75, 86, 92, 93, 94, 97, 106, 114, 118, 119, 121, 122, 124, 127, 129, 130, 131, 140, 144, 149, 150
Maryville Board of Aldermen, 150
Maryville College, 92, 144, 149
Maynard, Horace, 50, 51, 52, 55

McCampbell, William, 61
McCamy, James, 43
McCauley, James, **91**
McClellan, Major General George B., **51**, 52
McCook, Brigadier General Edward, 128, 129, 130, 131
McCown, Major General John P., 47
McCrea, Captain J. C., 71
McDowell, James P., 40
McDowell, Tom, 64
McGaha, Robert, 91
McGhee, James, 76
McKinney, Gordon B., 38
McKinney, James A., 47
McMahan, 62
McMahan, George, 144
McTeer, Harriet, 49
McTeer, Montgomery, 87
McTeer, Will, 49
McTeer, Will A., 80, 81
Meade, Jared, 97
Mease, George, 91
Meece, Robert, 60
Meek, Samuel, 36
Merriman, A. S., 65
Mexican War, 43
Miller's Cove, 16, 25, 95, 96
Miller, Samantha and Adalia, 49
Mims, Captain A. L., 43, 49
Mingus, H. T., 44, 45
Mingus, Sarah, 45
Mississippi River, 20
Mitchell, North Carolina, 133
Mobile, Alabama, 103
Mohawk Indians, 12, 13
Monroe County, Tennessee, 69, 71, 74, 76
Monsarrat, Captain, 58
Montgomery, Alabama, 32
Montgomery, Colonel William, 12
Montvale, Tennessee, 118
Moore, Evelina, 94
Moore, George, 99
Moore, John, 94
Moore, Levi, 96, 97
Morgan County, Tennessee, 52
Morgan, Brigadier General John Hunt, 127, 129, 130, 133

Morgan, Major Gideon, 45
Morgan, Major Washington, 45
Morganton, North Carolina, 117, 118, 119, 121
Morristown, Tennessee, 58, 127, 128
Mossy Creek, 127
Motley's Ford, 118, 119, 130, 132
Mount Le Conte, 48
Mount Sterling, North Carolina, 137, 143
Mount Sterling Bridge, 82, 137
Mount Sterling Gap, 27, 137,
Murphy, North Carolina, 27, 68, 69, 73, 96, 103, 122
Murrell, John, 91

N

Nantahala, North Carolina, 124
Nantahala Mountains, 14, 19
Nashville, Tennessee, 50, 60, 150
Need, John, 98
Nelson, T. A. R., 35, 39, 40, 50, 51, 52, 58, 61, 148
Netherland, John, 40
New Hampshire Baptist Gatlinites, 35
New Market, Tennessee, 144
New Rivers, 14
Newman, Wade, 68, 69
Newport, Tennessee, 15, 49, 58, 62, 63, 76, 114, 125, 126, 127, 128, 129, 130, 137, 145, 146
Newport Road, 62, 126, 128, 130
Newport, Tennessee, 15, 145, 146
Niles Ferry Road, 117
Nine Mile Creek, 73
Ninth Army Corps, 115
Ninth Infantry Corps, 128
Ninth Michigan Cavalry, 125
Ninth Tennessee Cavalry, 146
Nolachucky River, 14, 16, 80, 82, 127, 128, 129
Nolan, Allen, 143
Norris, Hugh, 91
Norwood, Robina, 44
Nuckles, James, 76

O

O'Neill, Jesse, 83
Oconaluftee, 18
Oconaluftee Gap, 126

Oconaluftee River, 14, 16, 18
Oconasta, 14
One Hundredth Ohio Infantry, 115
Osborn, Captain Thomas, 75, 76
Osborne Gap, 141

P

Paint Rock, 134
Palmer, Colonel John B., 127, 131, 132, 133, 134, 136, 139
Palmer, Colonel William, 125, 126
Pangle, Sarah Faubian, 87
Parrottsville, Tennessee, 57, 58, 75, 78, 90
Pearl Valley, 25
Pearson, Captain D. C., 72
Pendleton, North Carolina, 132
Pennebaker, Colonel Charles D., 118
Perham, Lieutenant W. T., 80
Philadelphia, Pennsylvania, 24
Phillips, N. G., 148
Pickens, Samuel, 39, 54, 57
Pickens, William C., 54, 56
Pigeon River, 15, 16, 76
Pittsburgh, Pennsylvania, 26
Point Lookout, Tennessee, 89
Pollard, Alabama, 103
Pope, Reverend Fielding, 144
Porter's Ford, 119
Porter, Colonel Edward, 118
Porter, W. H., 68
Preston, Colonel John S., 71
Pride, Dr. Samuel, 92
Provisional Constitution of the Confederate States, 34

Q

Quaker, 93, 149
Quallatown, North Carolina, 18, 19, 20, 21, 22, 27, 45, 125, 137, 139, 149, 150
Queen, Mary Moland, 89

R

Raccoon Creek, 19
Rader, Elkinah, 35

Ragan, Postmaster John H., **78**
Ragan, Robert, 87
Ragan, Robert Allen, 78, 79, 80
Raleigh, North Carolina, 31, 44, 60, 72, 98
Ramsey, Dr. J. G. M., **50**
Ramsey, John Crozier, 51, 59
Randolph, James H., 80
Ransom, Major General Robert, 116, 133, 136
Rawlings, John A., 97
Red Clay, Georgia, 21
Reece, Robert, 58
Removal Acts, 20, 21
Republican, The Maryville, 150
Revolutionary War, 15, 16, 17, 28
Reynolds, Brigadier General Robert, 103
Rhea, Lieutenant Robert, 72
Richmond, Virginia, 50, 53, 106, 136
Ridge, Major John, 20
Ringgold, Georgia, 104
Rixby, Mitchell, 73
Roadman, Robert S., 144
Roane County, Tennessee, 47
Roane, W., 77
Roberts, John, 84
Rockford, Tennessee, 119, 130
Rockford Cotton Mills, 75
Rogers, Reverend William H., 57
Rogers, S. A., 148
Rogersville, Tennessee, 118, 149
Rosecrans, Major General William S., 116, 117, **119**, 123
Rowan, Mrs., 74
Rumbaugh, Captain, 75
Russell, Isaac, 106, 107
Rutherford, General Griffin, 14

S

Sacred Ark of the Covenant, 35
Saffell, Thomas, 96
Salisbury, North Carolina, 27, 28, 70, 98, 138
Sanders, Brigadier General William P., 117, 118, 120
Savannah Creek, 26
Savannah River, 11, 14
Savannah, Georgia, 22, 24, 25, 106
Schermerhorn, Reverend J. F., 21

Schofield, Major General John M., **69**, 70
Schultz's Mill, 126
Schultz, George, 49
Scotch-Irish, 13
Scott's Creek, 16, 25
Scott, General Winfield, **20**, 21
Scott, William B., 150
Second North Carolina Mounted Infantry, 70, 133, 136, 138, 140
Second Manassas, 42, 47
Second Tennessee Cavalry, 43, 49, 76, 81, 96
Seddon, Secretary of War James, 127, 136
Selfridge, Lieutenant Colonel R. O., 130
Seven Days Battle, 42, 47
Seven Years War, 12
Sevier County, Tennessee, 16, 17, 22, 34, 35, 36, 37, 38, 39, 43, 48, 51, 54, 55, 56, 58, 59, 61, 62, 63, 76, 77, 78, 80, 81, 84, 86, 87, 91, 96, 115, 120, 124, 125, 126, 127, 128, 144, 145, 146, 147, 148, 149
Sevier, Colonel John, **15**
Sevierville, Tennessee, 14, 16, 17, 27, 34, 35, 48, 49, 56, 59, 75, 81, 93, 94, 114, 120, 124, 125, 126, 128, 129, 130
Sevierville Road, 125
Shackelford, Brigadier General James, 116
Shahan, Alonzo, 61
Shannon, Colonel John, 76
Sharpsburg, Virginia, 42, 47
Shawnee Indians, 12, 13, 17
Sheed, Reverend Henry M., 75
Shelton, Levin, 137
Sherman, Brigadier General William T., 52, **54**, 55, 104, 106, 118, 121, 122, 133
Shields, John, 69
Shook's Campground, 28
Shook, Jacob, 28
Silas, Uncle, 64
Siler, Jeffery, 103
Siler, Jesse, 25
Siler, Thomas P., 123, 124
Simerly, Henry, 107
Sixteenth North Carolina Infantry, 42, 43, 46, 47
Sixth Tennessee Infantry, 80
Sixtieth Tennessee Infantry, 43
Sixty-ninth North Carolina Infantry, 42, 43, 47

Sixty-ninth Tennessee Infantry, 43
Sixty-second North Carolina Infantry, 42, 43
Smith, C. D., 65
Smith, Dorcas, **89**
Smith, General Alexander, 75
Smith, James, 89
Smith, Joseph, 78
Smith, Major General Edmund Kirby, 45, **46**, 61, 63, 65, 101, 121
Sneed, Miles, 77
Soco, North Carolina, 18
Soco Creek, 18, 19, 137
Soco Gap, North Carolina, 138, 140
Spanish, 12
Sparks, Mr., 74
Spartanburg, North Carolina, 132
Stakely, David Vandyke, 36
State Adjutant General, 44
States Rights Party, 33
Stevenson, Major General C. L., 69
Stock Creek, 120
Stoneman, Major General George, 138, **139**, 140
Strawberry Plains, Tennessee, 36, 46, **53**, 54, 55, **57**, 95, 115, 128, 144, 149
Stringfield, Captain William Williams, 46, 47 **72**, 73, 137, 138, 139, 140, 144, 145, 147, 148, **149**
Strong, Dr. Joseph C., 77
Sturgis, Brigadier General Samuel D., 86, **87**, 125, 128, 129, 130, 131, 132
Styles, Louisa, 97
Sugar Fork, North Carolina, 64
Sugar Loaf Mountain, North Carolina, 26
Sullivan County, Tennessee, 53
Supreme Court, 20
Sutton, John, 44
Sutton, John M., 96
Swaggert, James, 75
Swananona, North Carolina, 14
Swannanoa Gap, North Carolina, 139

T

Tallapoosa River, 17
Tax-in-Kind Act, 85
Taylor, Captain James, 68

Taylor, Lieutenant C. H., 69
Taylor, M. D. L., 144
Tazewell, Tennessee, 103
Tecumseh, **16**, 17
Telford Station, 115, 116
Tellico, North Carolina, 15
Tellico River, 11
Telling, Lieutenant John, 134
Temple, Oliver P., 34, 36, 39, 40, 48, 53, 94, 97
Templer Lewis Scouts, 49, 62, 147
Tennessean, The Colored, 150
Tennessee River, 12, 14, 62, 71, 76
Tennessee Whigs, 50
Tenth Ohio Cavalry, 126
Terrell, James, 47, 149
Third Indiana Cavalry, 71
Third North Carolina Mounted Infantry, 70, 131, 133, 136, 140
Third Tennessee Cavalry, 43, 54
Thirty-seventh Tennessee Infantry, 43
Thomas's Legion, 45, 46, 47, 115, 134, 135, **145, 147, 149**
Thomas, Colonel William Holland, **18**, 19, 20, 21, 25, 31, 45, 46, 47, 48, 52, 55, 65, 66, 68, 72, 103, 115, 123, 124, 125, 126, 127, 131, 132, 133, 134, 135, 136, 137, 138, 139, 141, 142, **144**, 149, 150
Thomas, George, 52
Thomas, Isaac, 14
Thomas, Stephen, 66, 67
Thornton, Joe, 89, 90
Tillson, Brigadier General Davis, 140, 141, 142
Tinker, Ruth, 82
Tish, John, 75
Toole, J. E., 43
Toole, Polly, 131
Trail of Tears, 20
Treaty of Hopwell, 15
Treaty of Long Island, 14, 15
Treaty of Tellico, 15, 18
Trigg, District Court Judge Connelly F., 35, 147
Trundle's Crossroads, 35, 54
Tsali, 21
Tuckaleechee Cove, 16, 52, 59, 130, 131
Tuckasegee River, 11, 12, 14, 16, 18, 27, 131
Tuscaloosa, Alabama, 57
Tuscarora Indians, 11

Twenty-fifth North Carolina Infantry, 42, 43
Twenty-ninth North Carolina Infantry, 42, 43, 60, 123
Twenty-sixth Tennessee Infantry, 43

U

Underdown's Ferry, 54
Unita, Tennessee, 121
United States Congress, 20, 32, 44, 50

V

Valleytown, North Carolina, 46, 140
Vance, Brigadier General Robert B., 42, 60, 98, 123, 124, 125, 126, 127
Vance, Governor Zebulon B., 31, 64, 68, 104, 105, 123, 125, 127, 134
Vaughn, Brigadier General John C., 68, 69, 72, 73
Vicksburg, Mississippi, 43, 78, 83

W

Walden Creek, 59, 96
Wales, 26
Walhalla, South Carolina, 132
Walker's Battalion, 115, 116, 136
Walker, Colonel William C., 115, 116, 133
Walker, Felix, 19
Walker, James, 95
Walker, John, **92**
Walker, Lieutenant Colonel William C., 47, 66
Walker, Samuel, 95
Walker, W. A., 94
Walker, William, 92
Walker, William D., 67, 68
Wallace, J. G., 59
Wallace, Mary L. T., 97
War Department, 47, 55, 75, 105, 123, 125, 135
Ward, Nancy, 14
Warrensburg, Tennessee, 58
Washington Peace Conference, 32, 33
Washington, D. C., 21, 24, 52, 136
Watauga Association, 13
Watauga Enterprise, 17
Watauga River, 13, 14, 15
Watauga Indians, 14

Watauga Settlement(s), 14, 15
Wayah Gap, 14
Waynesville, North Carolina, 16, 19, 27, 64, 87, 93, 137, 138, 139, 140, 141, 142, 145, 149
Webb, James, 83
Webb, Mary Shrader, 147
Webster, North Carolina, 26, 27, 48, 137, 140, 142
Weir's Cove, 59, 125, 126, 130
Welch, Richard, 98
Welch, William, 19
Wells, Morgan, 137
Western North Carolina Railroad, 28
Western North Carolina Turnpike, 27
Wheeler, Major General Joseph, 72, 73, 104, 119, 120, **122**, 131
Whitaker, Captain Stephen, 47, 66, 142, 149
Whitaker, James, 42
White Oak Flats, 35
White Sulphur Springs, 141
White Sulphur Springs Hotel, 149
Whittier, North Carolina, 27
Williams, Brigadier General John, 116
Williams, James, 97
Williamson, Colonel Andrew, 14
Williamson, Mary Ann McGaha, 89
Williamson, Reuben, 84
Willich, Brigadier General August, 86, 129, 130

Wilmington, Virginia, 44
Wilson, Alfred, 86
Wilsonville, North Carolina, 128
Wolford, Brigadier General Frank, 117, 119, **120**, 128, 129, 130
Wood, Colonel William B., 53, 56, 59
Woods, Gipson, 90
Worcester, Samuel, 20
Worth, Governor Jonathan, 148

Y

Yadkin Bridge, 70
Yamassee Indians, 12
Yancy, Governor William, 35
Yazoo River, 83
Yeebrough, William, 107
Yellow Creek, 68
Yellow Spring Branch, 89
Yellow Springs, 88
Yett, Hamilton, 58
Yonaguska, 18, 19
Younce, W. H., 83

Z

Zollicoffer, Brigadier General Felix K., **49**, 50, 51, 53, 55, 56, 115, 116